Why Leaders Fight

The history of political events is made by people. It doesn't exist without us. From wars to elections to political protests, the choices we make, our actions, how we behave, dictate events. Not all individuals have the same impact on our world and our lives, though. Some peoples' choices alter the path that history takes. In particular, national chief executives play a large role in forging the destinies of the countries they lead. *Why Leaders Fight* is about those world leaders and how their beliefs, world views, and tolerance for risk and military conflict are shaped by their life experiences before they enter office – military, family, occupation, and more. Using in-depth research on important leaders and the largest set of data on leader backgrounds ever gathered, the authors of *Why Leaders Fight* show that – within the constraints of domestic political institutions and the international system – who ends up in office plays a critical role in determining when and why countries go to war.

Michael C. Horowitz is an associate professor of political science at the University of Pennsylvania and the author of the award-winning book *The Diffusion of Military Power*. He has published widely in academic journals and mainstream media outlets on topics including the role of leaders in international politics, military innovation and the future of war, and forecasting. Professor Horowitz has worked at the Department of Defense, is a term member of the Council on Foreign Relations, and is a member of the International Institute for Strategic Studies. He received a PhD in Government from Harvard University and a BA in Political Science from Emory University.

Allan C. Stam is Dean of Leadership and Public Policy at the Frank Batten School at the University of Virginia. His work on war outcomes, durations, and mediation appears in numerous political science journals. Several grants have supported his work, including four from the National Science Foundation. His books include *Win, Lose, or Draw* (1996), *Democracies at War* (2002), and *The Behavioral Origins of War* (2004). He is the recipient of the 2004 Karl Deutsch award, given annually by the International Studies Association to the scholar under the age of forty who has made the greatest contribution to the study of international politics.

CAMBRIDGE
UNIVERSITY PRESS

32 Avenue of the Americas, New York, NY 10013-2473, USA

Cambridge University Press is part of the University of Cambridge.

It furthers the University's mission by disseminating knowledge in the pursuit of education, learning, and research at the highest international levels of excellence.

www.cambridge.org
Information on this title: www.cambridge.org/9781107655676

First published 2015

Printed in the United States of America by Sheridan Books. Inc.

A catalog record for this publication is available from the British Library

Library of Congress Cataloging in Publication Data
Michael C. Horowitz
Why leaders fight / Michael C. Horowitz, University of Pennsylvania, Allan C. Stam, University of Virginia, Cali M. Ellis, University of Michigan, Ann Arbor.
    pages   cm. – (Presidents, kings, dictators, and war)
Includes bibliographical references and index.
ISBN 978-1-107-02293-5 (Hardback) – ISBN 978-1-107-65567-6 (Paperback)
1. Heads of state.   2. Political leadership.   3. International relations.   4. Military policy.
I. Horowitz, Michael C., 1978–   II. Ellis, Cali M.   III. Title.
JF251.S92 2015
303.3'4–dc23   2015011879

ISBN 978-1-107-02293-5 Hardback
ISBN 978-1-107-65567-6 Paperback

Contents

Figures

Photographs

Tables

Preface

History is made by people. From wars to elections to political protests, the world revolves around the way that people decide to behave. In particular, world leaders – the people that run countries big and small around the world – play a large role in shaping the destinies of their countries. This will not be surprising to anyone in the United States or any other place that features public political campaigns. Every four years in the United States, the country becomes preoccupied not just with the policy ideas of potential candidates for the presidency, but with what we can learn about how they would govern from their prior experiences. Whether it is the church Obama attended, Mitt Romney's business experience, or the fact that there has not been a single unmarried president since the Grover Cleveland administration (and even he married in office), the American public, like democratic societies around the world, cares deeply about the personal and professional backgrounds of its political candidates.

This is a book about those world leaders and how their experiences before they enter office shape how they think about the world and the choices they end up making when in office. It presents the most complete dataset on leader experiences ever created, the Leader Experience and Attribute Descriptions (LEAD) dataset, which contains data on more than twenty leader attributes, from military service to childhood to marriage and children, for every world leader from 1875 to 2004.

We focus in particular on how the background experiences of leaders shape the choices they make about whether to lead their countries into wars and start military conflicts, or avoid conflict and focus on other issues. Our findings show that leader attributes play a significant role in shaping how countries behave in the military arena – a role similar to or even exceeding, at times, that played by the international system or domestic political institutions.

From the perspective of academic political science, which has mostly ignored the role of leaders in international politics over the last several decades, until a recent renaissance, our findings, and the data underlying these findings, will come as a surprise. They also provide support for exploring the role of leaders in greater depth. Indeed, the results presented in this book suggest that there is a significant interaction between leaders, the constraints of the international system, and the constraints of domestic political institutions. Only by understanding how all three of these factors interact to shape how leaders and countries behave can we better grasp the complicated international political environment.

We are grateful for the support of a number of organizations and people, without which this book would not have been possible. A grant from the National Science Foundation provided crucial financial support for our research, helping us build the LEAD dataset. One or more of the authors presented initial research at a number of venues, including Bates College, Cornell University, the European Institute, Harvard University, Princeton University, Stanford University, the United States Military Academy, the University of California at Los Angeles, the University of Michigan, the University of Virginia, Yale University, and several political science conferences.

We benefited from the support of many research assistants at Dartmouth College, Harvard University, the University of Michigan, and the University of Pennsylvania, who helped us systematically catalog leader experiences over a several-year period. Thank you to Sam Berson, Limor Bordoley, Brandon Breslow, Shala Byers, Matthew Chiarello, Kathryn Clark, Shelli Gimelstein, Max Kepes, Sabira Khan, Amrit Malothra, Jeanne Michele Mariani, Jack Miller, Jason Murray, Hailey Palmer, Dhruv Ramadive, Tripp Rebrovick, Samuel Schwartz, James Sharp, Joana Sidarov, and Kyle Wirshba, among others.

A number of scholars provided significant assistance as we began thinking through these issues, especially Hein Goemans and Rose McDermott. Other scholars who provided important assistance include, but are not limited to, Thomas L. Whigham, Roderic Camp, Gregory Guenthner, Naomi Hunt, and two anonymous referees. All remaining mistakes and errors are our own. Finally, we would like to dedicate this book to RCH, EAS, and SME.

Introduction

Facing death at the end of an unwinnable war against the combined forces of Brazil, Argentina, and Uruguay, Paraguayan leader Francisco Solano López's reported last words were, "I die for my nation."[1] For Americans, López's sense of self-sacrifice might bring to mind the words of Revolutionary War hero Nathan Hale, whose life ended at the hands of British executioners. Hale's last defiant words, "I only regret that I have but one life to give for my country!" have inspired subsequent generations of Americans.[2] López's words and image persist as well. His efforts leading his small nation against South America's greatest powers secured him a place in the Paraguayan "Pantheon of Heroes," the building in Asunción where bronze statues memorialize Paraguay's greatest leaders. Almost 150 years after his death at the end of the War of the Triple Alliance in 1870, López remains an idolized figure in Paraguay.

A close examination of Paraguay's domestic and foreign policy under López reveals a country whose course and destiny resulted from the imposition of the preferences and beliefs of just one man. López had nearly complete control over Paraguay's domestic political institutions. The policy decisions he made that led to the annihilation of his people and the destruction of the Paraguayan state demonstrate how the will of a bold leader can shape its population.

In late 1864, under López's rule, Paraguay initiated the War of the Triple Alliance against Brazil, Argentina, and Uruguay. On December 13 of that year, López declared war against Brazil after a relatively small-scale Brazilian military intervention against Uruguayan farmers who had sought support from Paraguay. The farmers' request for assistance against Brazil's military provided the pretext that López had been waiting for; it was a war López wanted to fight.

---

[1] He said, "¡Muero por mi Patria!" Frutos 2007.   [2] McCullough 2005, 224.

IF THEY RULE A LEAK, UNEDUCATED AND UNWANTED GROUP OF COLANDS.

1

In response, Brazil, Argentina, and Uruguay formed the Triple Alliance to confront what they regarded as Paraguayan aggression.[3]

While Paraguay was a relatively powerful country at the time, particularly for its size, the combined material assets of the Triple Alliance far outweighed Paraguay's capabilities. Once mobilized for war, the members of the Triple Alliance were able to crush the Paraguayan military. More than six years of fighting decimated Paraguay, its infrastructure, and its people. The war resulted in the death of almost 60 percent of its population and nine out of every ten males.[4] In the last years of the war, military combatants from Argentina and Brazil were shocked to see Paraguayan women and children as young as twelve years old taking up arms in what had degenerated into an utterly futile fight. Across Paraguay, soldier and civilian alike starved. To get a sense of the devastation the war inflicted on Paraguay, the 25–30 million deaths the Soviet Union suffered in World War II represented roughly 14 percent of the Russian population, proportionately less than a quarter of the losses imposed on Paraguay. Relative to the size of the countries involved, López's war was the most devastating international war of the past three centuries anywhere on earth. In every other war since the signing of the Treaties of Westphalia in 1648, when a war's impending outcome was undeniable, the losing side has sought a settlement or surrendered unconditionally – every losing side except Paraguay.

Many factors explain both the war's path and its consequences, including politics among the Triple Alliance members, the state of Paraguay's economy, and European colonial influence. Ultimately, however, the story of the war is the story of López. What is interesting is not only that López initiated a war against multiple, ultimately far stronger, adversaries, each of whom tried to counsel him against it; many leaders in history have overestimated their country's capabilities or underestimated the power and resolve of their opponents. What defies conventional explanation is that, in the face of certain defeat with a shattered army, López had the opportunity to end the war several times on relatively generous terms and each time chose to continue fighting. Five years into the war with López's military and country in ruins, following a round of clear Brazilian victories, the Brazilian leader Conde d'Eu proposed settlement terms to López. A memoir written by one of López's closest lieutenants describes López's response: [5]

On 23 December of that year (1869), the Marquis de Caxias, with their allies sent a note to the Marshal López, president of Paraguay, in his headquarters in Ytá-Ibaté, requiring the deposition of the weapons of the Republic within 12 hours, thus avoiding useless shedding of more blood, and to take responsibility for this, in case of a refusal to surrender. López answered the summons, "This is the response of a free and independent nation to the enemies of Paraguay. What is the aim of the Triple Alliance with this demand of surrender? Perhaps they are actors in a just war of self-defense of

[3] Whigham 2002.   [4] Whigham and Potthast 1999.   [5] Resquin 1875.

unquestionable right. Not a thousand times? The powers of the wicked Triple Alliance from the secret treaty of May 1, 1865, signed in Buenos Aires, have brought this unjust war of usurpation of the territories of Paraguay, and the extermination of their populations, because they never had claim to these territories, despite the questions of the Brazilian and Argentine governments."[6]

After each round of Paraguayan losses and proffered treaty rejections, the armies of the Triple Alliance advanced further into Paraguayan territory. The area of land under López's control shrank with each defeat. Still López refused to accept a settlement. The war finally ended at Cerro Corá, in an outpost in northern Paraguay, when the Brazilian army surrounded López and his remaining forces, which were reduced to just 200 soldiers from some sixty thousand at the war's outset. Defiant until the end, a captured López refused the settlement terms, rejecting Brazil's demand for surrender by saying, "Therefore I will die with my country!" At this point, the Brazilian army was more than pleased to remove the intransigent dictator. Brazilian soldiers shot and killed López on the spot. A postwar treaty consummated in 1876 carved up Paraguay among the victors. Brazil and Argentina allowed a substantial fraction of the devastated country to retain its independence in order to provide a buffer state between the continent's two great powers.

What radical thoughts drove López's behavior? Although we have few letters and no long-term diary, hints from his upbringing point early on toward extreme and messianic autocratic behavior. A young López served in Paraguay's military when his father ruled as dictator, but he never saw combat. When López was only eighteen years old, his father appointed him a general.[7] Historian James Saeger notes that despite López's limited experience and lack of formal military training, he sincerely believed his teenage military service had bestowed in him extraordinary "military genius."[8] This delusional self-image drove much of his strategic thinking. López also lacked much in terms of life experience and perspective, growing up in his father's shadow in a geographically and socially isolated Paraguay. A trip to Europe in the mid-1850s may have proved critical in the development of his worldview. According to a British citizen who traveled with him, the trip revealed to López the wonder of Europe's military "parade and glitter." Just as Europe's militarists bathed in "false glory and proud memories of wars and warriors," ultimately leading to decades of increasingly destructive wars that culminated in World War I, López returned from the continent with a keenly romantic sense of what it meant to go to war.[9]

Following his European excursion, López became preoccupied and obsessed with honor and prestige. Once in office, he set out to win a glorious military victory for Paraguay. George Thomson, another English citizen in Paraguay at the time of the war, directly connected López's personal ambitions for

[6] Ibid.   [7] López 1845.   [8] Saeger 2007, 11.   [9] Masterman 1870, 91.

Paraguay's future through the war, writing that "[he] had an idea that only by having a war could Paraguay become known."[10] In his pursuit of personal and national glory, López repeatedly doubled down at every opportunity. Rather than accepting the ignominy of defeat, he continued to pursue a sense of honor that dictated the course of the war and the utter destruction of his country and people. Our puzzle lies not so much in the explanation of López's behavior as an individual leader; rather, it is whether we must think of leaders such as López as historians do, as idiosyncratic individuals whose personal choices are as inexplicable as they are extreme. Alternatively, can we somehow fit someone like López into a broader pattern, using early life indicators to develop something of a profile by which extreme leaders, both those who seek violence and shun compromise as well as those who prefer to appease aggressors and shirk from violence, are identifiable before the fact?

It is easy to take the role of leaders for granted, seeing them constrained by circumstances, by the international and domestic political contexts in which they operate. Prussian Prime Minister Otto von Bismarck, as responsible as any leader for the rapid rise of Germany to great-power status in the late nineteenth century, once famously stated, "Man cannot create the current of events. He can only float with it and steer."[11] However, many examples seem to suggest otherwise, beginning with American foreign policy in the first few years after the September 11, 2001, terrorist attacks in New York and elsewhere. In 2000, the U.S. Supreme Court delivered an extremely close election victory to Republican candidate George W. Bush over Democratic candidate Al Gore.[12] While any American serving as president of the United States likely would have invaded Afghanistan, as George W. Bush did in 2001, the 2003 invasion of Iraq was a different story. Even conservative advocates such as William Kristol referred to the War in Iraq as one of choice. George W. Bush was the one person whose choice it was that ultimately led to war against Iraq in March 2003.[13] Had the U.S. Supreme Court ruled differently and demanded a complete recount of the disputed election returns, which would have placed Al Gore in the presidency rather than Bush, would a President Gore then have done the same? Many think that Gore would have allowed diplomacy with Iraq to play out longer and would have counted on maintenance or tightening of the economic sanctions regime then in place to deter Saddam Hussein.[14] In 2014, few would deny that Vladimir Putin's personal preferences had played a critical role in motivating Russian aggression against Ukraine, from the invasion of the Crimea to Russian support for Ukrainian separatists in Eastern Ukraine.

Going back further in history, while the secession of the Confederacy may have been inevitable, due to the pernicious institution of slavery and a handful of other factors, a devastating civil war was not. Abraham Lincoln's victory in

---

[10] Thompson 1869, 25.   [11] Lee 1988, 89.   [12] Bruni 2000.   [13] Kagan and Kristol 2004.
[14] There are some who disagree, arguing that the same factors that led Bush to support war against Iraq would have driven a President Gore to declare war as well. See Harvey 2011.

the hotly contested 1860 election over John Breckinridge triggered the South's move toward secession and Confederacy.[15] Lincoln's leadership of the Union in the war is now the stuff of legend, considered a definitive example of a particular leader's choices bending the arc of history. Lincoln suffered critics on both sides. Liberals bemoaned his draconian policy choices, such as the arrest of the Maryland legislature to bar their vote on secession. Conservative critics felt he dallied after dramatic early losses before pressing the war. Perhaps the turning point in the war, the Emancipation Proclamation, was controversial as well. Lincoln summed up the depth of criticism he faced in an interview when he observed, "If I were to try to read, much less answer, all the attacks made on me, this shop might as well be closed for want of any other business."[16] One need not stretch one's imagination to believe that were it not for Lincoln, the history of the United States and perhaps democracy worldwide would have been quite different.

Leaders affect national policies in several ways. One of the more obvious is through their decisions about war and peace. Leaders are responsible for calibrating national policy when it comes to a country's grand strategy as well as how to treat particular countries. Leaders are ultimately responsible for their nation's involvement in or avoidance of war. Following the failure of Britain's appeasement policies from 1938 to 1939, Neville Chamberlain resigned as British Prime Minster, acknowledging Leo Amery's and other Conservatives' critiques of the Chamberlain government's policies. Amery, in the House of Commons, notoriously quoted Oliver Cromwell in demanding that Chamberlain step down following the failure of the Norway campaign: "You have sat too long here for any good you have been doing. Depart, I say, and let us have done with you. In the name of God, go!"[17] A short time later, in May 1940, as France was falling to the Germans, it was Winston Churchill who outmaneuvered Halifax and the Liberals on the British War Committee and, by carrying the day, committed the British to a total war against the Germans rather than settling for what Churchill viewed as a humiliating bargain.[18]

Leadership of the Lincoln or Churchill type is not restricted to democratic states nor great victories, either. While there is an enormous literature describing the role that Germany's offensive military doctrine played in the escalation of the crisis leading to World War I,[19] Germany's military policy flowed from the top. Kaiser Wilhelm II authorized the rapid mobilization strategy that helped lead to the rapid escalation of the July 1914 crisis. The Kaiser also made the final decision to mobilize the German army in the days following the assassination of the Archduke Ferdinand.[20] Kaiser Wilhelm II fits the profile of a leader predisposed to aggression, with a background that included military service – but not combat experience; it taught him to trust his expertise and

---

[15] McPherson 2003.   [16] Quoted in Burlingame 1987, 193.   [17] Louis 1992.
[18] Lukas 1991.   [19] Van Evera 1984.   [20] Mommsen 1990.

instincts as a military grand strategist but did not give him experience in the horrific downsides of war.[21] Along with childhood experiences that predisposed him toward risk-taking and insecurity fueled by resentment of his peers,[22] Kaiser Wilhelm II illustrates well one of the kinds of leaders most likely to initiate and escalate international conflict.

Leaders also make critical decisions such as whether to pursue key military technologies that carry long-term security implications. For example, chief executives' policy preferences play an outsized role in the decision to start or terminate a state's nuclear weapons program. Prior experiences in rebel and revolutionary movements make leaders more likely to pursue nuclear weapons than one might expect.[23] Leaders with prior rebel experience are acutely aware of how tenuous their hold on government is and even of the contingency of national sovereignty. This has made leaders from Charles de Gaulle to David Ben-Gurion to Fidel Castro to Saddam Hussein more likely to favor acquiring nuclear weapons. In each case, these leaders saw in nuclear weapons a technological fix they believed could secure their countries from invasion.[24]

China's pursuit of nuclear weapons under Mao Zedong provides a clear example of the link between success as a rebel leader and nuclear proliferation. One of Mao's top priorities when he entered office was avoiding the humiliation at the hands of outsiders that had plagued China since the nineteenth century. Mao, recognizing China's weakness compared with the United States and the Soviet Union in the 1950s and 1960s, did not want China again to fall hostage to the politics of the other great powers.[25] His prior experiences as a rebel, leading the Chinese Communists to victory against the nationalists and the Kuomintang in the Chinese Civil War, shaped his perspective on accomplishing his goal.[26] Without nuclear weapons, Mao worried that China would have to "kneel and obey orders meekly, as if they were nuclear slaves"[27] and that, since China did not have nuclear weapons, "others don't think what we say carries weight."[28] Independently of China's security concerns, which stemmed from the war against the United States in Korea and other crises in the region, especially over Taiwan, his prior experiences predisposed Mao to seek nuclear weapons.

Political executives also have responsibility for indirect influence over lower-level policies as well. Leaders typically select or approve the appointment of

[21] Lebow 1981.   [22] Ibid.   [23] Fuhrmann and Horowitz 2015.
[24] For more on nuclear proliferation, see Sagan and Waltz 1995; Singh and Way 2004; Gartzke and Jo 2005.
[25] Kennedy 2011, 119–22. See also Miller 2013a; Miller 2013b.
[26] This overall story is drawn in large part from Fuhrmann and Horowitz 2015. For more on Mao's rebel experience and how it shaped his worldview, see Schwartz 1951; Rice 1972; Goldstein 2005.
[27] Krepon 2009, 101.   [28] Lewis and Xue 1988, 36.

Harry Truman at the White House.
Source: Harry S. Truman Library and Museum.

their cabinet officials and other key officials. Decisions made by those officials trace back to the leader.[29] U.S. President Harry S. Truman explicitly recognized this by placing a sign on his desk in the oval office plainly stating, "The buck stops here."

While leaders bear direct responsibility for the policy choices they make, domestic political institutions also constrain the head of state when in office. Franklin Roosevelt in 1940 faced greater constraints in pursuing his preferred domestic policy of conscription and increasing the size of the U.S. Army than Hitler had in the early 1930s. Different types of political systems have more or fewer bureaucratic obstacles or veto points that prevent a leader from simply enacting his or her will. There are limits to the autonomy of any leader. Even the most authoritarian leaders, such as the Soviet Union's totalitarian leader Joseph Stalin or Iraq's Baathist President Saddam Hussein, are responsible to a selectorate, a group of people whose support is critical for the leader to remain in power. [30] If a leader strays too far from the policy preferences of

[29] In the United States, cabinet officials are appointed by the President and must be approved by Congress. While Congress sometimes blocks nominees (and with increasing frequency), the President generally has discretion on these selections.
[30] Tsebelis 1995.

the selectorate, the selectorate may rebel and try to remove the leader from office through a coup or other means.[31] During World War II, as the fighting on the Eastern front devolved into a horrifying war of attrition that Germany was bound to lose, Hitler's own officers made multiple assassination attempts. In Egypt in 2012, Hosni Mubarak lost the support of his military and stepped down in the face of rising antigovernment sentiment.[32]

WHY STUDY LEADER EXPERIENCES?

While common sense tells us that leaders play a crucial role in setting their state's course, sorting out in a systematic manner what explains how leaders will behave is more difficult. New research in behavioral psychology, however, suggests that individuals' early experiences profoundly shape their choices later in their lives.[33] This is consistent with thinking about leaders in the context of political campaigns. In the United States, for example, in every election cycle, the background experiences of American presidential candidates provide fertile ground for debate among the media, public, and the politicians themselves. Politicians point to their own past experiences as evidence of special competence and indicators of the policies they are likely to adopt once in office. In turn, the media picks through the backgrounds of candidates with a fine-toothed comb, searching for prior experiences that will shed light on the quality of decisions a candidate might make in office. In the 2008 election cycle in the United States, news sources focused on the church that then-candidate Barack Obama had attended, the pastor's sermons, and what they might mean for Obama's social policies once in office. Much was made of Obama's parents' divorce and the fact that he had been raised by a single mother. His foreign travels as a young man convinced some observers that he would have some special competence in foreign policy if elected. In comparison, some commentators focused on Obama's lack of military service and highlighted Senator John McCain's record as a Navy aviation veteran and prisoner-of-war survivor and wondered whether that suggested Obama was too weak, too inexperienced, or both for the job of being Commander-in-Chief.[34] In 2012, when Mitt Romney represented the Republican Party in the American presidential election, both his campaign and his supporters focused on his business background as an indicator of great managerial competence. Some detractors focused on his Mormon faith, claiming his adherence to a religion out of the mainstream made him suspect.

Four years before President Obama's first victory, the backgrounds of the candidates featured prominently in the campaign. The sitting President, George W. Bush, had served in the Texas Air National Guard but never in

---

[31] Bueno de Mesquita et al. 2003; Chiozza and Goemans 2011.   [32] Kirkpatrick 2011.
[33] Kolb 1984; Roberts et al. 2003; Xue et al. 2010; Wood et al. 2013.   [34] Press 2008.

a combat role.[35] His opponent, John Kerry, was a decorated combat veteran who had served in the Vietnam War. In a series of interviews, speeches, and columns, Kerry and his handlers explicitly suggested that his combat experience in Vietnam provided him with experiences that would make him a more effective wartime president than George W. Bush. During his speech in Boston accepting the Democratic Party's nomination to be their presidential candidate, Kerry even stated, "As President, I will wage this war with the lessons I learned in war."[36]

Moreover, the relevance of leader backgrounds is not simply limited to evaluating leaders during political campaigns. For example, after the September 11 attacks, as the U.S. government began considering its short- and long-term response strategy, according to one account, President George W. Bush's background came to the fore. In an interview with the television network CNN ten years later, the pilot of Air Force One that day, Colonel Mark Tillman, stated that George W. Bush's military background drove his reaction to the 9/11 attacks. Tillman said, "I saw a leader in action. In my mind, a military man. He had been trained in the military as well. He was able to make a lot of decisions . . . He was executing as a military man would do and make decisions right on the fly."[37] Bush's checkered past, including his limited military experience, had been an issue on the campaign trail during the 2000 presidential campaign.[38] Yet even that limited military experience, according to Colonel Tillman, shaped the way that Bush responded.

While several of these examples come from the United States, this is not a uniquely American phenomenon, nor is it one restricted to democratic states. Xi Jinping, General Secretary of the Chinese Communist Party, did not serve in the Red Army but received graduate education in engineering. Commentators in the Chinese press focused on his background as an engineer and what it might suggest about his viewpoint on China's economic and political trajectory.[39] When he visited the United States in 2011, members of the American media wondered how his trip to Iowa as a younger man had shaped his view of the United States and what that could mean for United States–China relations.[40]

The cover of this book highlights another leader whose early experiences shaped his later behaviour: Winston Churchill. A young Churchill attended Sandhurst Military Academy, fought in the Battle of Omdurman, went abroad as a war correspondent, and was first elected to Parliament in 1900. He described these experiences as critical to his worldview, stating, "I felt as if I were walking with Destiny, and that all my past life had been but a preparation for this hour and for this trial."[41] His experience promoting air power in World War I also shaped his perspective when he became a leader, encouraging his strong advocacy of air bombing by the British in World War II.[42]

[35] Rimer 2004.   [36] Kerry 2004.   [37] Crowley 2011.   [38] Kristof 2000.
[39] *Economist* 2010.   [40] Johnson 2012.   [41] Churchill 1948, 601.   [42] Overy 1995, 267.

In 2003, commentators discussing French opposition to the American-led invasion of Iraq argued that French President Jacques Chirac's military service in Algeria powerfully influenced the way he estimated and weighed the costs and benefits of armed conflict. Chirac himself even stated that his experiences in Algeria made him especially aware of the risks involved in a conflict such as the Iraq war.[43]

Background experiences matter in part because they form a mental Rolodex that both citizens and leaders turn to when making strategic decisions in the future.[44] Behavioral psychologists have long noted that humans tend to reason by analogy. When confronted with a difficult decision, we tend to look for a case or set of circumstances in the past that appears to be similar to the situation at hand and that might provide guidance for the current situation. Personal experiences provide particularly powerful "lessons of history." Compared with many domestic policy choices, international institutions provide relatively weak constraints compared with the rules and legal frameworks that shape executives' decisions regarding domestic policy. Moreover, leaders tend to face greater uncertainty and more incomplete information when coming to foreign-policy decisions compared with domestic ones, making heuristics based on past events particularly important. Background experiences represent a pool of lessons learned, shaping a leader's judgment about which strategies are more or less likely to succeed or fail. This means background experiences could shape leader personalities in ways that influence whether they attempt to act as transformational or transactional leaders.[45]

This is especially true for more poignant and intense experiences, and leaders are more likely to rely on them again later in life.[46] Both cognitive and behavioral psychologists note that intense or traumatic events, particularly early in life, shape adults' personalities and individual attitudes toward risk and rewards. On average, people who successfully pursue actions that the public would view as highly risky are more likely to try them again. It is not just that some people are inclined, for example, to think that bungee jumping is a great idea while others think it is extremely dangerous.[47] It is also that those who go bungee jumping or sky diving are more likely to think that those sorts of activities are worthwhile and that they are good at them. Similarly, those who participate in and survive a revolutionary war, such as Mao Zedong or David Ben-Gurion, are likely to emerge with beliefs that violence can solve political dilemmas. Those on the losing side of such wars often conclude the opposite. Background experiences, therefore, provide crucial markers to help predict which leaders are more likely to engage in risk-taking behavior on the international scene and which are not. But how do we sustain this claim?

---

[43] Starobin 2003.   [44] Khong 1992; Goldgeier 1994; Kennedy 2011.   [45] Nye 2013.
[46] Jervis 1988; Goldgeier 1994, 2; Simonin 1999; Wood et al. 2013.
[47] Gardner and Steinberg 2005; Cutchin et al. 2008.

WOMEN !

DEMONSTRATING THAT LEADER EXPERIENCES MATTER

While journalists and psychologists have long worked to connect leaders' background experiences to their professional behavior once in office, political scientists have been loath to do so. In part, this reflects their focus on modeling the systematic rather than the idiosyncratic factors influencing executive behavior. They would view Francisco Solano López as an intriguing, albeit destructive, individual outlier, one of numerous idiosyncratic cases. Political scientists view leaders, both those like López who are outliers as well as other, more prudential individuals, as factors we can safely ignore in our more systematic studies of world politics.[48] The nineteenth-century historian Thomas Carlyle wrote that "the history of the world is but the biography of great men."[49] He notably sidestepped the question of whether we might be able to say anything systematic about world politics by drawing on the biographies of all great men. We aim to turn this perspective on its head just a bit and, in so doing, recast the analytic presumptions that have guided political scientists for the past sixty years. If Carlyle is correct, then understanding international politics, and especially decisions regarding war and peace, requires an in-depth grasp of leaders. Who are they? What motivates their decisions? Do they really matter in systematic ways, or should people conclude as they have for the recent past that their role, however important, is idiosyncratic, restricted to the particulars of any event or set of events?

The claims of mainstream political scientists notwithstanding, leaders do matter in systematic ways that we can understand and make great use of. Leaders play a critical role in shaping international politics. Moreover, examining their early life experiences provides insight that enables us to predict their behavior in office, especially when it comes to starting military conflicts.[50] Each of us can probably think of examples of how our own upbringing and life experiences shape the course of our daily lives. Leaders are no different. Building on evidence from developmental psychology that demonstrates how prior life experiences affect how people behave later in life, this book shows that the formative experiences of political leaders influence everything from the way they evaluate the costs and benefits of using force to the types of military grand strategies they view as most likely to be successful.

When Kenneth Waltz laid out his three-image model of international relations, he suggested that first-image explanations, those focused on leaders,

---

[48] Schweller (2006) and Weisiger (2013) both describe Paraguay as a rationalist state with revisionist aims attempting to expand. It is López's continuation of the war, despite repeated offers to settle, and with ample evidence available to him that the war was going poorly, that especially suggests something uniquely important about López, as opposed to what any other leader of Paraguay would have done at the time.

[49] Carlyle 1935.

[50] Military conflicts in this context refer to interstate military conflicts. Intrastate conflicts are a promising topic for future research.

would prove too complex to lend themselves to the analytic instruments available to him and other political scientists. Unconvinced by Waltz's claim, we approach the question from multiple perspectives. To model how leaders shape international relations, we compiled a new dataset, the Leader Experience and Attribute Descriptions (LEAD) dataset, built specifically for this purpose. It contains information on the background experience of more than 2,400 leaders around the world from 1875 to 2004, from their upbringing to military service to education to age. Comparing the relative explanatory power of our first-image explanations (those focusing on leaders) with the second- and third-image ones (domestic politics and international system structure, respectively) the LEAD dataset enables us to create a Leader Risk Index that evaluates, solely on the basis of the background experiences of the leaders, the probability that a leader will engage in interstate military conflicts while in office. National leadership matters and leaders' choices vary in systematically predictable ways. A country's choice of leader will influence the militarized behavior of that country as substantially and as predictably as do its domestic political institutions and its relative military and economic power.

It is also important to recognize at the outset that the policy choices that our models predict are not destiny. Not every leader with a particular set of experiences will make the policy choices we predict. Nevertheless, the patterns we outline here and detail in Chapter 1 are consistent and substantial; they provide significant predictive leverage that exceeds the explanatory power of the most important traditional indicators of conflict and war, including the balance of power and institutionalized democracy.[51] While not every leader fits our model, including early life experiences in predictive models of international politics greatly enhances our ability to forecast and anticipate which countries will pose a danger to their neighbors and which are far less likely to do so. Some of the leader experiences we investigate increase the risk of war between states; others decrease the risk. We look closely at the factors that can dramatically reduce a leader's willingness to opt for war even in settings where most other leaders would choose to fight.

In the following chapters, we explore some of the implications of this statistical analysis by focusing on the biographies of particular leaders and detailing the particular background experiences that seem most important for understanding their choices and behaviors. We also focus on the historical context in which leaders serve. While some leaders serve during very dangerous periods in international politics, others face relatively benign security environments. By studying leaders from Herbert Hoover to Nikita Khrushchev, we show the way that leader attributes shape the behavior of countries both when

---

[51] Other than the immutable fact of geographic contiguity, states that neighbor one another are vastly more likely to go to war with one another than states separated by either water or other states (Diehl 1985).

the international security environment makes military action by a country more likely and when it does not.

We then move from looking at the totality of leaders' life experiences to focusing on those key experiences that matter across the universe of leaders. One of the most important is military service. Scholars from Samuel Huntington to Eliot Cohen have detailed how military experience influences the way people behave.[52] Leaders with prior military service are naturally more familiar with contemplating the use of force. Once in office, they are more likely to have perceived expertise and have greater influence with their country's military, even in a democracy.

The results show that military experience does matter, but not in the way that many may expect. Our research demonstrates that leaders with prior military service but no combat experience are among the most likely to initiate and escalate military conflict. Peacetime or rear-area military service absent experience in combat socializes participants to be more comfortable with the use of military force later in life. Combat experience can thus, at times, significantly dampens leaders' subsequent militaristic tendencies.

This relationship, though, depends to some extent on domestic political conditions, as well as the particularities of the individual. In authoritarian states, the relationship is different, reflecting the different demands that the selection process in autocracies presents compared with democratic systems. As Chapter 1 explains in greater depth, rising to power in an autocracy requires engaging in intensely risk-seeking behavior. Rising to power can require starting, leading, or participating in coups or rebellions. In autocratic states, those potential leaders who react to military service and especially combat experience by becoming more aggressive are more likely to rise to become chief executives later in life.

Prior military experience is but one of several observable factors that shape leaders' attitudes toward the use of military force. A leader's age while in office strongly affects the likelihood that the state will attack a neighbor.[53] While one might expect younger leaders, with associated higher levels of testosterone,[54] to be more prone to militarized behavior, in fact it is the opposite in most states, including democracies. On average, in most states, it is the older leaders who are more likely to start military conflicts. The reason has to do with the shorter time horizons and greater institutional experience of these leaders. Older leaders who want to leave a legacy have relatively fewer opportunities and so must act if they are to lead their country through a fight.[55] At the same time, older leaders in democracies are more likely to have experiences in other areas of government that provide them with the personal connections and consolidated

---

[52] Huntington 1957; Kim-Cohen et al. 2004.   [53] Horowitz et al. 2005.
[54] Mazur and Booth 1998.
[55] U.S. presidents from Theodore Roosevelt to Bill Clinton have noted that leading the country into war is necessary to be seen as a "great" president.

authority needed to overcome the institutional checks and balances that are the hallmark of democratic systems.

The general relationship between leader age and military conflict disappears in extremely autocratic regimes in which leaders such as Stalin, Mao, and Saddam Hussein exercised nearly complete control. In those regimes where building a stable power base over time is less important for the use of power by a leader, younger leaders who are willing and able to use violence during their ascent to power and who are also highly likely to use violence as a tool of state power once in office are also very likely to use force.

Similarly, as is often the case for those outside politics, those with troubled childhoods are more likely to have riskier profiles later in life.[56] Leaders who grew up in unstable households or who experienced war in their countries as a child, all other things being equal, are more likely to discount the benefits of the future and accept higher degrees of risk in the policies they favor. This makes them more likely, on average, to support risky military endeavors when they are in office.

Finally, we evaluate one facet of the relationship between gender and international conflict. We provide an in-depth assessment of several female heads of state, including Margaret Thatcher of the United Kingdom and Kim Campbell of Canada, showing how their backgrounds shaped their behavior in office. With two important caveats, the results show no significant differences in the behavior of male and female leaders in office when it comes to the use of military force. First, the extremely small number of female heads of state up to this point makes it very difficult to generalize about the effects of gender. As more female heads of state emerge over the next few decades, it will be possible to say more. Second, of the leaders who have served thus far, while the average woman has a risk profile similar to that of the average male, there has not yet been a female "outlier," a female leader so aggressive, like Hitler or Stalin, that she deviates significantly from the norm.

THE NEED FOR LEAD

International relations theory is not static; it evolves in response to real-world events, the availability of improved technology, and the ideas of new scholars. It has also been cyclical, with scholarly interest and support for certain perspectives on world politics going out of favor only to be rediscovered later. As theoretical developments in recent decades have focused on the importance of institutional and structural constraints, the study of individual agency has largely been ignored by mainstream international relations theorists. However, this has not always been the case.

Early international relations scholars, motivated by a desire to understand the causes of World War I, drew insights from military and diplomatic history

---

[56] Mersky et al. 2012.

as well as from international law and trade.[57] In the interwar period, the scholarly debate between realists and those arguing for financial interdependence focused on the level of the state and the power relations between pairs or small numbers of alliances.[58] With the outbreak of World War II, theorists recognized that the undoing of the European peace was due in large part to the exploitation of the peaceful preferences of many European leaders by individual leaders such as Hitler, Mussolini, and Tojo, as well as the temporary setback in interdependence caused by the Great Depression. Recognizing the role Churchill, Hitler, Roosevelt, and Stalin played in leading their countries, international relations theorists, writing from a diplomatic history perspective immediately after World War II, understood that leaders mattered.

In his canonical text on international relations *Politics Among Nations*, published shortly after the close of World War II, Hans Morgenthau laid out, with a focus on the importance of political leaders as both sources and manipulators of power, a theory of politics that is both reductionist but also extraordinarily nuanced. His theory of the balance of power was reductionist in that he argued persuasively that the relative balance of power between nations was the determinative factor guiding their relations. At the same time, his notion of power was far more nuanced than that of contemporary writers of today who focus almost entirely on readily measurable material attributes such as gross national product (GNP), iron and steel production, technology, and military manpower. Morgenthau noted that all these factors form the potential power with which leaders work. He argued strenuously that the caliber and nature of a state's leadership could make or break their future.

Much of the debate during the late 1940s and early 1950s focused on leaders and their personal attributes. Kissinger paid careful attention in his book *A World Restored* to the personal character of Lord Castlereagh and Prince Metternich, as reflected in their own letters and first-hand observations. Kissinger did not argue that Castlereagh and Metternich were solely responsible for the peace that resulted from the Congress of Vienna. Instead, he included personal information to illustrate how they were uniquely prepared to handle the gravity of the exogenous forces that created the difficult situation in which they found themselves.[59] Writings of the period embraced a nuanced weighing of numerous explanatory factors, even by some of the fathers of classical realism such as Morgenthau and John Herz.[60] During this period, prior to the advent of nuclear weapons, a nation-state could face a threat to its existence, but theorists and leaders alike did not need to consider potential threats to the existence of the entire system of states. Ivy Mike, the first functional fusion bomb,[61] changed both the nature of politics and the nature of international relations theory and scholarship.

---

[57] Wright 1955.   [58] Angell 1914; Carr 1946.   [59] Kissinger 1957.
[60] Morgenthau 1948; Herz 1951.   [61] Rhodes 1996.

History drove innovation, and scholarship grounded in diplomacy, military history, and political economy was largely swept aside by the nuclear revolution. Two factors converged in the postwar period. The invention of the fusion-based bombs – weapons three orders of magnitude more powerful than those that had destroyed Hiroshima and Nagasaki – shifted mainstream scholars away from a focus on the national interest and a state's ability to survive toward the possibility of global thermonuclear war, an event that would in all likelihood destroy the international system as they understood it. The need for theory development in light of the technological advances of nuclear weapons seemed to make the study of leaders irrelevant. In a world of massive retaliation, where a single warhead could eliminate an entire city and its population, great-power war was assumed to be obsolete, and individual leaders did not matter. In a world where power and war outcomes were binary, nuanced discussions about the nature of power and leadership were now also obsolete.

The second and not entirely coincidental feature emerging at the same time was the scientific revolution in the social sciences on both the theory building side and the analytics or evaluation side. Immediately before and during World War II, great advances occurred in game theory, computing, and econometrics. In turn, these three extraordinary intellectual innovations led to a call for the study of politics to become more scientific. John Von Neumann and others demonstrated that game theory could provide great insights into both states' behaviors in war and firms' and investors' behaviors in markets. A challenge for the game theorists arose from the problem of infinite regress, the problem of "I know that you know, that I know, that you know …" and so forth. To limit their worlds to a plausible number of reasonable equilibria, game theorists made powerful assumptions about the nature of choice and preferences and how they aggregate into stable equilibria. In doing so, they largely assumed away nuanced characterizations of decisionmakers' desires and differences, although doing so provided great payoffs for several decades.

On the computing side, again an area where Von Neumann made seminal contributions, the computer held out the prospect of doing econometric analytics in minutes or hours when previous calculations by hand might have required days or weeks. The prospect of being able to analyze political scenarios with data in the same manner in which economists modeled the economy and markets proved an irresistible combination to many political scientists, launching what is now known as the behavioral revolution. As with game theory, however, powerful simplifying assumptions were needed to be able to translate the world of politics into the models and tools of economics and econometrics. The subtle descriptions of history gave way to the crude measures of GNP and numbers of warheads. Beginning in the 1960s, the call for a more scientific approach, combined with the collective focus on system survival versus the pursuit of the national interest, led to a dramatic shift in focus from Morgenthau's highly nuanced notion of power to a binary one in which states either possessed the weapons or did not. The security literature moved away from what most of us think of intuitively as politics toward more technical discussions about missile gaps and throw-weights for those focused on security studies and to theories of functionalism and decolonization for others interested in comparative politics. In both cases, the evolving structure of the system, either in terms of material power as defined by nuclear weapons or, more ideationally, as defined by the collapse of colonialism and the puzzle of economic and political development, augured to discount the role of leaders and to empower that of the social scientist and technocrat. This intellectual revolution reached a logical endpoint when James Rosenau in 1971 famously characterized states as billiard balls in a powerful and influential book, *The Scientific Study of Foreign Policy*.[62]

In the late 1960s, the great-power confrontations in Korea, Vietnam, and elsewhere led policymakers to the conclusion that wars could be fought that would not necessarily escalate out of control and that massive retaliation and nuclear weapons would not stop limited wars from occurring.[63] With a focus on crisis decision making, leadership became important again, especially in the area of U.S. foreign policy.[64] As important as these early works were, however, they were primarily in-depth case studies and suffered from a lack of cross-national comparative data. This made the work peripheral to the expansion of large-scale data collection efforts on war and conflict that began around the same time.[65] As the "scientific" paradigm expanded, political realists, following Waltz's argument in *Man, the State, and War*, focused on increasingly stripped-down notions of the balance of power, especially its material basis. Critics of the realist approach turned to focus on international institutions and ideologically driven belief systems. Others turned away from positivism. In particular, those working in England and Northern Europe turned toward normative theory or more historically oriented work. Western European scholars began their multigenerational turn toward postmodern notions that evolved eventually into studies focused on socially determined identities and status competition.

Kenneth Waltz's *Theory of International Politics*,[66] published in 1979, became the most influential work of modern international relations, at least for political scientists in America. This single book shaped the way an entire generation of scholars as well as their critics viewed the puzzle of international relations. Waltz argued that the international system's structure, and its structure alone, was the feature of the entire system of world politics that was most worthy of study. Those convinced by Waltz took up the sword and spread the word. His critics focused on proving him wrong. Largely ignoring these debates, the game theorists and econometricians built increasingly baroque

---

[62] Rosenau 1971.   [63] Kissinger 1958.   [64] Hermann 1974; Etheredge 1978.
[65] Kadera and Zinnes 2010.   [66] Waltz 1979.

models of strategic interaction. The game theorists began focusing much of their efforts on the problem of limited information. Applied econometricians continued to search for increasingly sophisticated tools to address the inherent problems associated with analyzing observational versus experimentally generated data. For those most interested in studying the empirical implications of realism or other power-based explanations, there was no space for sophisticated discussion of leaders. In academia, leadership studies became something of an intellectual backwater, a research area that serious students and scholars would be counseled to avoid.

On the empirical side, the application of ever more sophisticated statistical models to the data collected during the 1960s and 1970s further marginalized the work of early studies on leadership.[67] This period did lead to important developments, such as more nuanced understanding of the security dilemma, insights incorporated into game theory as well as realism, and most important from an analytic view, the democratic peace literature.[68] Beginning with a series of papers first by J. David Singer, then Michael Doyle, and finally Bruce Russett, this literature was inductive and data-driven and descriptively emphasized the importance of institutional constraints. Scholars working at the level of individuals, lacking the same large-scale datasets, were again left behind.

By the 1990s, debates about the material balance of power, system structure, and domestic and international institutions dominated the intellectual discussion and analysis of international politics. Around the same time, scholars such as Robert Powell, Bruce Bueno de Mesquita, and James Fearon developed formal, rational choice models of the less formal arguments developed during the previous two decades. By bringing structure and rigor to the existing debates, rational choice theorists began to inhabit an increasingly important place in theorizing about international relations.[69] As noted, however, such models also had little if any room for individual agency, instead treating any actor – from heads of state to average citizens – as having essentially undifferentiated utilities and making decisions in pursuit of maximizing goals.[70] By the end of the millennium, leaders and their leadership roles were largely absent from serious scholarship focused on international relations.

We aim to show that this evolutionary process, which largely focused on system structure and institutions, drove out one of the most important determinative factors shaping international relations, regional politics, and the international system: political leaders. The analyses we present in the rest of this book bring international relations scholarship full circle to the close of World War II. From this perspective, power matters as it always has; governance, both international as well as domestic, matters in ways more important

---

[67] Kadera and Zinnes 2010.   [68] See Russett 1988, among others.
[69] Bueno de Mesquita 1981; Riker 1990.   [70] Cox 1999.

and nuanced than people understood sixty years ago. Leaders do so as well, and most important, they matter in systematic and predictable ways.

Focusing on political leaders provides a lens into international politics that none of our contemporary approaches alone can provide. Institutionalists, focusing on either domestic or international institutions, have little to say about the course of war, the democratic peace literature notwithstanding. Classical realism, while recognizing the importance of leadership, discounts any systematic relationship between institutions, domestic or otherwise, and the onset or course of war. Realists also view quality leadership as an idiosyncratic aspect of human behavior rather than something we can measure and test systematically. Structural or neo-realism tells us little if anything about the course of any single war or conflict. By focusing on leaders, while also accounting for system structure and institutional constraints, we can see for the first time a more complete picture of international relations. We can step back, take off our blindfolds, and see the complete elephant for the first time rather than describing it bit by bit.

In particular, analysis of the LEAD data provides a way to incorporate leaders into existing models of international behavior while maintaining a connection to real-world decision makers who drive global politics. This development comes at a particularly important time, as, to many practical observers, it seems that modern, international relations theory has sometimes lost touch with reality. The need for scholars to develop parsimonious and tractable models has moved the field away from the concrete world of diplomatic history and into the abstractions of math and statistics.[71] States do not trust or distrust each other; people do. Democratic institutions and ballot boxes do not fight wars; people do. With the development of evidence-based models of human psychology, we have an even greater understanding of what interpersonal relations actually mean and how to model them so that we can compare their explanatory power to the factors on which mainstream scholars myopically focus.

While we reintroduce leadership and individual leaders with their personal characteristics, strengths, and foibles as important components of the international system, we are not advocating a return to the days of psychobiography and the psychological personality studies of the 1950s and 1960s.[72] Instead, we study individual leaders just as systematically as scholars examine other components of the international system, such as state-level variables of GDP, regime type, prior conflicts, border length, and the other variables that comprise the current, positivist conflict agenda. The data we have collected allow us to do this for the first time. In combination with the in-depth biographical research

---

[71] Authors such as Whang (2010, 7), to take one example, take great pains to convince readers that particular equations indicate a time when some country somewhere will decide to fight back when they are challenged for some reason by some other country.

[72] See, for example, George and George 1964.

completed for this book, the evidence presented encompasses both systematic statistical analysis and case studies of individual leaders. This gives us more confidence in the results presented in the following chapters than we could have based on any single methodology.

ANTICIPATING OBJECTIONS

We make this extraordinary claim: Ignoring states' leaders, as the past sixty years of political science scholarship has mostly done, for the most part, ignores one of the most important features of international politics. Our critics will claim this to be an act of hubris, that attempting to bring the psychological background of political executives into a systematic scholarly discussion is folly. The inclusion of leaders and the experiences and backgrounds that account for the variation within their ranks has been criticized on several grounds. The LEAD dataset provides an important first step for addressing some of these concerns. By including world leaders from all countries during the period 1875–2004, we are attempting to remove as much potential selection bias from the underlying data as possible.[73] While the underlying historical records used in the dataset and the profiles here are certainly far from complete, the LEAD dataset brings individual-level variables into the same empirical focus as other widely accepted international relations approaches that focus on state power and political institutions.

The structure of the LEAD dataset gives us insight into the mechanisms underlying the state behavior we observe. In political science, there is a rich, largely descriptive literature on U.S. presidents, including statistical analyses comparing the presidents with one another. This comes largely from both the greater interest of American political scientists and significantly greater data availability. The Presidential Library system provides a rich and readily accessible source of primary data, which are being mined by scholars for new insights about the lives, thoughts, and insights of U.S. presidents. Notably, much of the work in this book on several of the leaders emerged from long hours spent in archives and presidential libraries in the United States, South America, and Europe.

A U.S. president does not operate in a vacuum, but instead is one of many players in the constantly changing makeup of the global system. In-depth study of U.S. presidents, or the leaders of any single country, gives only a partial view of their personalities and decision-making processes. For example, any study of John F. Kennedy would be incomplete without a discussion of his relationship

---

[73] Instead of deciding selectively who to include, we let the data speak for itself (Ludwig 2002; Keller 2005). The predominance of males in the dataset reflects the lack, until very recently, of female leaders. The greater number of country-years from Europe reflects the historical fact that European countries were independent for longer than most New World nations. See also Quirk 2010.

with Nikita Khrushchev. We cannot fully understand Ronald Reagan's foreign policy without understanding Mikhail Gorbachev. By assessing several leaders in depth and gathering data on all leaders, we can compare individuals directly using sophisticated statistical methods.

Finally, the inclusion of psychological variables has been criticized because they cannot be quantified in the same way as other war-related variables, such as material power. LEAD provides a rich set of covariates that are, as much as possible, not subjective judgments. We ascertain a leader's prior military service, for example, from biographical information readily available to all researchers.[74] Reducing human experience to variables such as those in LEAD has its drawbacks, but it is also an important step toward developing more valid explanations of interstate behavior. As Parsons argues, "If we want 'psychological explanation' to designate a distinct kind of causal segment, it must refer to claims about how action departs from simple rationalist expectations for hard-wired reasons."[75] Because this is the first systematic time-series cross-sectional evaluation of leader background variables, however, we anticipate a number of criticisms about the meaning of these variables and the conclusions we draw. Here, we catalog a few of the most prominent and respond in brief.

Leaders Do Not Have Exclusive Control over Martial Decisions

Why study leaders at all? After all, they operate within complex domestic and international bureaucracies that constrain their personal desires. Moreover, all state institutions have carefully developed routines for selecting or screening against particular types of leaders. This is the core of the institutionalist argument, that political constraints are sufficiently powerful to render variations across individual leaders meaningless. In the extreme, this argument implies that the political structure of Germany in the 1930s was so powerful as to overcome the potential preferences of any leader who would come to power during that time. An understanding of Hitler's goals and preferences, according to this type of argument, is not necessary to understand the onset of World War II. Any leader whom the international or the German state system would have selected at the time would have taken the same actions when facing the same exogenous threats and limitations.

Yet no reasonable student of World War II, from high school seniors to distinguished historians, would claim that Hitler, as an individual human being with distinct personal characteristics, did not matter in the initiation and escalation of World War II. It is not the fault of earlier theorists for leaving out leaders, but our new theory and data removes the excuse. The role of individual leaders, nested within other institutional variables, needs to be taken

---

[74] Shirkey and Weisiger 2007.   [75] Parsons 2007, 138.

seriously. Even in constrained environments, such as democracies, the evidence indicates that leaders matter.

Background Experiences Are Not Determinative of Future Actions

As we know from the leaders profiled in the chapters that follow, not all orphans go on to become militaristic adults, and not all combat veterans from war become embittered advocates for peace or hawkish aggressors. However, the preponderance of our data shows that there are some correlations that deserve further study. We do not actually know what effect these experiences have on any given individual's psyche. The literature we reference and some of the cognitive studies now under way show promise for sorting out these questions. Consider, however, the role of military experience. The purpose of any modern military is, temporarily at least, to subsume soldiers' individual variation in order to achieve a violent goal that requires the coordinated participation of many people. The remarkable consistency across time and cultures, states and eras of military training – drill, order, discipline, and marksmanship – results in a very similar experience for varied individuals. This is what our data show again and again. Leaders who have seen combat are more cautious about military engagements than those who served but did not see combat.

We are not suggesting that individuals always trump their circumstances. The chapters that follow will give due weight to the importance of systemic and institutional factors that constrain leaders or enable certain kinds of behavior. Nonetheless, ignoring individual agency is similarly counterproductive. While international relations are about the relations between states, individual leaders, individual people, their decisions and policy choices are what most profoundly influence these relations. It is shortsighted to claim that any theory of international conflict is fully developed if it treats state leaders as automatons. We know that this is simply not true and that overlooking these leaders, their unique characteristics, and individual agency ignores important sources of explanatory power.

Leaders Don't Matter; They Just Reflect the Times They Are In

Skeptics of our overall argument might suggest that leaders simply reflect the times they are in, that they do not have an independent effect on national policy. Robert Jervis argued strongly that the American invasion of Iraq in 2003 would have occurred regardless of who was in office.[76] There are two variants of this claim. The first is that the backgrounds of leaders do not matter

---

[76] Jervis 2013.

at all, that leaders simply represent the interests of their parties and are subject to powerful constraints. In short, they are just responding to what is happening in the world. At the extreme, this argument seems implausible, because it suggests that it would not matter whether Nuri el Maliki or Al Gore led either Iraq or the United States in 2003.

The more sophisticated version of this objection is that leaders are selected on the basis of their background attributes.[77] When countries face the risk of war, they choose a leader with background experiences designed to handle the situation. There is some truth to this claim, and we lay out an approach that allows us to take this possibility into account. However, the naïve version of this argument simplifies things in ways that obscure the true importance of leaders.

Whether it is through an election (which can include several levels of screening with primary and general elections, along with party conventions, the need to raise vast sums of money, and the like), a violent fight for power in a revolution, a bloodless coup, or a backroom succession agreement in an autocracy, all leaders enter office through a screening process. A potential leader has no control over part of that screening process. For example, opposition party candidates do well when the domestic economy performs poorly. In the U.S. Congress, the party out of power almost always gains seats in the House of Representatives during off-year elections. The factors to which voters or other candidate screeners attend are rarely related to the willingness of leaders to start military conflicts. More commonly, potential leaders' competence or perceived ability to manage the state's economy lies at the heart of the matter. As Bill Clinton's campaign advisor James Carville famously wrote on a bulletin board during the 1992 presidential campaign, what matters is "[t]he economy, stupid."[78]

During periods in which the international system appears to be particularly dangerous, as was the case in Europe before World War I, many states will choose leaders who, the selectorate believes, will keep the country safe. These choices are typically not prospective either. Even then, it is seldom the dominant factor determining who becomes a leader. Leaders perceived as delivering strong economic growth and candidates who seem most credibly able to improve the domestic economy very often stand the best chance of entering office, especially in democracies.

In the 2012 U.S. presidential election, 60 percent of the public, according to a CNN exit poll, stated that the economy was the most important issue influencing their vote choice.[79] Even if the selectorate is aware that a leader might have particular background characteristics that make him or her more or less inclined to international military aggression, those characteristics are rarely the ones that actually drive the selection of that leader.

---

[77] For an interesting take on how selection processes are critical, see Mukunda 2012.
[78] Rosenthal 1992.   [79] Abdullah and Van Kanel 2012.

To the extent that background experiences influence how different types of governments select leaders, they do so in a few ways. First, the type of political "competition" necessary to become a leader will enable those with different sets of background experiences to rise to power. For example, in autocracies, leaders often come to power through coups or rebellions, which are inherently risky activities. Those with background experiences that make them more likely to employ violence are equally more likely to rise to the top in autocracies. Second, as not all people are affected in the same ways by the same early life experiences, different types of governments are more or less likely to select people whose experiences shape their preferences in particular ways. For example, democratic states do not tend to favor those who react to their experiences by becoming extreme risk-takers.

For years, international relations scholars have been arguing for the integration of multiple levels of analysis, in both theory and empirical analysis.[80] We now have an increasing scientific understanding of the psychological basis of human behavior and its links to human development. Like other traditional realist variables, such as material capabilities, the backgrounds of leaders are measurable. With the LEAD dataset, we can now account for the psychological predispositions of political executives. Arguing that leaders "matter" is nothing new for those who actually work in politics or who have engaged in international negotiations. Who sits across the negotiating table or who is making the decisions plays a huge role in determining what outcomes actually occur at the bargaining table. This is a new approach, however, for political science.

---

[80] Ray 2001; Rasler and Thompson 2010.

I

How Leaders Matter

INTRODUCTION

Explaining the importance of studying leaders in an international relations context requires returning to a topic briefly mentioned previously, the treatment of leaders in existing international relations research. Current scholarship generally understates the importance of leadership in determining countries' foreign policy goals and strategies.[1] While political scientists generally recognize that leaders can and do shape a state's foreign policy, they have also been deeply skeptical that there is anything systematic in the ways we can understand leaders' personal preferences in world politics. For the past sixty years, these scholars have focused on the ways in which political institutions and the distribution of power within the international system shape states' choices, and in so doing, they have largely ignored leaders. At the same time, the general trend among historians has been to focus less on political leaders and diplomatic history and more on social movements and previously underrepresented groups within societies. While the shift in academic focus away from leaders was originally a reaction to psychoanalytic arguments that lacked nuanced data, it has led many to ignore numerous studies of individual leaders' policy preferences and the psychological foundations of those beliefs.[2] The turn to social history has therefore come at a cost: an entire generation of academics and students has little appreciation of the ways – both idiosyncratic and systematic – leaders shape the world in which we live.

---

[1] Hermann 1980.
[2] Including but not limited to Hermann 1980, 2003, 2001; Barber 1992; Greenstein 1992; Post 2003; Dyson and Preston 2006; Bar-Joseph and McDermott 2008.

RESEARCH ON LEADERS WITHIN INTERNATIONAL RELATIONS: FALSE REVIVAL?

A renaissance in the study of leaders in political science, and especially international politics, seems under way. However, the growth in research on leaders that has occurred over the last several years has largely taken place in the confines of the dominant paradigms described previously. Nearly all current research on leaders and international conflict focuses on the ways domestic institutional arrangements shape and constrain the choices of leaders rather than demonstrating how variation in leaders' individual attributes affects state behavior.[3] According to much current scholarship, the person who resides in an office, whether Barack Obama, Joseph Stalin, or Neville Chamberlain, is largely irrelevant. What matters most are the institutional constraints influencing the probability that the leader will survive a given situation and the ways those odds shape the willingness of the leader to support or oppose particular policies.

The most widely cited current institutionalist theory of international relations, the selectorate model of decision making, argues that the primary goal of leaders is to survive in office.[4] Leaders are responsible to a selectorate or group of people who influence whether or not they can stay in office and, if removed from office, whether or not they will physically survive. The size of the selectorate differs by regime, with democracies generally having larger selectorates than autocracies. All leaders, even the most authoritarian, face a selectorate. Iraqi leader Saddam Hussein, who ran one of the most tightly controlled political regimes of the last half-century, relied on a small group of key individuals to stay in power. Hussein's family, especially his sons Uday and Qusay, the Iraqi Republican Guard, and Hussein's tribe in Tikrit represented an important constituency that even Hussein had to satisfy to stay in power.

Selectorate theory asserts that, from the perspective of the leader, the welfare of the country is a distant priority compared to staying in office and personal survival. There may be no relationship between a state's welfare and its leader's political and physical survival. It is in the interest of a leader to improve the general welfare of his or her country in some cases, but certainly not in all or even most cases. The best way to understand the decisions of leaders, according to the selectorate way of thinking, is to look at the effect of the policy options they face on their probability of staying in office, or surviving if they are removed from office.[5]

Autocratic leaders who win their wars or who do not suffer decisive defeat survive in office much longer, while those on the losing sides commonly find themselves out of office and, under certain circumstances, pay for defeat with their lives. Conversely, in openly competitive political systems, rarely if ever do

---

[3] For recent examples, see Chiozza and Goemans 2011; Croco 2011; Weeks 2012.
[4] Bueno de Mesquita et al. 2003.   [5] Chiozza and Goemans 2003.

former leaders face death for poor performance while in office. Debs and Goemans find that this helps explain which international crises become wars.[6] The concessions leaders are willing to make to avoid war depend on how fighting a war will influence the probability of their staying in power and the probability of survival if they are forced from office.

Given that autocrats face stronger punishments, including a higher probability of death when forced from office, they are reluctant to make concessions in crises. This, in turn, makes crises involving autocracies more likely to escalate to war than those involving democracies. The anticipation of this dynamic plays a critical role in leaders' decisions to initiate international disputes.[7] The leaders in this selectorate model are generic, almost interchangeable; every leader when faced with the same incentives makes the same decision. From this perspective, the interaction of states' institutional structures with the international balance of power produces the ebb and flow of international politics.[8] In each of these stories, the leaders matter in that they are responsible for the decisions that create the policies, but all leaders make the same choices when placed in similar situations. In all of these models, the leaders themselves are "dispensable" black boxes, to paraphrase Fred Greenstein.[9]

The scant existing research on leaders themselves, although useful, generally treats individual leaders in isolation, rather than examining the leader attributes that systematically shape foreign policy across space and time. Our enterprise, examining the formative experiences of leaders and how they shape leader's behavior when they take office, is a new and radical approach to the systematic study of international relations. Rather than assuming that leaders residing in the same institutional settings will behave similarly, we unpack a leader's risk-taking propensity by coding risk-inducing or -inhibiting formative experiences and evaluate how different leaders, although facing the same institutionally induced incentives, will behave differently.[10]

WHAT DOES IT MEAN TO SAY THAT A LEADER IS RISKY?

This book describes leaders who are more likely than others to start international conflicts as "risky," using the term "risk" in a common usage way.

---

[6] Debs and Goemans 2010.   [7] Chiozza and Choi 2003; Chiozza and Goemans 2004, 2011.
[8] Similarly, Sarah Croco (2011) finds that leaders' sense of personal responsibility influences whether they are willing to settle for an outcome short of a decisive victory or to go for broke during a conflict. In related work, Jessica Weeks (2012) demonstrates the way military regimes produce particularly risk-prone leaders.
[9] Greenstein 1969, 51–5.
[10] For an early discussion of the limitations of research on leaders and the potential promise of future research, see Byman and Pollack 2001. Also, see Abdelal et al. 2006; Saunders 2011. Exceptions exist in research focused on leader selection and the link between leaders and economic growth. See Jones and Olken 2005; Besley and Reynal-Querol 2011; Besley et al. 2011.

In the United States, based on the aggregation of all deaths associated with all motorcycle and automobile trips in a single year, riding a motorcycle increases one's risk of death in an accident thirty-five times, compared with driving an automobile over the same route.[11] Based on the willingness to accept the increased risk associated with riding a motorcycle, we then refer to these riders as more risky, or risk-acceptant, than automobile drivers. In much the same way, some political leaders are more risk-acceptant than others. When we characterize a leader as "risky," we mean that they have a greater propensity to use force than others do when placed in similar situations.

Importantly, this notion of risk distinguishes it from uncertainty. Uncertainty describes the unknown properties of a gamble; relative risk refers to the known odds of each outcome occurring. When the odds are unknown or unclear, we describe the outcome as uncertain. Risk is an objective characteristic of any crisis or war. Riskiness or risk acceptance is personal, describing the potential willingness of a leader to tolerate the risks associated with the outcomes of a decision. Just as some people are willing to accept the higher risk of death associated with riding a motorcycle, some leaders are willing to make choices likely to trigger the possibility of attack, thereby accepting the risk of removal from office or of international sanctions, while other leaders in the same situation are not.

Like risk, uncertainty is on a continuum and refers to our confidence in being able to forecast the odds of the outcomes associated with decisions. In our usage, leaders can then be risk-acceptant in two ways, either by accepting objective risks differently (like a well-informed motorcycle rider) or by being willing to act in the face of uncertainty when others are not. In a February 12, 2002, Department of Defense news briefing, Secretary of Defense Donald Rumsfeld famously stated:

Reports that say that something hasn't happened are always interesting to me, because as we know, there are known knowns; there are things we know we know. We also know there are known unknowns; that is to say we know there are some things we do not know. But there are also unknown unknowns – the ones we don't know we don't know.[12]

Noncooperative game theory models commonly assume that actors have full information. One attribute of models that explicitly allow for uncertainty is that the number of equilibria, the range of rational possible outcomes, expands dramatically. In the real world, individuals rarely have full information on which to base their decisions. All leaders spend considerable resources on intelligence services, from cloak-and-dagger spies to multibillion-dollar satellite programs in an attempt to reduce the general uncertainty they face. Regardless of their intelligence agency's efforts, when making high-stakes decisions, leaders seldom have sufficient intelligence to be certain that no "unknown

---

[11] NHTSA's National Center for Statistics and Analysis 2007.   [12] Rumsfeld 2002.

unknowns" remain. Some leaders will ultimately choose to act in the face of uncertainty, while others will not.

The Psychological Definition of Risk

We are using the term "risky" the way that psychologists tend to think about it; we are referring to individuals who are more likely to make choices in which high costs as well as high potential gains are at stake in situations where others would hesitate to act. Disinhibition, the lack of restraint in group settings, is one characteristic of "riskiness."[13] Other risk-acceptant activities include sensation seeking, aggression, and impulsivity.[14]

When individuals are consciously pondering any given choice, they weigh the benefits against the perceived costs. A sensation-seeking shoplifter, for example, is looking for the psychological thrill of pocketing an item while running the risk of arrest. Uncertainty about the consequences is only part of the conscious as well as unconscious calculation for such a person. Although the risk, or odds, of getting caught in any given store is roughly the same for all would-be thieves, the calculation that the shoplifter makes is highly subjective: How much do they want the item along with the associated thrill of the risk of being caught? A higher perception of risk (and higher uncertainty) may heighten the individual's personal preference for a given choice. This is the sense in which psychologists and laypeople think about "risky."

The Economic Definition of Risk

In economics, the concept of risk is somewhat narrower. Economists think of an individual's preference for risk fundamentally as the preference for the outcome of a hypothetical gamble. This is a sophisticated approach to a basic idea: Is a bird in the hand worth more than two in the bush?

Imagine a situation in which one would receive a certain $10 payoff with one choice, or a 50/50 chance of a $25 payoff with another choice. Some people would definitely take the $10; economists describe these people as *risk-averse*. These individuals value certainty, even if they are worse off on average for it. Others are indifferent between the two options; they are *risk-neutral*.[15] Some will take the gamble, giving up the guaranteed $10 for the possibility of getting more. These so-called *risk-preferring* individuals[16] are the ones we describe in the book as "risky."

Consider how two different leaders might assess the possible outcomes of massing troops at their country's border (a mid-level militarized interstate

---

[13] Nigg 2000.   [14] Zuckerman and Kuhlman 2000.
[15] By mathematical explanation, a risk-neutral individual's utility is linear or, for a given gamble c, $E\{U\{c\}\}=E\{c\}$, while a risk-averse individual's utility is concave, or $E\{U\{c\}\}=U\{E\{c\}\}$.
[16] With a convex utility function, $E\{U\{c\}\}>U\{E\{c\}\}$.

dispute) because they feel a military presence would deter a future threat. The leaders facing this decision could either send the troops or keep them at home. In this gamble, the $10 payoff is keeping the troops where they are, avoiding unnecessary expenditures and confrontation with the leader's allies, and keeping the public calm. The $25 payoff would come if sending the troops resulted in the neighbor removing the threat, which might be, for example, dismantling nuclear facilities. This would be a big win for the leader: the public would feel safer, and the threat that precipitated the crisis would be eliminated.

The risk-averse leader would keep the troops home, just as the risk-averse Neville Chamberlain chose to appease Adolf Hitler while Winston Churchill chose to confront him. Perhaps in the future, another leader may feel forced to deal with the threat, but uncertainty, public opposition, and cost could all ultimately work to change our risk-averse leader's mind. The gamble is just not worth it. Leaders like this generally show up in the LEAD dataset as noninitiators, although they do occasionally engage in wars when the risk of inaction becomes too great.[17] Woodrow Wilson, for example, finally chose to lead the United States into World War I once German U-boats started attacking American ships, which reduced public opposition to participating in the war.

In most crises, a risk-neutral leader would pass the buck. This leader would feel that keeping the troops home is equivalent to the chance that sending them to the border might actually work to deter the threat. Other issues might become more distracting, going to the top of the agenda while the border threat is put aside. If the threat becomes too great, however, the leader would take action. Importantly, he or she would take action sooner than the risk-averse leader would. So risk-neutral leaders also show up as initiators in the dataset, and they are quicker to reciprocate threats than risk-averse leaders.

What would the risk-acceptant leader do at the border? Always preferring the $25 payoff, the leader would mass the troops. Even when the 50/50 chance means possibly getting nothing, the higher payoff is an irresistible lure to attack or at least initiate martial actions that look like militarized interstate disputes.

Why, therefore, do some individuals prefer risk, while others are risk-averse or risk-neutral? The efficacy of beliefs is important.[18] This can come from military experience. Some leaders believe they know more about the functioning and power of the military because of their own experience with that institution, and it makes them more aggressive. Leaders who were in the military but did not see combat can also come to idealize the military experience. This same experience can make others cautious, however; both John Kerry and John F. Kennedy served in the U.S. armed forces and were combat veterans. Their experiences with the military bureaucracy made them

---

[17] The analysis is not directly comparable, because economic utility functions are based on the ordinal utility of money – $25 is always better than $10. Obviously, the range of issues important to a leader is much more complex than this.

[18] Kennedy 2011.

more cautious, as they had seen their friends and fellow soldiers sacrificed for the grand strategy of the war mission.

Risk preferences can matter even when the expected values for two choices are the same. Imagine an identical game, but where the payoff is either $10 or a 50/50 shot at $20. In this case, the expected value of the "gamble" (rolling the dice on getting either $20 or $0) is identical to the "safe" choice of $10, because a leader who takes the bet values the taking of risk (as opposed to the first example, where from a strictly rationalist perspective, an expected value calculation could suggest taking the "gamble"). Leaders who take the gamble in this scenario value the upside from making a risky choice, because there is not an expected value return to taking the gamble. Similar to the first scenario, efficacy beliefs can matter in shaping whether leaders believe they are, in fact, making a risky choice.[19]

A THEORY OF HOW LEADERS' EXPERIENCES SHAPE INTERNATIONAL CONFLICT

Research in political psychology powerfully demonstrates how leaders' personalities influence their policy choices when in office, potentially leading to different types of risk taking on the part of the states that the leaders control.[20] Other scholarship focuses on executives' leadership styles or their normative beliefs, both of which can affect state behavior internationally.[21] Saunders shows how individual beliefs concerning the root causes of danger in foreign countries, something driven by personality, led to different military intervention strategies on the part of Presidents Eisenhower and Kennedy in the 1950s and 1960s.[22]

What does this mean in the aggregate? Over the last few decades, to better understand what makes people more risk-acceptant or disinhibited, psychologists have developed a five-factor model of personality that includes neuroticism, extroversion, openness to experience, conscientiousness, and agreeableness. Using this model, Gallagher finds that those who are more open to new experiences and who seek excitement engage in more risky behavior as leaders.[23]

Yet existing research often fails to address where these personality traits come from. What shapes our behavior as adults? Individual personalities and attitudes flow from two main sources that also significantly interact: nature and nurture. A combination of situational incentives, life experiences, social forces,

---

[19] In fact, to the extent that efficacy beliefs reflect reality, and leaders have different capacities in different situations, holding all else equal, it is theoretically possible that a choice that is "risky" for one leader is not "risky" for another leader.

[20] Kowert and Hermann 1997. See also Levy 1997; Nicholson et al. 2005.

[21] George 1980; Foyle 1999; Hermann 2001; Boettcher 2005.   [22] Saunders 2011.

[23] Gallagher 2010; Gallagher and Allen 2013.

and neurobiological dispositions interact to result in our actions and choices. This is true for society's general rank and file as well as for leaders. So far, however, studies that explore human behavior have focused on the incentives that proximate settings provide as well as the emotional reactions these settings provoke.[24] There is an important lacuna, however, because not everyone behaves the same way when put in the same situation. Rather, differences in preferences as well as differences in individuals' willingness to perceive and accept risk profoundly influence the choices and reactions that different humans make and have in any given setting.

What then shapes our preferences and attitudes toward risk? A well-established literature in psychology and psychiatric genetics suggests that a complex interplay of genes and environment or personal life experiences account for individual behavior and attitudes. Developmental psychologists have found that children are born with dispositions or innate inclinations that their experiences then shape and enhance over time. To give an example from a university setting, the study skills that students develop and the strategies they use when preparing for tests have both short- and long-term implications. In the short term, successful studying will make a student more likely to take the same approach for each exam. In the longer term, perceived success with a particular approach to studying can become the way, later in life, a student approaches researching other questions, from buying a house to preparing for a presentation at work.

Indeed, it is widely understood that some combination of innate dispositions and personal experiences guide human behavior in stable and predictable ways.[25] In this view, "environment" is a complicated thing. No one experience or event will solely determine one's attitudes and behaviors. At the same time, not all events are equal in their power to shape our individual and collective actions. At the very least, environment includes the situation at hand, parenting, schooling, training, and even the in utero environment (hormones in the womb). All of these environmental factors shape our preferences, attitudes, and personal dispositions toward risk and what society considers appropriate behavior.[26]

People and their personalities are the result of more than a simple collection of their experiences, but experiences matter a great deal in shaping their attitudes during subsequent periods.[27] Prior experiences affect how people view the potential costs and benefits of actions and the types of strategies they view as likely to succeed.[28] As David Matthews writes, "[H]uman beings perceive what goes on about them within a *frame of reference* determined by their total previous experience."[29] This is true for political leaders as well as for the general population.

---

[24] Oxley et al. 2008; Medland and Hatemi 2009.
[25] Eaves et al. 1989; Loehlin 1992; Martin et al. 1997; Boomsma et al. 2002; Plomin 2008.
[26] Hatemi and McDermott 2012.   [27] Matthews 1954, 2.   [28] Mumpower et al. 2013.
[29] Matthews 1954, 3.

For example, an individual's attitudes or values about society-wide attributes such as support for capitalism or socialism are shaped powerfully by one's previous life experiences.[30] In recent research, Ludeke and Krueger have found that tendencies toward authoritarianism have a genetic basis but can be influenced by environmental conditions.[31] At the other end of the spectrum, willingness to engage in aggression in ways that would typically fall outside social norms, including the use of violence, results in substantial part from the environment or is manipulated by it.[32]

Leaders' prior experiences inform their "sense of personal efficacy," the view they have of their capabilities. The higher the level of knowledge a leader believes he or she has about a given situation, something drawn in part from prior experience, the lower the level of uncertainty about the appropriate policy response.[33] Andrew Kennedy similarly finds that efficacy beliefs drawn from past experiences shape the future foreign policy behaviors of leaders.[34] These background experiences serve as the key reservoir of knowledge to which a leader turns when making strategic decisions. The international-political realm is often a difficult decision making environment, in which a leader has incomplete information. In terms of the strategies likely to succeed or fail, background experiences form a pool of lessons learned. This is especially true for more poignant and intense experiences, and leaders are more likely to rely on those experiences again later in life.

Essentially, while we sometimes look at particular decisions by leaders and point to "personality" as a cause of action, those traits are learned behaviors conditioned from the past experiences of those leaders.[35] Experiences in the context of an individual's underlying "type" in turn shape personality, and learned behaviors along with a combination of innate attributes and formative experiences play a role in the ways in which leaders consider the risks and likely payoffs involved in pursuing particular strategies.

For example, Franjo Tudjman, who was the father of modern Croatia but who was also regarded by some as a war criminal, bore a great deal of

---

[30] Boomsma et al. 2002. Economists have been working this vein for some time in trying to sort out the factors that affect an individual's support for or antagonism toward socialism. Individuals who suffered from severe economic shocks such as long spells of unemployment or intense relative poverty are less supportive of capitalism and more supportive of socialism (Machel 1996; Hatemi 2013).

[31] Ludeke and Krueger 2013.

[32] Some aspects of our personalities appear to be determined almost entirely by our genes or some not yet understood gene–environment interaction. Executive functioning, for example, is considered to be almost entirely inherited (Friedman et al. 2008).

[33] George 1980, 5 and 27.

[34] Goldgeier 1994; Kennedy 2011. See also Khong (1992) to see how societal experiences shape behavior.

[35] Goldgeier 1994, 2 and 4.

responsibility for the way Croatia emerged from the Balkan Wars and also for the frequent suffering of minorities within Croatia's borders:

Shaped by his experiences as a Partisan, a Communist, a scholar, and a dissident, the middle-aged Tudjman was a patriot who still reflected the theories, ideals, and the prejudices of a young man from a small town in the Croatian Zagorje. So while he condemned violence, looting, and destruction, he warned that the number of dead would multiply if there was no peace – a realistic admonition, not a moral injunction by a man who viewed reality in geopolitical terms and shaped his policy according to what he perceived as the political, military, and diplomatic realities of the real world, not the spiritual realm.[36]

By 1991, when the Balkan war began in earnest, "Tudjman was already an old man ... his character formed in another era. But he was also a wounded man; defamed and denigrated for much of his adult life, he viewed the world as a hard place full of weak people and sudden, unexpected misfortune."[37]

The beliefs and personalities of leaders may play a critical role in filtering how their life experiences are translated into policies. Background experiences, however, "heavily influence" where the beliefs and behaviors of leaders come from.[38] Thus, understanding leaders' behaviors and the choices that guide state behavior requires studying these experiences. Complicating everything is that leaders have a number of crucial experiences, not only one, as they rise to power. Focusing on specific events such as a parental divorce or serving in the military makes it hard to evaluate the relative importance of the entirety of our leaders' backgrounds in the context of the overall set of factors that influence the militarized behavior of a country. Some leader experiences may matter in one leadership context, while others may not. This does not necessarily tell us much about the relative impact of a leader's overall life experiences, unfortunately. Some particular characteristics are associated with greater risk propensity, but when combined with other experiences that are associated with lower risk propensity, the two effects cancel each other out. We therefore need to find a more comprehensive approach. Thus, to really understand leader backgrounds and how they relate to the risk of international conflict, it makes sense to look at the "whole" leader or the combination of leader background experiences that cause a leader to be more or less risky.

WHICH LIFE EXPERIENCES MATTER?

Research indicates that the experiences people have in adolescence and early adulthood can have a unique impact on personality, aggression, and disinhibition, or risk propensity later in life. This is especially true for adverse or dangerous early life events.[39] The developmental years of adolescence and early

---

[36] Sadkovich 2006c, 276. [37] Ibid., 259. [38] Matthews 1954, 4.
[39] Roberts et al. 2003; Caspi and Roberts 2005; Roberts et al. 2007.

adulthood are critical to social reinforcement, neurological development, and patterns of cognition, emotional perception, and preference structure.[40] Late adolescence and young adulthood are also when societal conditioning on the political orientation of an individual operates most strongly.[41]

Evaluating a range of experiences during that period sheds interesting light on the future beliefs of leaders and how those beliefs translate into policy actions. Other experiences can matter as well. In fact, psychologists suggest that a range of background experiences, from military service to education to prior occupation to family life, should influence the future calculations of leaders. This section lays out a set of key experiences, captured in the LEAD dataset, that should influence the future military behavior of leaders.

The Role of National and Rebel Military Experience

There are many reasons to suspect that military experience might have a particularly powerful and systematic impact on leaders' behavior once they reach office. First, military service offers a potentially direct connection between a behavior someone would engage in prior to entering office – fighting a war – and something they might do while in office – initiating a militarized dispute or war. Second, military experiences can be particularly acute or traumatic and often occur during late adolescence or early adulthood. It is also not the case that only those with more risk-acceptant personalities go into the military. Those who enter militaries do so for many reasons,[42] and experimental research by Roberts suggests that those experiences then have an independent impact on personality and risk-taking propensity.[43] Third, frequent debates in the United States since the Cold War between military and civilian leaders over the use of force lend credence to the idea that military and civilian elites may think differently about military options in the face of crisis.[44]

There are reasons to believe that those with experience in the armed forces are more prone to militaristic behavior. Military service, after all, generates expertise in the use of violence and socializes participants to think about the use of force as a potentially effective solution to political problems. This can crowd out in a policymaker's mind other potential solutions for dealing with military challenges, in turn leading to a perceptual bias in favor of using military force.[45] Samuel Huntington maintained: "The military man is held to believe that peace is stultifying and that conflict and war develop man's highest moral and

---

[40] Cutchin et al. 2008.   [41] Niemi and Hepburn 1995, 9.   [42] Dempsey 2009.
[43] Roberts et al. 2003.   [44] Feaver and Gelpi 2004.
[45] See Posen 1984; Snyder 1984; Walt 1987, 162. Some argue this leads to biases in favor of offensive doctrines, but that does not necessarily imply biases toward using force in the first place, just biases toward using force in a particular way if the situation occurs (Snyder 1984; Feaver and Gelpi 2004, 26).

intellectual qualities; he favors aggressive and bellicose national policies."[46] Ties to the military also create parochial interests in favor of using force and decision making biases toward rapid escalation.[47]

More generally, military experience serves to educate participants in a way that makes them more emotionally comfortable with force. For example, in the period immediately before World War II, American army planners viewed the world through a military-tinted lens. "Like their colleagues the world over, they saw international affairs as an eternal Darwinian struggle for survival."[48] Concern with the militaristic attitudes of those in the armed forces in the United States goes back to the founding of the nation. Alexis de Tocqueville wrote, "A great army in the heart of a democratic people will always be a great peril."[49]

Exposure to combat specifically represents a foundational and potentially traumatic experience that can influence future beliefs about violence.[50] Some microlevel data suggest that exposure to combat makes people more risk-acceptant. In survey research, Brunk et al., focusing on retired military officers in the United States, found that those who had participated in combat were significantly less sensitive to risk.[51] In Burundi, Voors et al. used variation in exposure to combat at the village level as a way to measure risk attitudes among villagers. They showed that people in villages exposed to combat, including combatants themselves, have higher levels of risk seeking and discount the future more.[52]

While much of this literature focuses on the United States, military regimes worldwide are more likely to initiate military conflicts than other types of regimes.[53] The normalization of violence for leaders in military regimes, especially given that they often come to power through violence, makes them more likely to use force once in office. It is not necessarily the case, however, that participating in a military organization makes someone more likely to favor the use of force later on. An alternative perspective originated with Huntington, who found that military experience actually leads to conservatism around the use of force.[54] Although military leaders are more likely to view the world through a threatening lens,[55] Huntington believed they are risk-averse in the actual use of force because they view other states based on their capabilities, rather than their intentions. "The military man normally opposes reckless, aggressive, belligerent action ... war should not be resorted to except as a final recourse ... the military man rarely favors war."[56] Military

---

[46] Huntington 1957, 60.   [47] Sechser 2004, 750–1.   [48] Maiolo 2009, 107.
[49] De Tocqueville 2000, 622.   [50] Voors et al. 2010.   [51] Brunk et al. 1990, 101.
[52] Voors et al. 2010, 1–2.   [53] Brecher 1996; Colgan 2013.   [54] Huntington 1957.
[55] See, for example, survey data from the Triangle Institute for Security Studies (TISS) showing that those with military experience tend to view China as a greater threat than those without military experience (Feaver and Gelpi 2004).
[56] Huntington 1957, 69–70.

experience leads to a desire for greater armaments and preparedness, not a greater desire to use force.

Similarly, the sociologist Morris Janowitz argued that a lack of civilian knowledge about the military leads to the flawed perception of professional militaries as militaristic. In fact, military officers are often more realistic and conservative about the use of force than their civilian counterparts. Statements by then-General Eisenhower after World War II reflect a military operational code that viewed war not as inevitable but as a last resort in extreme circumstances.[57] Conservatism results for several reasons: military forces are the ones that will actually die in conflicts; setbacks can be career ending or worse for senior military officers; and military leaders often perceive civilians as naïve, perpetually underestimating the costs and risks of armed conflict. Alternatively, civilian leaders, lacking knowledge about how force is used or an accurate understanding of the costs, are more prone to risky adventurism or "chicken-hawk" aggressiveness.[58] This military conservatism argument extends beyond the United States. According to Huntington, for example, prior to World War I, German generals "generally viewed" war "as the last resort of policy."[59] Even in the early Nazi period, German generals favored a slow buildup of German military forces to deter foreign influence over Germany and at times discouraged Hitler's rapid adventurism.[60]

Existing research, however, fails to differentiate military service itself from actual participation in armed conflict. Separating prior service from combat participation provides a new way to think about the effect of prior service on the willingness to use military force.[61] Essentially, different experiences within the military might drive different attitudes. Differentiating between those with combat experience and those without provides a way for us to resolve the perennial dispute between the military conservatism and militarism schools of thought. The militarism argument is predicated on the idea that exposure to the military leads to socialization that makes support for the use of force more likely. The causal logic of the military conservatism argument, however, is not just about military experience as a whole, but about the exposure to risk and potential psychological trauma experienced by those in the military. Direct exposure to combat could trigger the type of conservatism that would accentuate planning and armaments but not the use of force.

---

[57] Janowitz 1960, 274, 4, 230–1, 274.

[58] Betts found that, excluding commanders actively deployed in the field, high-level military officers in the early Cold War were not more supportive of deployments or warfare than their civilian counterparts, although they were more supportive of escalation once war began (based on author's reanalysis of Betts' appendix table A; Betts 1977, 4–5, 216). See Horowitz and Stam 2014. See also Janowitz 1960, 259; Sirota 2011.

[59] Huntington 1957, 101–5.

[60] Hitler eventually replaced those generals. See Huntington 1957, 119–21, 114.

[61] Feaver and Gelpi (2004) is an exception to this pattern. Existing work also tends to focus on active-duty personnel. See also Horowitz and Stam 2014.

For example, some research shows that while making people less sensitive to risk, previous exposure to combat also makes some people more altruistic, in ways potentially similar to the way veterans in the Feaver and Gelpi survey became more hesitant about the initial use of force in many scenarios.[62] Brunk et al. also find that, while combat veterans are more risk-acceptant, they are also more restrictive about the situations in which they think the use of force is appropriate.[63] These findings are supported by experimental psychological research on risk propensity, which shows that exposure to fear-triggering events generally has a restraining influence on later risk-seeking behavior.[64] As an experience likely to trigger fear in most individuals, direct exposure to combat should therefore generate more sensitivity to risk later.

The French general and president Charles de Gaulle recognized that for soldiers "war is, first and last, the purpose of their lives."[65] He also stated that that military men do not necessarily "approve of the principle of war. It would not be difficult to show that they, of all men, are only too well aware of its horrors."[66] In Janowitz's survey of military personnel, one respondent cited "recent combat experience," which led to "intimate knowledge of the horrors of modern warfare," as the force behind military conservatism.[67]

Microlevel survey evidence of the general population also demonstrates a potential causal link between combat participation and lower levels of support for some types of military action. In 1975, the second wave of a panel study by Jennings and Niemi included several questions about military service, including a question that allows us to differentiate those who deployed to Vietnam from those who just had some form of military service.[68] The population surveyed had all been high school seniors in 1965, making the Vietnam War the first war in which they could have deployed. The third wave of this study, in 1982, then included a question about respondent attitudes concerning American foreign policy. While the specific focus of the question was not the use of force, foreign policy attitudes are a reasonable proxy for those beliefs. The results showed that those who deployed to Vietnam were significantly more skeptical of an active American foreign policy than those who had served in the military but had not deployed.[69]

Additionally, data from the Vietnam Era Twin Registry shows that, in identical twins where one fought in Vietnam and experienced combat trauma and the other served in a noncombat capacity, the twin who fought was far

---

[62] Voors et al. 2010.   [63] Brunk et al. 1990.   [64] Lerner and Keltner 2001.
[65] De Gaulle 1960, 102.   [66] Ibid., 102.   [67] Janowitz 1960, 230.
[68] While not all who deployed to Vietnam would have had direct exposure to combat, all would have been in a combat zone, to some extent. Even this imperfect measure allows us to differentiate in some way within the "veteran" population.
[69] Jennings et al. 1991. Also, see an assessment of Feaver, Gelpi, and Reifler's survey data in Horowitz and Stam 2014.

more likely than the other to engage in high-risk behaviors.[70] In the twins dataset, the combat veterans who lived through traumatic experiences were dramatically more likely to suffer from substance abuse and to engage in gambling and violence over the two decades after their experiences in Vietnam.

The attitudes of survey respondents do not necessarily reflect the reality of the way they would behave, however.[71] Respondents tend to fill out surveys thinking about the application of their values at some nebulous future point, but more practical, short-term concerns tend to motivate their behavior in any given situation. Average survey respondents might also differ from leaders in some systematic way. Thus, while research on personality and risk attitudes suggests that intense experiences like military service should powerfully affect a leader's behavior, and the survey data cited here demonstrate a plausible causal link between combat experience and attitudes toward conflict, we need to look at the actual behavior of leaders to determine the relationship.

Taken as a whole, these ideas suggest that the effects of being in the military in general should be different from the effects of being in the military and participating in combat. In particular, those leaders with prior military service but no combat experience should actually be the most prone to react to that experience by becoming more aggressive and more likely to use force. They believe they have the expertise and experience about the use of military force necessary to make good associations, they may have positive efficacy beliefs associated with their military experience, and they have not been exposed to the danger of combat. A quick survey of world history finds many supporting examples, from Kaiser Wilhelm II, who led Germany into World War I, to Saddam Hussein, to Mobuto Seko, the leader of the Democratic Republic of the Congo from the 1960s through the 1990s.

The literature on military professionalism also provides a way to differentiate between the socialization of military personnel in different types of political regimes, as well as the relationship between prior military service and the selection of leaders into office. Classic military professionalism involves accepting the view of war as an inherently Clausewitzian political process, with military aims and interests subservient to political ones. Thus, professional militaries should be those in which the conservative values of military professionalism, as outlined by Huntington and Janowitz,[72] should shine through most clearly, and the military is subservient to the political leadership.

In political regimes run by the military, classical military professionalism is by definition, impossible, because the military is not subservient to the political leadership. Such states will naturally tend to select leaders who lack those values as well. Consistent with previous findings about military regimes,[73] non-professional militaries, by not embedding deference to political authority, are

---

[70] Koenen et al. 2003; Stam et al. 2012.   [71] Gilens 2001.
[72] Huntington 1957; Janowitz 1960   [73] Weeks 2014.

more likely to select and promote leaders who interpret their own experiences in ways that lead to militarized behavior. The microlevel data demonstrate a positive relationship between combat exposure and future militarized behavior. This result is particularly strong in nonprofessionalized militaries, as the path to power is more likely to be through coups or other irregular means.

The greater the level of professionalism in an officer's military education, the more likely that he or she will be willing to cede control to civilian authorities, according to existing research.[74] These findings about the relationship between civilian authority structures and military decision making as well as the beliefs about the proper role of the military in society may affect political elites' expectations of civil control over the military as well. In democratic states, for example, individuals with military education are more likely to be sensitive to the political and social constraints on the use of force. In states in which civilian–military relations do not hinge on civilian control of the military, military education is likely to have little effect on state policy.[75]

This relationship demonstrates the interaction between how countries select their leaders and the backgrounds of those leaders. In nonmilitary regimes, such as democracies, the military personnel who become civilian political leaders tend to be the least militaristic.[76] For example, as described previously, it was Dwight Eisenhower who became president of the United States after World War II, not Curtis LeMay or Douglas MacArthur. Both LeMay and MacArthur advocated preventive war against American adversaries. In LeMay's case, during the Cuban Missile Crisis, he counseled President Kennedy to ignore Secretary of Defense McNamara's more cautious advice and to invade Cuba, which would likely have precipitated a nuclear war between the United States and the Soviet Union. MacArthur's insubordination during the Korean War precipitated a dramatic escalation of the war when U.S. forces crossed the Yalu River, thereby triggering a large-scale Chinese counterinvasion. The domestic political institutions in nonmilitary regimes are more likely to select out those more aggressive military leaders from successfully pursuing higher office. In 1968, LeMay ran as the U.S. vice presidential candidate beside George Wallace, whose campaign ran a distant third place to Richard Nixon and Hubert Humphrey. In democracies with professionalized militaries, those who react to being exposed to war by becoming more aggressive, particularly if they have seen combat, are unlikely to rise to become head of state. In dictatorships, where violence and aggression is necessary to gain power, the reverse is often true.

[74] Calhoun 1998; Trinkunas 2001.
[75] While we do not control for this possibility to the fullest extent in this book, future iterations will use coding schemes like Geddes's to account for variation in nondemocratic regimes and civilian control of the military.
[76] Janowitz 1960, 4.

Military Success and Failure

Service in the regular armed forces or a rebel group is one form of military experience that shapes leaders' attitudes. Another aspect of military experience that shapes leaders' later views is the ultimate outcome of the war or revolution in which they participate, especially for those who see combat. While he did not become head of state, U.S. Secretary of State Colin Powell's skepticism about limited military interventions after the Vietnam War flowed from his first-hand experiences in the U.S. military during America's struggles and ultimate failure there.[77] A different outcome in Vietnam would likely have led to a different set of beliefs on the part of Powell and others regarding military force.

The U.S. experience in the 1991 Gulf War likely altered the views of a generation of policymakers such as George W. Bush, Donald Rumsfeld, and others who, observing the quick coalition victory over the Iraqi army, assumed that a more ambitious goal of regime change would be relatively easy to accomplish in 2003. Critics of the Bush administration included many whose military lessons of history drew more heavily on the failure in Vietnam rather than the success of 1991. More generally, success or failure on the battlefield influences the efficacy beliefs of leaders. Mao Zedong and Jawaharlal Nehru demonstrate how success with certain strategies earlier in life predispose leaders to use those strategies repeatedly once they become national leaders.[78] Success or failure in war is a particularly important experience for many. Elites use analogical reasoning based on previous experiences when they evaluate the costs and benefits of potential conflicts.[79] Prior success or failure conditions whether or not a leader views the use of force as likely to succeed. Studies using experimental neurological data suggest that the higher the level of risk and success in previous events, the higher the later likelihood of an individual engaging in subsequent high-risk behavior.[80] Those with prior military success should be more likely to consider militarized behavior when in office.[81]

This discussion of military service does not cover the full range of ways that military experiences could vary and influence future behavior. Such a list might also include such factors as the position in which someone served (officer vs. enlisted) and their branch of service (Army vs. Navy).[82]

The Role of Rebel Military Service

Many heads of state have prior experience in rebel groups, and some come to power directly as part of rebel movements. Participation in a rebel group is

---

[77] Powell and Persico 1995.   [78] Kennedy 2011.   [79] Khong 1992.
[80] Xue et al. 2010, 709.
[81] This prediction is not in contrast to prospect theory, because the conflicts that leaders fight in office are rarely the same conflicts that they fought when they were in the military.
[82] Jennings and Markus 1977.

another type of experience that predicts more risk-acceptant behavior once a leader takes office. Simply participating in a rebel movement signals that an individual is more risk-acceptant than usual and is willing to take action to upset the status quo.[83] Success as a rebel also likely reinforces this innate proclivity.[84] For example, consider Mao Zedong's transition from a rebel leader to the national leader of China. In its early years, Mao's China experienced high levels of violence, both internal and external. Research by Andrew Kennedy suggests that, among other factors, Mao's prior successes as a rebel leader predisposed him to think, once he entered office, that similarly martial behavior would be successful.[85]

Two related factors, which are difficult to disentangle, drive the links between rebel experience and later military behavior. In part, people of a particularly risk-acceptant type are drawn to rebel movements, as they are willing to take extraordinary risks to alter the political status quo. Psychology research indicates, however, that these types of experiences do not just involve particular personalities. These sorts of high-intensity and high-risk experiences reinforce the individual's innate tendencies and in turn heighten rather than dampen the willingness to countenance behaviors that other people would judge too risky to accept.

For would-be rebels, their grievances with the existing nation-state apparatus are so large that they decide the optimal strategy is to take up arms. They are making a choice that will have consequences for the rest of their lives and, once the rebels are in power, for their neighbor states. Engaging in rebellious or seditious activity is an extremely risk-acceptant choice. Rebel groups, unlike national militaries, are constantly threatened by state authorities and are more likely to be eliminated than to achieve their goals. The risk propensity of the rebels, therefore, will potentially translate into more revisionist behavior if the rebellion succeeds and its leader achieves the goal of taking control of the state.

After all, revisionist behavior on an international scale is likely to involve the threat or use of military force. This argument is consistent with research by political science professor Jeff Colgan, who finds that revolutionary regimes are more likely to start military conflicts.[86] However, those leaders with prior rebel experience tend to be more risk-acceptant in general, even if they do not immediately rise to power following a successful rebellion. The research also suggests that there is a relationship between the indirect effects of revolutionary regimes and the background characteristics of the leaders who control them.

---

[83] No analogue to the military conservatism hypothesis exists for former rebel leaders. Former rebel leaders might be less aggressive internationally than an average leader, but that might occur because they are generally still engaged in some degree of conflict at home (Stanton 2009).

[84] Pickering et al. 1997; Corr 2004.   [85] Kennedy 2011.

[86] Colgan 2010. See also Colgan and Weeks 2015.

Education

Education represents an important personal development characteristic that may influence the behavior of leaders. Unfortunately, the literature on the ways in which the education of leaders influences their behavior once they become leaders is remarkably limited. The literature on the links between education and violent behavior presents mixed theoretical claims as well as mixed empirical results. Many studies focus on education and the incidence of violence within particular cultural contexts, such as the level of education of suicide bombers. In each area, the links between an individual's education level and his or her willingness to participate in political violence are tenuous at best. Elsewhere, during the Irish Troubles in Ulster, higher levels of education tended to moderate views about the efficacy of violence.[87]

In related work, other scholars make broader arguments about the relationship between political leadership and education, often focusing on the education of the followers as much as on that of the leaders. Ranis and others working in political and economic development focus on the development of human capital. The greater the investment in individuals, the less likely they are to advocate political violence.[88]

Higher levels of education may also increase the opportunity costs of political violence for likely participants, thereby lowering support for political violence.[89] In the Sri Lankan context, state educational systems have the potential to indoctrinate varying beliefs about the efficacy and desirability of political violence.[90] In this view, the role of education will be context specific. During the lead-up to the war between the United States, its allies, and Iraq, for example, the Gallup organization, along with numerous other polling organizations, asked Americans and Europeans about their support for the then-impending war. In each setting, on average, individuals with higher levels of education were less likely to be supportive of the war.

In related literature, political psychologists focus on the nature of elites' belief systems. There are significant gaps between citizens' and political leaders' beliefs about the appropriateness of the use of force and about several other policy areas such as foreign aid and support for unilateral versus multilateral force.[91] Some studies find significant support for arguments linking education and gender to choices in the three strategic domains of force, engagement, and containment.[92] In all cases, individuals with higher levels of education are more likely to support a moderated set of policies.

Some microlevel survey data on the U.S. population also support the notion that higher levels of education lead to more dovish preferences. In 1998 and 1999 surveys of military officers, civilian elites, and the mass public, researchers

---

[87] Paxson 2002.   [88] Ranis 1987; Le Billon 2001.   [89] Collier et al. 2004.
[90] Goodhand et al. 2000.   [91] Page and Barabas 2000.   [92] Herrmann and Keller 2004.

asked respondents about their level of education.[93] Controlling for those who did not serve in the military, the results show a clear linear trend with higher levels of education making respondents less likely to view China as a threat and less likely to think that the use of military force against China would be an effective policy action.[94]

If this line of thinking about the relationship between education and the propensity to support the use of military force is correct, we should expect to see that the education level of a leader should be inversely proportional to his or her propensity to initiate or escalate militarized disputes. The higher a leader's educational level, the lower the probability that the leader will use force against his or her neighbors.

There is also a line of argument focused on the importance of early childhood education on later behavior. Research conducted by the United Nations Educational, Scientific and Cultural Organization (UNESCO) shows that effective early childhood and primary education is critical for stable emotional development and behavior later in life.[95] Unstable early educational experiences can lead to future discipline problems for children, distancing them from their parents, and to higher levels of aggression both at the time and later in life.[96] Poor primary school environments or failure to move children into primary school in a timely manner can hinder childhood social development and lead to more aggressive behavior later in life.[97]

Prior Occupation (Job)

A leader's occupation before his or her entry into politics is one of the clearest ways to conceptualize the socialization of a leader. In addition to prior military service, there are other occupations related to an individual's future riskiness. Caspi and Roberts, among the mostly widely cited psychologists who study life experiences and personal development, find that one of the best predictors of risk behavior is prior occupational experience. Occupations, especially during formative years in the late teens and early twenties, serve as primary socializing factors for all individuals.[98] While there is a selection effect, in that people with particular personalities are more likely to choose particular professions, the impact of occupation on risk propensity is not simply endogenous to personality.[99] Instead, experimental data demonstrate that those experiences have an independent impact on behavior.

There is not a great deal of literature to suggest the way that particular occupations may influence later risk propensity. For example, perhaps being a lawyer would make someone more aware of competing arguments, making him

[93] Gelpi and Feaver 2002.
[94] Collins and Holsti 1999; Gronke and Feaver 2001; Grieco et al. 2011.   [95] Kaga et al. 2010.
[96] Loeber and Hay 1997.   [97] Yoshikawa1994, 1995; Huesmann and Guerra 1997.
[98] Caspi and Roberts 2005.   [99] Zuckerman and Neeb 1980; Stewart and Roth 2001.

or her less likely to engage in militaristic behavior. However, it is also possible that being a lawyer could give someone greater confidence in the ability to change the status quo. Then there are occupations often associated in popular lore with resistance, such as labor activism and creative occupations. We might expect that those with labor experience or those who engage in creative pursuits that challenge conventional thinking might be more likely to support risky activity when they get into office. Future leaders with these backgrounds are trained to challenge the status quo, a trait that might make them more inclined when they enter office toward military action that challenges the status quo.

However, understanding the effects of prior occupation demonstrates that it is important to consider leader attributes holistically, as well as breaking them down individually. A positive relationship between creative occupations or labor backgrounds and militarized dispute initiation could just reflect the fact that people from those occupations are more likely to choose violent rebel activity.

Age

Prior research demonstrates a significant relationship between the age of leaders and their behavior in international conflict situations.[100] The relationship is not what most people would expect at first glance. History and popular portrayals often depict younger leaders as aggressive and older leaders as wise, cautious, and experienced. A young Louis XIV of France initiated several wars in office, including France's attacks on Spanish assets in the War of Devolution in 1667–1668. As a young man, before dying at the age of thirty-three, Alexander the Great assembled the largest empire the world had ever seen.

One explanation grounded in physiology points to testosterone. Blood levels of testosterone decline over time for nearly all individuals, but especially for men. This is relevant from an international conflict perspective, as biological research demonstrates a positive relationship between high levels of testosterone and physical and emotional aggression. As aging men experience declining levels of testosterone, they often become less likely to engage in aggressive behavior or to make decisions objectively viewed as risky. Thus, we would expect young leaders, with relatively more testosterone, to be more likely to engage in militaristic actions.

Prior research suggests, however, that absent controlling for the institutional setting, older leaders are actually substantially more prone to militarized behavior.[101] Older leaders have more experience and time to build relationships with their selectorate, giving them a greater ability to influence national policy. This is especially true in the foreign policy arena, where executives already have more freedom of action than in domestic politics.

---

[100] This section builds on Horowitz et al. 2005.   [101] Horowitz et al. 2005.

More important, older leaders may have shorter time horizons, making them more likely to undertake risky gambits. We know from psychological research that time horizons play an important role in decision making. The passage of time decreases the utility that individuals believe they will receive from a given action. In experimental settings, subjects generally chose short-term rewards over longer-term benefits, even when the longer-term benefits are larger.[102] Leaders who expect to live for several decades are likely to have longer time horizons than older leaders. They are more likely to believe that they can stay in office for longer periods, for example, and see their preferred policies implemented in their lifetimes.

Older leaders, in contrast, may be more interested in creating a legacy and may be worried about the possibility of losing office due to death or declining health. Older leaders often make riskier choices; they may be more concerned with building a legacy faster, making them more likely to engage in militarized behavior to "secure" their nation. Ratings of American presidents demonstrate that building a successful legacy generally requires being involved in and succeeding in international crises.[103] Older leaders are often more likely to be in office for longer periods of time, meaning they will develop greater efficacy beliefs about their ability to control international situations.[104] Older leaders are also more likely to experience significant health issues that affect their judgment and further shorten their time horizons. As McDermott notes, "Illness provides specific, predictable, and recognizable shifts in attention, time perspective, cognitive capacity, judgment, and emotion, which systematically affect impaired leaders."[105] Psychologists have shown that concerns with legacy creation and short time horizons may have led Menachem Begin of Israel toward more aggressive behavior near the end of his time in office.[106]

Family Background

Leadership research from other disciplines suggests that family history plays a very large role in socializing the behavior of future leaders.[107] Experiences in families, like occupational experiences, provide a reservoir of examples of successful and unsuccessful behaviors that leaders draw on once they get into office. Family backgrounds play a critical role in shaping the way people view the world and evaluate the costs and benefits of different types of actions. Benazir Bhutto, one in a line of Pakistani prime ministers, grew up in a family culture of strategic thought and debate as conversations within her family often reflected the concerns of the day. How much did this influence her behavior when she entered office?

---

[102] Prelec and Loewenstein 1991; Loewenstein and Prelec 1992.   [103] Horowitz et al. 2005.
[104] For more on efficacy beliefs, see Kennedy 2011.   [105] McDermott 2008, 2013.
[106] Post and Robins 1993, 202.   [107] Harvey and Barbour 2009.

The relative importance of upbringing in shaping the future ideas and preferences of adults harkens back to the age-old debate between nature and nurture. Studying the upbringing of leaders and their own subsequent family structures most clearly brings the relative role of genes and the environment to the forefront of the discussion. While researchers across disciplines will likely never reach complete consensus on this issue, psychological research on aggression, as well as studies in other fields, concludes that both genes and the environment play an important role in shaping personality development.

Background experiences form a critical vector that shapes the relational world with which a child interacts, encouraging the development of some traits and constraining others.[108] Early life experiences also influence the overall confidence and assuredness of a leader, which we know from experimental research makes aggressive behavior more likely.[109] Essentially, the family is a "microcosm of society," to quote Valerie Hudson.[110] The family is where children first learn the strategies and behaviors that they will employ as adults. Aggression appears in early childhood as a natural behavior. The key question is whether social learning leads to its control and regulation in children.[111] For most children, control and regulation develop at an early age. For others, they do not, and environmental factors often play a mediating role. Aggression then stabilizes in most people. An adult's propensity to engage in aggressive behavior correlates strongly with tendencies toward aggressive behavior during childhood. Research in behavioral genetics provides strong evidence supporting the heritability of raw aggression.[112] In meta-analyses of twin studies, it appears that an individual's personal genetic makeup and the interaction of those genes with an individual's environment accounts for roughly 40 percent of an individual's underlying aggressiveness. The substantial majority of an individual's aggressive tendencies results from their life experiences and the environment in which he or she grew up.

Very little existing research on leaders, even that which focuses on leader personalities, evaluates leaders' upbringing in a systematic fashion. Some research on leaders does look at the link between their personalities and behavior. For example, Barber used the energy and effect levels of leaders to predict the character and worldview of presidents.[113] Klonsky investigated how developmental factors such as parental warmth and parental discipline influenced the growth of leadership characteristics in children.[114] The findings showed that family background significantly influenced later behavior and that gender differences played an important role. Intense socialization made boys more likely to develop leadership traits, while women developed leadership

---

[108] Hartup 2005, 12.   [109] Johnson et al. 2012.   [110] Hudson 1990, 585–96.
[111] Tremblay and Nagin 2005, 93.
[112] Keenan and Shaw 1994; Coccaro et al. 1997. The same research also demonstrates a link between genetics and other, more general, behavioral issues (DiLalla 2002).
[113] Barber 1972.   [114] Klonsky 1983.

traits when they had more intrafamily responsibilities. Other factors such as social class and family size also drove leadership development.

There is very little international relations research that focuses on leader backgrounds, and there are no stable findings to point to. There is even less work that focuses on family backgrounds or family structure. Much of the work focuses on gender roles. While intrinsically interesting, this literature is less relevant for our purposes simply because of the exceedingly small number of female heads of state in the 1875–2004 period. However, we draw on research in other fields to build our argument about the relationship between the family backgrounds of leaders and their later behavior.

Much psychological research, public media analyses, and parents themselves presume that family influence directly impacts the later behavior of children. Freudian ideas about early childhood development continue to influence these theories and research, but there is very little work on how this might influence later behavior in the conflict realm. However, there are reasons to think that an individual's approach to violence and conflict learned as a child might influence the way that individual interacts with the world as an adult. Research on aggression highlights the commonality between all types of aggression, whether it is the aggression of an infant, an aggressive act by a soldier in a war, or an aggressive decision by a leader to use force.[115]

The link between age and violent crime suggests not only the role of testosterone mentioned earlier, but also the effect of learned behavior.[116] In some cases, social learning embeds aggression as a potentially more successful strategy than the alternatives. While the translation to international politics will be indirect, at best – and much more indirect than that argued in other chapters – in some ways, it will be the most deeply rooted in the psychology literature.

A significant body of research in psychology and sociology demonstrates that the early childhood period is critical for personality development, including the development of aggression and risk propensity. For example, researchers have found significant links between childhood experiences and criminal behavior of adults.[117] It is possible to overstate the effect of the early childhood period, however. The legacy of psychoanalysis, the politics of the child welfare movement, and the ease of access to research have encouraged researchers to focus on children, even though other developmental periods are theoretically important as well.[118] We therefore focus on the entirety of the upbringing period, rather than just early childhood.

Parental Stability

Most people are consciously aware of how the behavior of their parents influenced their behavior growing up and likely continues to influence their

---

[115] Tremblay and Nagin 2005, 84–5.
[116] Dabbs et al. 1987; Dabbs et al. 1995; Baron-Cohen 2004; Tremblay and Nagin 2005, 86–7.
[117] McCord 1979.   [118] Hartup 2005, 11.

behavior today. Parents serve as the primary role models for children, especially during the critical period of early childhood development. Recent research shows that, even accounting for genetic factors, parenting plays a large role in influencing the temperament of children.[119] For example, Easterbrooks and Goldberg's widely cited work suggests that whether the father is present or not significantly affects toddler development.[120] Children raised in dysfunctional families with lower incomes, even controlling for other factors, are substantially more likely to engage in violent behavior, starting at a very young age.[121] Numerous studies find that children with "parents who have low income and serious problems living together," among other factors, are much less likely to learn to regulate their aggressive behavior in early schooling, making aggression later in life more likely.[122] The early childhood period is critical for embedding lessons about the utility of violent, aggressive behavior.

While it is not uncommon for those with high levels of early childhood aggression to return to lower aggression levels in adolescence and later, essentially aging out of early tendencies toward violence and aggression, it is extremely rare for those with low levels of early childhood aggression to become more aggressive later in life. Thus, early childhood aggression is a key predictor of aggression later in life.[123] Low socioeconomic attainment on the part of mothers also makes high levels of aggressiveness in their children more likely. While developmental psychologists speculate that the relationship may be genetic rather than environmental, because more aggressive teen women are more likely to have children early and attain lower socioeconomic levels, it is still possible to predict future aggression on the basis of external factors associated with maternal parenting.[124] The more stable the family upbringing of a leader, the less likely it is that his or her upbringing will teach the likely success of risk-prone strategies that will trigger aggressive behavior.

Childhood Wealth

Psychologists and sociologists have long noted the link between early childhood socioeconomic status (generally thought to be some combination of wealth and social status) and the development of particular personality traits.[125] Nevertheless, the literature on socioeconomic status and childhood development is not without controversy. It is often very difficult to disentangle the effects of economic status from other correlated factors. There are also generally wide arrays of childhood development experiences even within particular economic cohorts.[126]

---

[119] Romano et al. 2005.   [120] Easterbrooks and Goldberg 1984.   [121] Lambert 2004.
[122] Tremblay et al. 2004, e50.   [123] Farrington 1991.
[124] Nagin and Tremblay 2001, 394–5.
[125] For a review of the literature, see Conger and Donnellan 2007.
[126] Bradley and Corwyn 2002.

Low socioeconomic status contributes to deviant and aggressive behavior through two main pathways. The family stress model suggests that low socioeconomic status leads to other hardships that make future success more difficult and that increase the prospects for deviant behavior. The family investment model, in contrast, suggests that the inability of lower income families to invest fully in their children is what influences their behavior.[127] For our purposes, diagnosing the specific causal pathway is not critical. Instead, what matters for our purposes is whether a particular set of background experiences, regardless of how or why they happen, makes certain types of preferences or behaviors more or less likely.

Social and economic factors in early life have a powerful effect on most adults' lives. Controlling for other factors, low socioeconomic status during childhood leads to greater acute stress and lower achievement in school and beyond.[128] Independent of social status, growing up in a lower-income household also leads to higher levels of aggression among children, even persisting into adolescence.[129] Lower levels of wealth, especially when children are aware of the relative difference between their status and that of their peers, can lead to resentment and antisocial behavior. Parental support is a critical intervening factor between economic hardship and children externalizing that hardship through aggression. This suggests it is important to consider both the stability of the home life for a future leader and the family's socioeconomic conditions.[130]

Parental Occupation

Some early work in this area explored the relationship between parental occupation, particularly the father's occupation, and subsequent occupational choices made by children. In a survey of more than 125,000 people, Werts and Watley found that both sons and daughters tend to excel in their father's employment fields.[131] This proved true across a wide variety of domains, including scientific, artistic, oral, musical, literary, and leadership areas and skills. The more diverse the tasks and problem-solving opportunities that parents deal with at work, the faster the cognitive development of their children.[132] The causal logic here is not just genetic – that parents conditioned to succeed in particular jobs will naturally have children with those traits. Instead, parents incorporate the strategies they learn at work into their parenting at home.[133]

Gender

One of the most discussed elements of the link between biology and aggression relates to gender. Researchers have found that, especially in baseline and

---

[127] Conger and Donnellan 2007.   [128] McLoyd 1998.   [129] Tremblay et al. 2004.
[130] Conger and Donnellan 2007, 179.   [131] Werts and Watley 1972.
[132] Parcel and Menaghan 1990.   [133] Kohn and Schooler 1982; Bradley and Corwyn 2002.

unprovoked conditions, males tend toward aggression more than females. As noted earlier, men have higher average levels of testosterone and from early life receive signals from society to be more aggressive than women. Bluntly put, gender matters and does so particularly for men, who make up the vast majority of political executives. For example, some researchers have shown that after viewing images of attractive women, men were more likely to support aggressive military actions, while women showed no such effect from observing attractive men.[134] Some research on the relationship between gender and international politics suggests that more "feminine" attributes lead to more peaceful behavior, although this claim has been vigorously disputed.[135] This would lead us to expect that male heads of states should be systematically more aggressive, for example, more likely to engage in militarized behavior, than female leaders.

However, according to academic research, in conditions of provocation, the difference between the aggressiveness of males and females declines.[136] Thinking about the implications from the perspective of leaders and international politics, while in some cases countries may engage in unprovoked aggression, history reveals few "bolt from the blue" attacks. In the "normal" conditions in which militarized disputes arise, gender research suggests that we may not find enormous differences. Those cases would all count as "provoked" in one way or another, meaning they would not fit into situations in which we would expect gender differences to play a role in relative levels of support for military action.

The issue of leader selection also potentially complicates the study of gender in leaders. It is possible that the women selected to be head of state, such as Margaret Thatcher, often have personality traits generally associated with men. If the only women selected to be heads of state have personality traits commonly associated with men, then even if gender differences exist across the population, we will be unable to observe them in international politics. Additionally, the way society treats women in general may be more significant than the influence of the individual head of state. For example, some research suggests that societies with greater levels of gender equality participate in fewer severe international crises.[137]

Birth Order

Conventional wisdom in popular culture suggests that there is something about birth order that influences the way people behave. Birth order advocates suggest that older siblings are more likely to bully or dominate younger siblings. Only children can be selfish and demanding. Young siblings are disruptive,

---

[134] Chang et al. 2011.

[135] Our point is not that Tickner makes this claim, but that she engages with that argument and describes it clearly (Tickner 1992; Fukuyama 1998).

[136] Bettencourt and Miller 1996.   [137] Caprioli and Boyer 2001.

refusing to simply follow along the normal family hierarchy in order to attract parental attention away from older siblings. If true, there may also be implications for international politics. To the extent that birth order may fundamentally influence personality, it should also affect the way leaders behave when confronted with crises.

The challenge is that, even within the field of birth order research, there is significant disagreement about whether birth order really matters. For example, in the early 1980s, Ernst and Angst conducted a comprehensive review of the existing literature on birth order.[138] Evaluating more than 1000 studies, they concluded that there was no existing statistical relationship demonstrating a linkage between birth order and behavior. In contrast, Frank Sulloway's book, *Born to Rebel*, published in 1996, contradicted much prior work and found a substantial link between birth order and later behavior.[139]

The essence of Sulloway's argument about childhood behavior is that children compete for parental resources and attention, and the way their parents respond teaches them fundamental lessons of behavior that last through adulthood. Furthermore, children have incentives to create their own niches within the family (as the leader, negotiator, etc.) to justify the allocation of resources, creating lessons that become permanent shapers of behavior.[140] Evolutionary pressures to acquire resources force children to develop behavioral niches used to justify their particular allocation of resources. Since first-born children are generally larger and have more experience, the distribution of resources tends to favor them. Younger siblings, forced to deal with a family environment tilted toward the older siblings, must innovate and adapt in order to survive. Therefore, the need to establish a productive relationship with their parents forces behavioral differentiation among children that carries over into adulthood.[141]

Forer argues that the first-born child is more likely to be authoritarian as he or she grows up in a household based on the exercise of raw power, because the child will model the behavior of the parents.[142] While younger children may also model parental behavior, their inherent power disadvantage, given their relatively smaller size and life experience, means the first-born will learn how to lead in an authoritarian manner. Forer states that this personality tendency learned during childhood carries over into adult behaviors:

---

[138] Ernst and Angst 1983.   [139] Sulloway 1996.   [140] Harris 1998, 366.

[141] Stewart argues that structural political change can also be explained by birth order dynamics. Large-scale changes, such as the expansion of America that occurred after the election of Andrew Jackson, a last-born son, are likely to be initiated by last-born children, extended by intermediate and first-born children, and synthesized by only children (Stewart 1992, 87). While to some extent this is beyond the scope of this study, Stewart's theory does not seem to stand up to closer scrutiny. The theory would predict that the American Revolution/founding of the Republic would be led by last-born sons. However, Presidents Adams, Jefferson, Madison, Monroe, and Quincy Adams were all first-born sons and leaders in the initiation of the American Revolution.

[142] Forer 1976.

Such direct translation of raw power over other people reveals itself in modern society as violence and destructiveness, and the strain is as old and deep as the story of Cain and Abel. These examples begin to show how the position of birth and the interrelationship among family members determine the way in which striving for dominance manifests itself in behavior and personality. Children observe their parents' interaction, relate to the push and pull of discipline, and maneuver for a dominant position among the other siblings.[143]

Forer's work thus identifies a critical difference between the likely *political* behaviors of a first-born or later-born child. In a given situation, a first-born child is more likely to apply raw power to try to influence others. A later-born child, growing up in an environment in which his or her reliance on the exercise of power based on physical capabilities could not have guaranteed him or her material benefits learns to rely on manipulation, persuasion, and tactics for gaining control.[144]

Many scientists studying birth order have concluded that it has almost no effect on personality and that the effects that do exist are quite limited.[145] Rodgers and others conclude that previous correlations found between birth order and intelligence and birth order and personality are simply that: correlations. Human psychology and the desire to generalize from a perceived experience within the family to society at large causes the "birth order trap,"[146] or the belief that birth order has a larger causal effect than is, in fact, the case. Other causal variables, such as age, class, and gender, explain behavior much better than birth order.[147]

However, despite the evidence against birth order effects, "birth order theories, like some other belief systems, have remained essentially immune from falsification, even when consistently contradicted by the available evidence."[148] The stickiness of beliefs about birth order could have important implications for the way national leaders are perceived and the way intelligence agencies assemble profiles of leaders and predict their behavior.

HOW LEADERS OPERATE WITHIN POLITICAL SYSTEMS

Now that we have outlined which early leader experiences are most likely to influence later behavior, we return to the question of the interaction between an individual leader and the domestic political context in which that leader operates. Leaders operate within the constraints of a political system, rarely having the capacity to rule by fiat. Even Chairman Mao and General Secretary Stalin worked within the constraints of Communist Party Central Committees. Many authoritarian leaders face institutional checks and balances – albeit typically weaker ones than those in democratic systems – that make it difficult to enact

---

[143] Ibid., 112.   [144] Ibid., 113.   [145] Steelman et al. 2002, 256.   [146] Rodgers 2001, 506.
[147] Ibid., 506; Rodgers et al. 2000, 599.   [148] Somit et al. 1996, 6.

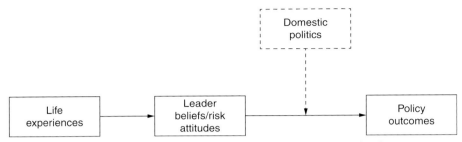

FIGURE 1.1. Theoretical relationship between leader experiences and policy outcomes.

policies exactly when and how they wish.[149] Therefore, examining the effect of leaders' personality attributes on policy requires outlining the ways in which the beliefs that follow from those attributes might translate into policy. Figure 1.1 demonstrates, conceptually, how leader beliefs operate through domestic political institutions to influence the policy process.

The causal sequence in Figure 1.1 illustrates the link between leader experiences, domestic politics, and national policy. It also reveals the critical role that domestic political institutions play in shaping the context in which leaders operate. Domestic political institutions interact with leaders in at least two different ways relevant to understanding the effect of leader experiences. First, institutional rules place constraints on leaders already in office. Second, they play an important role in the selection of subsequent leaders.

Different domestic political institutions constrain leaders differently. As previously referenced, all leaders face some sort of domestic political audience, or selectorate, that is responsible for keeping them in office. If a leader loses the support of that critical constituency, he or she is likely to lose office.[150] Following several years of poor economic performances and the Cuban Missile Crisis debacle, Leonid Brezhnev and other members of the Communist Party Central Committee conspired to remove Khrushchev from office. The Central Committee had been critical to Khrushchev's hold on power, and when Brezhnev and his co-conspirators convinced a majority of the Committee that it was time for a change in leadership, Khrushchev realized that his time as leader of the Soviet Union had come to an end.[151]

In general, we would expect that states with numerous checks and balances on executive power would constrain an individual leader's ability to act on personal preferences to a greater degree. Essentially, in states with larger selectorates, which are generally democracies, leaders have less flexibility to simply enact the policies they want.[152] To some extent, this is different in the foreign-policy realm.

---

[149] Cheibub et al. 2010.   [150] Bueno de Mesquita et al. 2003; Chiozza and Goemans 2011.
[151] Taubman 2003.   [152] Narang and Staniland 2013.

Political theorists commonly characterize the U.S. Constitution as an "invitation to struggle" for the president and Congress.[153] While this is almost certainly true in the domestic political realm, in foreign policy the powers of the U.S. president, as well as of many executives in other states, have been increasing for several generations. Presidents, such as Bill Clinton after 1994, prevented by a hostile Congress from enacting their domestic political agenda, often turn to foreign policy as a realm in which they will have greater freedom. Clinton's decisions to intervene in Bosnia and Kosovo and deploy aircraft carriers to the Taiwan Strait, all of which occurred while Republicans controlled Congress, demonstrates the freer hand democratic leaders have in foreign policy.

Leaders who operate in less constrained political systems seem to have a greater ability to enact policies more to their liking. This is likely especially true in two types of regimes. Heavily autocratic regimes, especially personalist regimes, should feature significantly smaller selectorates. In these types of regimes, leaders such as Adolf Hitler and Saddam Hussein have greater flexibility in making policy decisions than more constrained leaders in other regimes. Until he stepped down in 1964, Khrushchev enjoyed far greater freedom to enact foreign policy for the Soviet Union. He had significant responsibility for the gambles over Berlin and Cuba.

In the Archigos dataset of world leaders from 1875 to 2004, on which the LEAD dataset introduced in the next chapter is based, more than 550 leaders exited office through irregular means such as a coup, civil war, or other internal conflict.[154] Another 66 leaders lost office due to the decision by a foreign power to impose regime change on a country. Of those more than 600 leaders who lost power through the use of force or more extreme political machinations, only about nine percent led democracies. Over ninety percent of the leaders who lost power in this manner led nondemocratic regimes,[155] and more than twenty-five percent of the irregular or foreign-imposed regime changes occurred on the watch of leaders of extremely autocratic regimes.

Now, consider entry into office. The role that domestic political institutions play in determining whether leaders are selected for office is just as relevant. More than forty-seven percent of the leaders who entered office through "regular" means were democratic leaders, compared with only nine percent who were autocratic leaders. Extremely autocratic leaders made up, alternatively, about twenty-seven percent of all leaders who entered office through irregular means. More than thirty-nine percent of the world's more autocratic leaders entered office through irregular means. This total is likely low; it excludes back-room internal violence and other extreme actions that leaders in some autocracies must go through to put themselves in position for "selection" to the highest office.

---

[153] Corwin 1948.   [154] Chiozza and Goemans 2011.
[155] For more on data on political regime types, see Marshall et al. 2014.

Saddam Hussein exemplifies a leader whose life experiences predict risky behavior and who became a head of state precisely as a result of his aggression. His rise to power through the early Baath party was punctuated by violence, murder, and assassination along with a stint in the Iraqi military that did not expose him to combat, but left him confident of his military expertise. Once in power, Hussein turned to war as a policy tool against neighboring Iran in 1980 and against Kuwait in 1990.

States that select leaders through violent means may also be more likely to engage in violence. For example, in 1994, the Rwandan civil war exploded in a spasm of violence that left somewhere between 250,000 and 1,000,000 dead in less than 100 days. The leaders of the Rwandan government who plotted the genocidal response to a rebel invasion from Uganda had come to power two decades earlier in a violent military coup.[156]

Given that more autocratic leaders may come into office through violence and irregular means – and are more likely to be replaced through those same practices – we should not be surprised to find that autocratic regimes are more likely to feature leaders who are more risk acceptant. Taking up arms against the government in a leadership role is an inherently risky activity, as is plotting a coup or other back-room violence against the current leader. Those more likely to undertake those measures are systematically more likely to come into office in autocratic regimes, meaning that we would expect those with a higher level of baseline risk propensity to become, when in office, autocratic heads of state.

One example of practices leading to risk-acceptant leaders, although it relates to the selection of military leaders rather than of heads of state, comes from the eighteenth- and nineteenth-century Prussian military. While dueling had been officially outlawed in Prussia and surrounding states by that time, no less an authority than the philosopher Immanuel Kant wrote that dueling "receives leniency from the government, and it is made a matter of so-called honor in the army to take action against insults into one's own hands."[157] The dueling culture was especially strong in the Prussian military. Young officers engaged in duels as a natural response to challenges to their honor, such as insults to their character. Dueling served a secondary benefit of ensuring that those officers who survived would be cool under fire in battle. While the fatality rate from dueling had declined, part of the point was to demonstrate character by the ability to take and deliver blows to the face. The persistent risk of death meant that those who emerged from this dueling culture tended to behave aggressively and bore strikingly visible facial scars that made it easy to determine who had been willing to engage in dueling. In the infamous Insterburg dueling incident in 1901, Lieutenant Blaskowitz felt compelled to respond to a dueling request the day after his wedding, suffered a fatal wound, and died. His

---

[156] Prunier 1995; Newbury 1998; Mamdani 2001.   [157] Kant 2006.

superiors, up to the rank of general, were apparently aware of the incident but chose not to stop the duel.[158]

This pattern of behavior, dangerous in its own right, ensured that those selected for leadership positions in the Prussian military were precisely those who had not shied away from dangerous duels. Indeed, this was the purpose. A Bavarian minister of war in 1912 described dueling as "a basic pillar of the army." The logic of his argument was that peacetime dueling prevented "the dangers of the loss of habit of belligerent virtues."[159] In fact, German historian Ute Frevert argues that no less an authority than the Prussian minister of war at the outset of World War I, Erich von Falkenhayn, believed that dueling "forced a distinctly belligerent behavior upon men."[160]

[158] F.R. [*New York Times* correspondent] 1901, SM6.   [159] Frevert 1998, 51.
[160] Ibid., 60. Thanks to Hein Goemans for this insight and example.

2

Systematically Evaluating Leader Risk

By the time of his election to the presidency of Croatia at age sixty-nine, Franjo Tudjman had already lived a long, dramatic, and tragic life. Born at the end of World War I, he was a young man living dangerously as one of Tito's partisans in World War II. He was an ardent believer in Tito's vision for Yugoslavia, rising quickly through the military ranks. Tudjman spent his forties and fifties learning and writing prolifically about Croatian history, frequently clashing with the Communist government as his nationalist beliefs solidified. Sent to prison at age fifty, Tudjman was released by the authorities after he served ten months of a two year sentence. His incarceration proved to be an opportunity. As one writer notes: "Tudjman exploited his prison time, casting himself as a martyr for the Croatian cause, and wrote extensively on his experiences and his vision for Croatia."[1] By his early sixties, Tudjman had been in and out of prison for his extreme nationalist advocacy, finally being released for good at age sixty-two for health reasons.

Tudjman's health concerns did not stop him from finalizing and carrying out his nationalist plan. In 1987, when he was sixty-five, Tudjman began traveling around Canada and the United States to solicit support from Croatian diaspora communities. By the time he became president of Croatia in 1991, he had a very specific nationalist legacy that he wanted to create. His vision for the country was so exclusivist that in his mind it necessitated a war to ethnically cleanse the nation. As a leader with the mentality of a true believer Tudjman took a paternalistic role toward the citizens of Croatia.[2] Tudjman's life experiences combined to drive his self-efficacy about his martial decisions. "Yet if Tudjman saw himself as the hard-headed father of the contemporary Croatian state, he was also the idealistic, and disappointed,

---

[1] Macdonald 2003, 100.   [2] Ramet 2010.

58

child of the former Yugoslav state."[3] Tudjman's life spanned much of the scope of modern Yugoslavia. "Born four years after the creation of the Kingdom of the Serbs, Croats, and Slovenes, he died eight years after Yugoslavia's dissolution. He embodied the ideals and faults of many members of the first generation: the ideologies of Croatia's ruling elite and its dissident intelligentsia."[4]

This is how a man approaching seventy overcomes his physical and psychological limitations to start a war and to reshape a nation. Tudjman had beliefs that were set in stone and a passionate desire to implement them. He had the experience with military bureaucracy to know what he could accomplish. He spent years garnering the support of powerful allies, the relatively wealthy Croatian diaspora, the conservative church, and disaffected conservatives in the military, who responded positively to his self-serving intellectual arguments about the need for an independent Croatia.

By all measures, Tudjman had repeatedly beat the odds and lived to tell about it. Why, then, did he decide to live out his golden years preparing for and conducting a brutal ethnic war that would destroy his nation? Like younger leaders Alexander and Caesar, Tudjman believed in his ability to achieve great rewards even when taking actions that others might regard as risky. These rewards were not for him alone. In Croatia in 2000, the average life expectancy for males was less than seventy-four years and likely even lower in 1990. Tudjman knew he would not have much time to enjoy the trappings of power in his new country. Despite his designs on power, Tudjman retained the electoral system that had put him in place. He eschewed a turn to dictatorship, even for his son, whom he appointed to the Croatian intelligence service.[5] Instead, what Tudjman wanted was even more motivating than personal glory. He wanted a legacy as the father of a new nation.

Franjo Tudjman was not a typical person or leader; rather, he exemplifies the kind of state executive who not only wants to govern but also wants to change the world. A leader such as Tudjman does not view the global system as a constraint on his behavior but rather as a series of aggravating barriers to overcome or bypass in order to achieve his preferred policy objectives.

Leaders with particular background experiences such as prior rebel service or tumultuous childhoods develop efficacy beliefs that make them more likely to make assertive decisions that the average person would view as risky. Put simply, they become more likely to start wars and may also overestimate their probability of success. However, leaders do not make their decisions outside an institutional context or setting. They rise to power and rule in a particular international system that might be more or less dangerous depending on their country's allies and adversaries, economic situation, and other factors. They also behave the way they do not only because of one particular life experience,

---

[3] Sadvokich 2006b, 276.   [4] Sadkovich 2006c.   [5] Dawisha and Parrott 1997.

but also because of the combination of their experiences, some of which may prime them to behave in relatively more dangerous ways and others of which may promote caution and prudence.

Political scientists generally employ two different analytic approaches for determining how leaders' background experiences influence international politics: quantitative and qualitative analysis. Each presents advantages and disadvantages. Quantitative analysis using either the population of leaders or a statistically representative sample allows us to make powerful inferences about the central or general tendencies of leaders' experiential attributes associated with the use of force against neighboring states. Additionally, a statistical approach also enables us to estimate in a systematic fashion the relative explanatory power of leaders' background experiences compared with competing explanations of state behavior. However, the ability to make these kinds of comparisons comes at a cost. Our ability to measure nuanced differences among leaders is quite limited, restricted to behavior or experiences observable using the same criteria for all leaders at all times. Because of the relatively small numbers of each, we also cannot draw inferences about the classes of leaders who may be particularly disruptive to the system or may be particularly pacifistic. Similarly, our ability to make statistical inferences about the general tendencies of female leaders is necessarily constrained by their small numbers. Therefore, we also turn to qualitative analysis, investigating both archival materials as well as previously published biographies of individual leaders who are representative of certain classes of leaders.

This chapter combines quantitative and qualitative analysis to begin assessing the factors that make leaders more likely to go to war. We begin our analysis with a description of the data we gathered on more than over 2,000 heads of states along with an estimate (using a new method) of when and how their life histories influence their policy choices and consequently international politics. To the extent that scholars of the behavioral social sciences study leaders' experiences and links to policy, they tend to focus on such experiences as military service, prior occupation, and age in isolation from one another. In other words, existing work focuses on estimating the independent effects of a leader's early military experience, age in office, or potentially traumatic life experience on the leader's subsequent behavior. To understand how leaders affect the nature of the system as a whole, we need to move beyond the individual independent effects of singular life experiences to analyze simultaneously each leader's full set of formative experiences. Some factors may increase a leader's inhibitions on the use of force, while others may reduce them. Only by accounting for numerous factors simultaneously can we begin to address a leader's general or overall risk aversion or acceptance compared with other leaders present in the system at the same time, as well as in the past or future.

The solution to this challenge is to create a "Risk Index" that combines an array of a leader's background experiences into a unique risk score for every head of state around the world from 1875 to 2001. Each leader's individual aggregate risk score representing the combined effects of myriad experiences then becomes a new source of data from which to estimate the relative impact of leaders.

Can we build a model of leader behavior that incorporates the various background experiences of leaders and predicts which leaders are most likely to initiate military conflicts when in office? This chapter shows that the answer is yes. Not only do leaders such as Tudjman have life histories that suggest they are prone to aggression, but a statistical model built from those background experiences highlights Tudjman, in particular, as one of the most dangerous leaders of the last generation.

We then compare leader-focused models of international conflict with models built from institutional or structural features of the system, such as the dyadic balance of power or democracy. Once one controls for leader-specific risk attitudes, factors such as the balance of power and the democratic peace, on average, play a diminished role in explaining the interactions between states. This is not to say that balances of military power and domestic political institutions do not matter, not at all. Rather, in order to understand best how the international system and the distribution of power affect politics among nations, we need to understand which leaders will view a given type of power distribution as a green light to move ahead with plans for aggression and which ones will see the same distribution of power as a constraining force.

BUILDING A DATABASE OF LEADER BACKGROUND ATTRIBUTES

As mentioned earlier, the analysis in this book relies on a new dataset, the Leader Experience and Attribute Descriptions (LEAD) dataset, assembled specifically for this purpose. Several years ago, political scientists Giacomo Chiozza, Kristian Gleditsch, and Hein Goemans assembled a list of all heads of states from all countries from 1875 to 2004.[6] Their data list, Archigos, contains information on the dates and means by which the leaders entered office – for example, a regular entry, such as a democratic election, or an irregular entry, such as a coup – and exited office. Scholars have used this leader list to better understand how domestic political institutions or international political circumstances affect the environment faced by a leader.

With the benefit of a grant from the National Science Foundation, we added to the basic architecture of Archigos by gathering background information on each of the leaders from 1875 to 2004. The result is the LEAD dataset, which draws from several different types of sources, including leader-specific encyclopedias, military-history encyclopedias, databases of prominent leaders, national

---

[6] Goemans, Gleditsch, and Chiozza 2009.

TABLE 2.1. *Important Leader Background Experiences Captured by the LEAD Dataset*

Military Background	Educational Background	Occupation
Military service	Level of education	Law
Combat	Type of primary	Military
Rebel	education	Business
Rebel combat	Boarding school	Creative
Military education		Career politician
Prior war victory		Labor
(in combat)		Police
Prior war loss		Teacher
(in combat)		Journalism
Prior rebel win		Engineering
(in general)		Medicine
Prior rebel loss		Religion
(in general)		Activist
		Aristocrat
		Science
		Blue Collar
Upbringing	**Family**	**Subjective Experiences**
Considered	Age	**(excluded at present)**
"illegitimate" child	Gender	Wealth
Orphan	Married	Social status
Parents Divorced	Divorced	Mental health
Royalty	Married in power	Physical health
Birth order	Number of children	
Father's occupation	Polygamist	
Mother's occupation		

Some variables not included in models for data reasons. See the Technical Appendix.

as well as presidential archives, and individual biographies.[7] The LEAD dataset includes forty different variables covering the military, educational, occupational, and family backgrounds of heads of state. Table 2.1 shows the scope of the data and the variables included.[8]

As one might expect, the proportion of leaders with some particular combination of these characteristics varies widely over time. For example, of the 2,500 leaders in the LEAD dataset, there is substantial variation in the proportion of leaders who served in the military before taking office. Figure 2.1 shows the distribution of military service by decade. The data show a dramatic decline over the last few decades in the percentage of leaders with prior national

[7] Data sources also included Lentz (1994, 1999). We also cross-checked our data, when available, with other sources, including Ludwig (2002), Cheibub et al. (2010), and Besley and Reynol-Querol (2011). Only minimal differences existed, and we conducted additional research to resolve all disparities.

[8] For details on the specific coding of any of these variables, see the Technical Appendix.

FIGURE 2.1. Distribution of military service over time, 1870–2001.

military service. This trend reflects, in part, the general shift from conscription militaries to all-volunteer forces. States with volunteer armies have a smaller and generally declining proportion of individuals who serve in the military, something that is certainly now true in the United States, as well as much of Western Europe. During the era after the European revolutions of 1848, the wars of German unification, and the American Civil War, 35 to 40 percent of all world leaders had served in their countries' militaries. Today that figure is approaching 10 percent. It also reflects a declining belief that military service is a necessary attribute for national public service.

Trends in warfare and changing system structures and concomitant stability suggest potentially cyclical patterns of leader militarism. From a broad historical perspective, the 1870s, the period in Europe of the classical balance of power as led by the world system leader, Great Britain, ushered in an era of relative world peace. During the balance-of-power period, the number of leaders with military backgrounds plummeted, as opportunities for military leadership diminished greatly along with the perceived need for leaders to possess military experience. World War I brought this period, which was characterized by militarily inexperienced leaders, to a dramatic close. Beginning with the Balkan crises in the late nineteenth century and first decade of the twentieth century, the proportion of states led by leaders with some military experience rose steadily for two decades, returning to levels not seen for forty years. The second era of militaristic leaders then persisted until the 1970s, when the World War II generation of leaders began to pass from the scene. In the 2000s, the international system has fewer leaders with military experience than at any time since the 1870s. The implications of this seismic shift in leadership experiences are unclear. On the one hand, lower levels of leader militarism seem to lead to reduced risk of war. On the other hand, systems with very low levels of military experience also appear to present opportunities for exploitation by exceptionally militaristic leaders.

Other leader attributes show much less variation over time. For example, the percentage of female heads of state in any decade never exceeds 6 percent. The highest percentage of female leaders was in the 1990s (5.1 percent). It is possible that that number will be higher for the complete decade of the 2000s, but it had declined again to 2 percent for the period of 2000–2004, the last year for which we have complete data.

Interestingly, while human lifespans increased significantly from the late nineteenth century to the dawn of the twenty-first century, from an average of about forty-six years old around 1900 to around seventy-four years old in 2000, the average age of leaders also does not vary much over time. The median age of leaders in our sample never exceeds fifty-nine years or drops below fifty years in any decade. This suggests that there is a "sweet spot" of sorts for men in their mid-fifties when leaders are more likely to become heads of state, probably similar to the age at which people are likely to become CEOs or leaders in other arenas as well. A potential bias of this finding, however, is the number of long-serving autocratic leaders who spend the entirety of their fifties in office, but enter and exit at much younger and older ages, respectively. Figure 2.2 shows the median age of leaders in our dataset, by decade.

FIGURE 2.2. Distribution of leader age over time, 1870–2001.

TESTING THE RELATIVE IMPORTANCE OF LEADERS

Unfortunately, there is no single dataset that adequately tracks the myriad ways that leaders use their militaries to gain influence and power. Using the LEAD data to statistically evaluate the relative importance of leaders for international conflict thus requires a strategy of triangulation, using several different well-known databases of international military conflict. The main dependent variable of interest for the models presented here is the initiation of military disputes, drawn from the Militarized Interstate Dispute (MID) dataset. We also look at the initiation and conduct of wars using a dataset of interstate wars from the decades-long Correlates of War (COW) Project, along with a variety of other sources.[9]

One key distinction, in two of the datasets we employ, is between militarized disputes and war. The issue is largely one of scale. The initiation of a dispute or a war is the point at which a state challenges another state (the defender) by threatening or using military force, either in a level of violence short of war or through escalation to actual armed conflict.[10] When Iraq's head of state, Saddam Hussein, threatened Kuwait in the summer of 1990 and moved troops toward the border with Kuwait, Hussein initiated a militarized dispute. Japan's attack on the United States at Pearl Harbor on December 7, 1941, is an example of the initiation of a war, as was the U.S.-led invasion of Iraq in 2003.[11]

We also make several technical choices detailed in the Technical Appendix. An example of these sorts of coding decisions focuses our attention on leader entry and exit. Many countries have more than one leader in a given year. For example, every time there is a presidential transition in the United States, two people serve as chief executive of the United States at different times but for at least part of a single calendar year. For those situations in which there is more than one leader in a given year and neither leader started a military conflict that year, we use only the information for the leader who served in office for the most days that year. However, if one of the leaders started a military conflict that year, we include both leaders.[12] Details about other choices like this are in the Technical Appendix.

---

[9] MID 3.1 (Ghosn and Bennett 2003). COW 4.0 (Sarkees and Wayman 2010). See also Reiter and Stam 2002; Horowitz et al. 2011.

[10] Using these data restricts our analysis end date to 2001, the last year for which data on these disputes are available. Initiation is a dichotomous variable coded as 1 if Side A initiated a conflict in a given dyad year and a 0 otherwise.

[11] The initial statistical tests for our tests use the leader-year (MONAD) as the basic unit of analysis, meaning there is one observation per leader, per year, with a few exceptions. First, because militarized disputes do not happen that often in the grand scheme of international politics, we want to make sure we do not miss any. In years in which the leader of a country started more than one militarized dispute, we included each dispute observation in the analysis. The resulting dataset slightly oversamples those leader years with MIDs. We utilize this design due to the relative rarity of MIDs in the international system; including only the highest-hostility MID for a leader year does not change the results.

[12] While we show in the Technical Appendix that neither one of those choices changes the results, we make them because they help ensure we have the largest pool possible of military disputes with which to test our argument. One limitation in the MID data just described is that most of

WHICH LEADER ATTRIBUTES MATTER?

As a first step, we compare the way different statistical models predict the initiation of militarized disputes. The statistical model used to create Figure 2.3 uses only our variables, the set of leader background experiences that we think may influence the probability of conflict. It shows the coefficient for each leader experience variable and then the 95 percent confidence interval, graphically depicting the relative significance of particular experiences in this setup.

These estimates help assess which leader variables have the greatest explanatory power. Factors or experiences to the right of zero are associated with more militaristic or risk-acceptant leaders; those to the left of zero are likely to be associated with less aggressive leaders or those less inclined to use military force. The data support the intuition from Chapter 1 that prior military experience plays a critical role in influencing the later militarized behavior of leaders.

Other factors stand out as well. While the age of a leader in isolation might independently look as though it has very little independent influence on a leader's behavior in office, as we will see in Chapter 4, when we take into account the institutional setting, age has a powerful effect, but it depends greatly on the type of regime in which the leader is working. Older leaders in democratic states, perhaps because they have shortened time horizons and also potentially because of the time they have taken to build institutional support in office, pose a greater risk to their neighbors.[13] In authoritarian systems, it is the younger leaders who are most likely to be a threat to their neighbors.

The results also suggest mixed results with regard to the effect of gender. However, as is the case with age, closer examination reveals important exceptions and interactions. One challenge is that there are too few female leaders to make detailed statistical inferences. While the average risk associated with male and female leaders is roughly the same, with men being slightly less risk acceptant on average, there have not yet been female "outliers," or female leaders who have been among the most dispute prone or most supportive of extreme violence in wars. We delve further into this question by profiling a female leader who, in the popular media, exemplifies a more conflict-acceptant leader, Margaret Thatcher.

Many would argue that Margaret Thatcher exemplifies a leader prone to aggressive behavior despite facing a relatively benign security environment. Most famously, her military actions during the Falkland Islands War surprised her contemporaries, unnerved her opponents, and became a source of speculation for later students of this conflict.[14] From a system-level perspective, why would England have cared about the provocations of the Argentina

---

the events in the dataset, while they do entail the use or threat of force, are relatively minor events. Leaders may matter disproportionately in more important uses of force. To be sure our results hold up for both militarized crises as well as larger multiyear wars, we conducted a second set of analyses that show our analysis holds even when focusing on the initiation of wars.

[13] Horowitz et al. 2005.   [14] Lebow 1983.

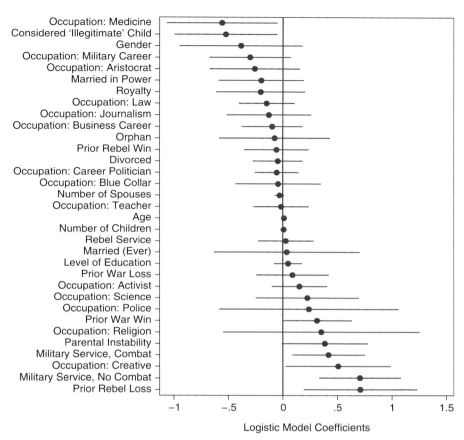

FIGURE 2.3. Statistical model of leader background variables.

dictatorship over such a small and distant outpost of the former empire? Great Britain's behavior seems particularly puzzling only if one ignores the interests, preferences, and predictable attributes of its leader at the time. Certain personality characteristics of Thatcher herself, based on key background experiences, provide important insight into her behavior.

Her biographers and former staffers describe her as extremely intense, driven, and hard working. In an obituary printed in *The Guardian*, Anne Perkins said that Thatcher was "a political phenomenon. She was the first woman elected to lead a major western power; the longest serving British prime minister for 150 years; the most dominant and the most divisive force in British politics in the second half of the twentieth century." Thatcher was also a global figure, "a star in the U.S., a heroine in the former Soviet republics of central Europe, a point of reference for politicians in France, Germany, Italy and Spain."[15]

[15] Perkins 2013.

Throughout her life, Margaret Thatcher demonstrated tremendous resolve and determination. Born to modest circumstances in a middle-class family, she incorporated her father's values of thrift and hard work into her political career. She was an ideological true believer who, unlike her predecessors, did not seek compromise and consensus with her opponents, regardless of which party they hailed from. Trained as a chemist, she switched to law in preparation for a political life, passing her bar exams just a few weeks after giving birth to twins. Although not a combatant, World War II and its aftermath in Britain shaped her outlook on international relations during her formative years by reinforcing the danger of backing down in the face of military challenges.

In one aspect, Thatcher demonstrates the importance of upbringing and family in driving a would-be leader's later behavior. Throughout her political career, she referred repeatedly to her father, Alfred "Alf" Roberts, as her most important moral and personal influence. Her father was a town councilman, alderman, and mayor over the course of twenty-seven years and owned a grocery store in which Margaret worked as a teenager. Thatcher stated later that she learned her work ethic as well as her sense of moral conviction and belief in public service from her father.[16] As Berlinski puts it, "[E]ven if her political philosophy clearly emerged from other influences as well, her class background – that frugal, industrious, Methodist upbringing – was crucially important to informing her worldview."[17]

Thatcher attended a middle-class public British grammar school (not to be confused with British "public" schools, which educate the nation's elites). As a child, she was consistently described as driven and perfectionist and received high marks in all courses.[18] She eventually achieved sufficiently strong scores to attend, on scholarship, Somerville College at Oxford, where she became active in Conservative Party politics and graduated with a degree in chemistry.

Two distinct aspects of Thatcher's adult education thus informed her political life and worldview. First, with a background in chemistry rather than politics, Thatcher grew up with a more disciplined worldview and one with which, in the classroom at least, she need not confront competing viewpoints.[19] Second, her time at Oxford uniquely gave her insight into the social background of her largely upper-class political colleagues and opponents. It "reinforced her righteous sense of persecution"[20] to see the condescension of England's upper crust in school. Together, these aspects of her education made Thatcher more willing, during military crises, to accept risks that other leaders might not accept. Once she had decided on her preferred course of action, informed by her belief that she was right and her opponents were wrong, she was impossible to dissuade.[21]

---

[16] Campbell 2001, 30.   [17] Berlinski 2011, 17.   [18] Campbell 2001; Berlinski 2011.
[19] Although this case can be taken too far; see Campbell 2001.   [20] Ibid., 50.
[21] Berlinski 2011, 109.

These attitudes were on display throughout her career, including during the lead-up to the 1991 Gulf War. In her memoirs, Thatcher describes a conversation in 1990 with then-U.S. President George H.W. Bush. In the conversation, Bush appeared to be having second thoughts about the extremely aggressive line of diplomacy that the United States and Britain were taking. Thatcher describes how she urged Bush to remain steadfast:

In the evening of 26th August President Bush telephoned me from Kennebunkport. I told him how pleased I was with Security Council Resolution 665, which had been passed the day before, enabling us to enforce the embargo. We must use our powers to stop Iraqi shipping. This was no time to go wobbly. Information we had gleaned from secret sources must be published to show up sanctions busting. The President agreed. I told him that the only area in which I thought we were not doing well was in the propaganda battle. We were now probably going into a longish period to see whether sanctions would work and we must not let the faint hearts grow in strength.[22]

Thatcher came of age during World War II; although she did not serve in the military or the women's auxiliary, she nonetheless observed the effect of the war on Britain, particularly the material difficulties of the postwar years. Her experiences as a home front civilian in wartime, several biographers argue, drove her desire to save and restore declining British prestige. As Campbell notes:

Margaret was not quite fourteen when the war began, nearly twenty when it ended; it overshadowed her entire adolescence and was overwhelmingly the formative influence on her political development and specifically her approach to international relations. She came to political awareness in the mid-1930s at just the moment when international crises – the Abyssinia, the Rhineland, Spain, and Czechoslovakia – began to dominate the news. Her first political memory was the so-called "Peace Ballot" organized by the League of Nations in 1934.[23]

Margaret Thatcher also helps illustrate the challenges involved in systematically examining the role of gender in international conflict. There is a belief among some that many female heads of state demonstrate characteristics that are stereotypically "male." If true, this would suggest that female leaders become heads of state only when they have behavioral characteristics more like those of men. Thatcher never described herself as a feminist and surrounded herself almost exclusively with highly competent men. She was aware of her unique position as a woman, however, and consciously used her image and relationship with males to her advantage in political arguments.[24] Berlinski explains that, depending on the situation, she selectively used roles of "The Great Diva, The Mother of the Nation, The Coy Flirt, The Screeching Harridan, Boudicea the Warrior Queen, The Matron, The Housewife" to persuade people to her side.[25] Given her unique position of power as

[22] Thatcher 1995, 24. [23] Campbell 2001, 38. [24] Berlinski 2011, 85. [25] Ibid., 72.

the first female prime minister, many of her political opponents felt highly constrained in their dealings with her, feeling that they would look worse if they publicly attacked her. In combination with her "moralistic certainty," her clear purpose and "unblinking single-mindedness" helped her prevail domestically and internationally.[26]

Institutionally, as head of state in a parliamentary system, Thatcher took power while her party, the Conservative Party, was in the majority. At the time, the opposition Labour Party was relatively weak. There was one institutional bureaucracy, however, with which Thatcher had a strong rapport: the armed forces. Although most British military commanders had first-hand experience with war while she did not, Thatcher accorded them respect and sought to protect them from defense budget cuts.[27] Campbell describes how this served her well during the Falklands War:

[A] part of her reached out, adopted and idealized the tough young soldiers, sailors and airmen who became "our boys" … The forces recognized "Maggie" as a politician with a difference, a fighter like themselves who actually understood them better than would-be peacemakers, who sought a diplomatic settlement to prevent the loss of life which would be inevitable in retaking the islands by force.

Common to professional soldiers worldwide, British soldiers looked forward to the chance to prove themselves.

They had not been training all their lives to have their one chance of action denied them. To the men in the South Atlantic "Maggie" was not just a civilian Prime Minister playing politics with their lives. She was a leader they were proud to fight for 'with a passion and loyalty,' the military historian John Keegan has written, "that few male generals have ever inspired or commanded."[28]

When British and Argentine relations collapsed in a haze of misunderstanding, both willful and inadvertent, the Falklands crisis escalated to a level that Thatcher and her advisors had not anticipated but were willing to seize on for domestic political gain.[29] At the time, her status as prime minister, in the eyes of both the public and her party, was at a nadir. Quite simply, the junta's decision to grab the Islands from Britain put Thatcher's political survival at risk. This created a strong additional incentive for her to stand firm in the crisis.[30] She believed that the domestic policies to which she was so deeply committed would fall by the wayside if Britain gave the appearance of backing down. Berlinski notes, "Failure in the Falklands would have been the end of Thatcher, Thatcherism, and the rollback of socialism in Britain."[31] Thatcher was also aware that Argentina had no real allies in the region and that the lone superpower in the hemisphere, the United States, would be unlikely to block her plans. The other world great power at the time, the

---

[26] Campbell 2004, 140.   [27] Dorman 2002.   [28] Campbell 2001, 191.   [29] Lebow 1983.
[30] Campbell 2001, 184.   [31] Berlinski 2011, 169.

Soviet Union, was loath to take on any military commitment that could lead to a direct confrontation with the United States, having been more than chastened by the Cuban Missile Crisis.

All of these experiences helped reinforce what became Thatcher's defining characteristic as a leader: her perceived iron will. The Falklands crisis most clearly demonstrated this determination and its connection to her background, which made her view Argentina's aggression as inherently unacceptable.[32] In addition, her lack of military experience may have also influenced her decisions. Somewhat paradoxically, in a crisis that rewarded bold choices,

[i]n one way Mrs. Thatcher's inexperience of war was a positive advantage. Practically every senior politician, soldier and diplomat involved in the Falklands was convinced that no male Prime Minister, except perhaps Churchill, would have done what she did when she ordered the task force to sail and then backed it to reconquer the islands, accepting the certainty of casualties if it came to a shooting war. Most of the men around her had personal experience of war ... A man, they all believed, would have been more vividly aware of what war involved.[33]

Most with negative experiences during Great Britain's limited wars after World War II might have concluded that engaging the Argentines would not be worth the risk. Thatcher did not welcome casualties, but understood that they were an inevitable part of warfare – and justified given the stakes.[34]

Thatcher's rule illustrates key components of personal leadership as they interact with systemic and institutional characteristics. She acted forcefully to fully commit British forces to a challenging operation with the potential for both high risks and high rewards. Our Leader Risk Index, described below, places her in the lower 50 percent of dangerous leaders when it comes to the initiation of conflict. While Thatcher did initiate a few militarized disputes while in office, her most famous uses of military force, such as responding to Argentinian aggression in the Falklands, were defensive.[35] This was consistent with the personality attributes described above: an "iron will," resolute in the defense of her beliefs and values.

From a system perspective, Thatcher also illustrates a leader whose personal characteristics inclined her toward militaristic behavior even though the international situation she faced was not particularly dangerous. Looking at her case in depth does reveal the role that personal attributes played in driving British policy.

---

[32] Besides the Falklands, Thatcher was also responsible for MID #2226, the "Baltic Sea Maneuvers" against the Soviet Union that occurred in conjunction with other allied forces in March 1980.

[33] Campbell 2001, 191–2. [34] Ibid., 191–2.

[35] This also suggests an interesting path for future research in differentiating between the leader attributes that make the initiation of conflicts more likely versus those that make leaders more likely to be steadfast in responding to military aggression.

Margaret Thatcher with Admiral Sir Terence Lewin leaving Falklands Islands
Thanksgiving Service at St Paul's Cathedral, 1982
Source: Express Newspapers

CONTROLLING FOR OTHER FACTORS THAT INFLUENCE
NATIONAL MILITARIZED BEHAVIOR

Shifting from Thatcher in particular back to leaders in general, understanding
the relative importance of leaders as an independent force shaping the international system requires assessing their relative importance compared with
other factors that influence international politics. Classical realists such as Hans
Morgenthau argued that the balance of power was the most important deter-
minant of state power and, as such, the most important factor shaping interstate relations. Neo-realists such as Kenneth Waltz have long asserted that the
structure of the power relationships among the greatest powers, and in particular the number of the great powers or poles within this system, is the key to
understanding the stability of the system and international politics.

Institutionalists rebut the claim that power almost exclusively determines international behavior, arguing that both international and state domestic institutions, when shared among multiple states, can trump the material balance of power. For example, continuing a line of argument that goes back to philosopher Immanuel Kant, they argue that democracies have shared interests, ways of viewing the world, and means of signaling their interests and ways of resolving their differences that make them unlikely to go to war against each other. In the case of the post–World War II strategic environment, institutionalists argue that security institutions such as the North Atlantic Treaty Organization (NATO) and economic institutions such as the International Monetary Fund (IMF) play an important role in shaping states' interactions. Controlling for the presence and absence of these factors in the statistical models allows us to consider the arguments other scholars view as central to questions of war and peace.[36]

We therefore expand from a statistical model with leader attributes to a model that uses variables that more "traditional" models use, such as material power and domestic institutions.[37] Accounting for important realist arguments about the balance of power requires variables that measure the relative material power of a country and its prior war experiences. More powerful countries, for example, might be more likely to start militarized disputes just because they have more expansive interests. Similarly, states that have been involved in wars in the past are more likely to exist in dangerous neighborhoods where wars might be more likely to occur. Therefore, we want to compare our model of international conflict, based on leader attributes, with a model that includes a set of material power, state satisfaction, domestic politics, and prior military conflict variables designed to control for these factors.[38]

Table 2.2 shows the initial results. The top list of leaders shows, solely on the basis of leader background variables, the ten most "militaristic" leaders

---

[36] We generated the data for these variables using EUGene (Bennett and Stam 2000).

[37] See the Technical Appendix to see the full regression results. The table relevant shows the regression coefficients from three statistical models. The first uses only leader background variables to predict militarized disputes. The second uses unit-level variables such as material power, regime type, and whether a leader entered into office through regular or irregular means. The third model combines the first two and adds the additional controls for tenure in office and other factors impacting the country as a whole. This allows us to see the relative effect of the leader background variables even when controlling for other factors. Note that several of the leader variables are significant even when we control for generational, as opposed to individual, experiences (Last War Win/Loss/Draw) and the possibility that risky leaders are selected because a country expects to face a militarized dispute in the short-term (Time in Office, 5 Year MID Challenge Lag).

[38] Correlates of War material capabilities score (*CINC*), state satisfaction (*TauB*), and the prior success and failure of the state itself in its last war (*Prior Success, Prior Failure*). The results we present below are also consistent with additional control variables including major power status, trade openness, the number of contiguous states, and the system concentration of power, among others (Singer 1987; Bueno de Mesquita et al. 2003).

TABLE 2.2. *Top Ten "Riskiest" Leaders: Leader Risk versus System Risk*

Leader Risk Top Ten

Country	Leader Name	Leader Risk Score
China	Deng Xiaoping	0.69
Iran	Ayatollah Khomeini	0.69
U.S.	Ronald Reagan	0.68
Croatia	Franjo Tudjman	0.67
France	Georges Bidault	0.65
China	Mao Zedong	0.63
South Africa	Jan Smuts	0.63
Iraq	Hassan Al-Bakr	0.61
U.S.	John F. Kennedy	0.60
U.S.	Gerald Ford	0.58

Leaders Facing High System Risk Top Ten

Country	Leader Name	System Risk Score
U.S.	Dwight Eisenhower	0.83
Russia	Yuri Andropov	0.82
China	Jiang Zemin	0.82
Russia	Leonid Brezhnev	0.81
U.S.	Warren Harding	0.81
U.S.	John F. Kennedy	0.81
Russia	Nikita Khrushchev	0.80
Russia	Konstantin Chernenko	0.80
U.K.	Salisbury (3rd Marquess)	0.79
U.S.	Woodrow Wilson	0.78

according to our model.[39] Note that they are drawn from several different countries, with no single country accounting for most of the more risk-acceptant leaders in recent times. The bottom list of leaders shows the ten riskiest leaders according to a power and institutions model that excludes our leader-background variables. Most of the factors we control for do not vary a great deal over time. For example, during the entire period of our data, over 140 years, the United States is listed as a democracy. During that same time, however, leaders of the United States have changed regularly. The bottom column suggests that the United States should be the most militaristic state and that Dwight Eisenhower was the most conflict-prone leader in the entire period under examination. More generally, the list on the bottom simply

---

[39] To generate this column, we generate the predicted probability of militarized dispute initiation for each leader, and then sort by those predicted values.

suggests that the most powerful countries are the most prone to conflict. However, history reveals a more complicated pattern. This is initial evidence that taking leader-specific risk factors into account improves our ability to understand when states are likely to pose a threat to their neighbors and start conflicts.

The Leader Risk Index illustrates several points about the importance of leader background experiences for predicting national militarized behavior. First, the diversity of countries in the top ten reflects that leaders in many countries have started conflicts. Second, neither the Leader Risk Index nor the System Risk Index gets every leader right, as a glance at both lists shows. The key is that the lists are different, demonstrating that the Leader Risk Index does not just pick up nation-state characteristics. Third, the Index helps explain the behavior of many leaders. For example, while containing conflict data only through 2001, the Risk Index accurately categorizes Vladimir Putin as in the top 10 percent of leaders most likely to start armed conflicts.

Additionally, the Risk Index scores demonstrate that some of the most conflict-acceptant leaders may not be the most famous. For example, one of the highest scoring leaders is the leader introduced at the outset of this chapter, Franjo Tudjman of Croatia. Overlooked by theories based on perspectives that exclude leaders, as the Introduction to this chapter shows, the case of Tudjman shows how life experiences can sometimes play a significant role in influencing national policy and making conflict more likely.

Historian James Sadkovich argues that Tudjman's defining characteristic was his obsession with a Croatian nation-state.[40] Tellingly, Tudjman had a series of rebel and military experiences that, as predicted by the Risk Index, made him more likely to favor aggressive actions once in office. Beginning at age nineteen, Tudjman worked with Tito's partisans against the Nazis and Ustasha during World War II. His father and brothers founded the partisan movement in their home region of Zagorje.[41] He worked as a propagandist, promoted a newspaper titled *The Voice of the Croatian Zagorje Region*, and eventually rose to the rank of major in the Yugoslav People's Army.[42] He spent his last year of the war at the General Staff in Belgrade.[43, 44]

Tudjman rose quickly through the ranks of Tito's communist military, becoming a major general at age thirty-eight, the youngest ever in Yugoslavian history. In 1961, he left the army and founded the Institute for the Study of

---

[40] Sadkovich 2006b.   [41] Husic 2007.   [42] Ibid.

[43] Tudjman is also illustrative of some of the complicated measurement challenges involved in coding the background experiences of leaders, even leaders from the recent past. The uncertainty for Tudjman involves whether he served in the military but did not see combat, or whether he saw combat as part of an active duty military unit. According to Binder (1999), he did not see combat, although Sadkovich (2006a) implies that he did. We code Tudjman as having served in the military but not having participated in combat.

[44] Husic 2007.

the Workers' Movement in Croatia (Institut za historiju radničkoga pokreta Hrvatske; IHRPH), which later expelled him for excessive nationalism. Although retired from the military, he retained his martial stature throughout his political career. Hedl illustrates how he used this imagery later as president:

He did not imitate Tito by copying only his opulent lifestyle, however. He proclaimed himself a "Vrhovnik" (commander), inventing a rank that did not exist in the Croatian army in an attempt to mimic Tito's title of "marshal." Tudjman also personally designed a uniform that was tailored for him and that he wore at military parades, as Tito had before him. In a single day he awarded himself nine high-ranking medals, an event that reminded many people of Tito, who bestowed on himself the Medal of National Hero three times.[45]

Tudjman received a Ph.D. from the University of Zadar (although political reasons may have factored into the decision to award him a doctorate) and began writing increasingly ardent Croatian nationalist tracts.[46] His published works sought to reinterpret Croatian history in ways that legitimized a separate Croatian state. His agitating ended with his expulsion from the Communist Party in 1967 for advocating the recognition of Croatian as a separate language.[47] It is from this work, much of it revisionist, that he sowed the seeds of Croatian nationalism that would eventually result in the Bosnian War. After his expulsion, during his years as a dissident, Tudjman actively courted the Croatian diaspora community, making frequent trips to Canada, the United States, and Western Europe.[48]

As the Cold War ended and Yugoslavia fell apart in the late 1980s and early 1990s, Tudjman and Serbian leader Slobodan Milosevic met in 1991 to plan the division of Yugoslavian provinces Bosnia and Herzegovina between their nations.[49] In terms of domestic institutional constraints, Tudjman made his own rules, even creating his own party, the Croatian Democratic Union.

Thus, when Yugoslavia collapsed and the new country of Croatia was created, he ran for president in 1990, appealing to nationalist themes. The voters rewarded his efforts by handing him an overwhelming victory.[50]

---

[45] Hedl 2000, 107.   [46] Hedl 2000.   [47] Binder 1999, A1.   [48] Hockenos 2003.

[49] One thing the international community failed to realize at the time was that the war in the former Yugoslavia grew out of secret meetings in which Serbia and Croatia argued over the division of Bosnia in a post-Yugoslavia world. Rogel (2004, 29–30) writes, "Something not known at the time was that both Serbia and Croatia had express designs on Bosnia. Presidents Milosevic and Tudjman had met in September 1991 and secretly agreed to divide their neighboring republic. Memoirs and interviews with key players in the Yugoslav breakup have confirmed this collusion. Croatia's Tudjman, moreover, conceded as much when he drew the former Yugoslavia's new boundaries on a napkin for a British statesman at a dinner party in London in May 1995." This also suggests that existing theories of international politics underestimated the risk of conflict, which may be one reason our leader model seems to do so well compared with a more traditional model, in this case.

[50] BBC News 1999.

Franjo Tudjman.
Source: Davor Višnjić/PIXSELL.

According to Plotz, he rigged parliamentary elections to guarantee power for his party: "For example, he guaranteed Bosnian Croats, who are wildly nationalistic, 12 seats in the parliament – even though they don't live in Croatia."[51] His age had given him a lifetime of experience working with the military bureaucracy and other key institutions.

All of this made him particularly powerful, institutionally, when he assumed office. With his single-minded focus on creating a Croatian state, he advanced his nationalist ideology beyond the fragile institutional limits of the former Yugoslavia. He built a selectorate that included ethnic Croats both inside and outside Croatia. Shortly after his election, he pushed through a Croatian nationalist constitution, fired most Serbian civil servants, and renamed public places after Ustashi leaders.[52] Eventually, systematic ethnic cleansing in the Bosnian War succeeded in removing non-Croats from the selectorate of the general populace. Given this situation, he governed largely with the consent of the remaining public.

In 1991, war in the Balkans was still preventable. Structuralists may argue that the breakup of the former Yugoslavia was a trigger that would have driven any leader to war. Nevertheless, Tudjman began his overseas nationalist

---

[51] Plotz 1999. [52] Meier 1999.

fundraising campaign in 1988, two years before the beginning of the breakup in early 1990.[53] The president of Slovenia at the time, Milan Kučan, opposed a militaristic end to Yugoslavia and pushed for democracy and elections as the solution.[54] There were few external systemic or structural factors to predict that Croatia, specifically, would be particularly belligerent.

Tudjman initiated several military conflicts during the Balkan wars of the mid-1990s. Three of these were fatal clashes against Yugoslavian (primarily Serbian) and, later, Bosnian opponents. Tudjman's military aggression against ethnic Serbs began in 1991, shortly after his election.[55] By the end of 1991, Serbian military forces under Milosevic besieged the Croatian cities of Dubrovnik and Vukovar, leading to the deaths of more than 8,000 Croats during the fighting, while displacing an additional 200,000 internal refugees.[56] Tudjman agreed to a cease-fire, which lasted only until Bosnia declared independence in early 1992. Appealing to claims of historical Croatian borders, Tudjman took the opportunity to seize territory and plunged into an even more destructive phase of war. By 1993, according to Plotz,

> Bosnian Croat militias – directed by Tudjman from Zagreb – imprisoned thousands of Bosnian Muslims in concentration camps, shelled towns, murdered civilians, and barred humanitarian relief convoys. The Croats laid siege to Mostar, penning 50,000 Muslims inside, cut off food and water, and launched an artillery bombardment.[57]

Would another leader of Croatia have acted so aggressively? The presence of more pacific leaders in other parts of the former Yugoslavia suggests that the dissolution of the state was not a sufficient condition for war. The fact that Tudjman had to tear apart families, villages, and regions to achieve his ethnic-cleansing goals further implies that this was a difficult task with significant costs – not every leader would have made the same calculus. Tudjman, unlike most plausible alternative leaders, had extraordinarily rigid beliefs, along with a passionate desire to implement them. The combination of preferences and personality traits proved a devastating combination.

Franjo Tudjman represents a leader who, our Risk Index suggests, would be aggressive, and he was, despite the fact that traditional structural indicators do not predict war. Tudjman faced a relatively pacific international security environment according to indicators at the systemic level. Instead, the powerful personality of one fanatical leader worked to eliminate external barriers to achieving his personal nationalist goals. Tudjman illustrates the importance of including a systematic understanding of leader backgrounds at the individual level of analysis in order to advance our understanding of the outbreak of war.

However, is Tudjman an exception? If that is the case, our naïve model, exclusively based on leader backgrounds, would not do as well at identifying risk-acceptant leaders as the model that incorporates material capabilities and

[53] Hockenos 2003.   [54] Bennett 1997.   [55] Hayden 1992, 212.   [56] Binder 1999.
[57] Plotz 1999.

domestic factors. Yet that is not the case. Table 2.3 shows the leaders who initiated the most military conflicts (MIDs) when in office (the top 2 percent), along with two additional columns: the prediction of our leader risk model regarding that leader and the prediction of our system risk model involving that leader. For each, Table 2.3 shows the percentile into which the leader fell for that given model. The closer it is to 99 percent, the more accurate. For example, the Leader Risk column shows that Ayatollah Khomeini fell into the 99th percentile for our leader risk model, meaning our model accurately predicts that he would be among the most dangerous leaders in the dataset.

The list of the most conflict-prone leaders, in reality, reveals that, more like the leader model than the power-institutions model, the ten most dangerous leaders come from several different states. Also, of the ten leaders who started the most military conflicts according to our data, the Leader Risk Index accurately predicts eight of them as in the top two percent of leaders most likely to start military conflicts.[58] This demonstrates that some of the riskiest leaders in world history, including Mao Zedong, Joseph Stalin, Saddam Hussein, and Adolf Hitler, were among the most dangerous not only because of their domestic institutional setting or the international security environment, but also because of their life background experiences.

That a naïve model of militarized dispute initiation containing information only on the background experiences of a leader predicts the riskiest leaders as well as a model based on material power and domestic institutions is very suggestive. This is not to say that the leader attribute model is better – far from it; however, these results do show the potential explanatory power of our approach.[59]

To conclude this chapter, we focus on two leaders who are both, by our leader risk model and a system risk model, predicted to engage in aggressive military behavior. Such leaders should be war prone in any context, and the interaction of their personal characteristics and their external environment makes them especially dangerous – in fact, some of the most dangerous leaders in the dataset. The inclusion of leader background experiences and beliefs is particularly important when looking closely at cases in which international conflict is expected to occur and does in fact occur. Through these case studies, we can unpack different explanations for conflict and show the relative importance of an individual, even when other theories would also predict that the same behavior would occur.

The Cold War provides grist for the mill for both the traditional theory and our new explanation. For traditionalists, the Cold War is the ultimate case in

---

[58] These results end at 2001. Therefore, most leaders from the last decade, such as George W. Bush of the United States, do not show up in either list.

[59] Robustness tests such as comparing successful predictions and likelihood ratio analyses demonstrate the value added of incorporating leader backgrounds into our understanding of international conflict.

TABLE 2.3. *The Most Conflict-Prone Leaders, 1875–2001: Comparing Leader versus System Risk*

Country	Leader	Leader Risk Prediction (By Percentile)	System Risk Prediction (By Percentile)
Iran	Ayatollah Khomeini	**99%**	97%
Germany	Adolf Hitler	98%	**99%**
China	Mao Zedong	**99%**	**99%**
Iraq	Saddam Hussein	98%	96%
Russia	Josef Stalin	**99%**	98%
Russia	Leonid Brezhnev	**99%**	**99%**
Italy	Benito Mussolini	98%	93%
Russia	Nikita Khrushchev	**99%**	**99%**
Germany	Wilhelm II	94%	96%
Russia	Nicholas II	95%	97%
Russia	Boris Yeltsin	89%	97%
North Korea	Kim Il-Sung	97%	90%
India	Jawaharlal Nehru	91%	92%
Democratic Republic of the Congo	Mobutu Sese Seko	73%	88%
Taiwan	Chiang Kai-shek	94%	83%
U.S.	Ronald Reagan	**99%**	98%
Libya	Muammar Qaddafi	90%	88%
China	Deng Xiaoping	**99%**	**99%**
Syria	Hafez Al-Assad	94%	89%
U.S.	William Clinton	81%	98%
Indonesia	Sukarno	92%	57%
Austria	Francis Joseph I	87%	76%
Morocco	Hassan II	87%	79%
Egypt	Gamal Abdel Nasser	**98%**	94%
Pakistan	Ayub Khan	96%	96%
South Africa	Louis Botha	86%	89%
Ethiopia	Mengistu Marriam	90%	89%
Rhodesia	Ian Smith	86%	73%
Yugoslavia	Slobodan Milosevic	92%	89%
Uganda	Idi Amin	96%	85%
U.K.	Neville Chamberlain	82%	95%
U.S.	Dwight Eisenhower	96%	**99%**
Russia	Vladimir Lenin	82%	98%
U.K.	Salisbury (3rd Marquess)	88%	98%
U.S.	Woodrow Wilson	89%	**99%**
France	François Mitterand	94%	89%
Cuba	Fidel Castro	59%	79%
Turkey	Turgut Özal	91%	91%
Portugal	Caetano Veloso	84%	94%

Table 2.3. (*continued*)

Country	Leader	Leader Risk Prediction (By Percentile)	System Risk Prediction (By Percentile)
U.K.	Winston Churchill	96%	96%
Syria	Abid Shishakli	91%	90%
Iran	Akbar Hashemi Rafsanjani	89%	97%

* Percentages in **boldface** indicate leaders in the top 2% of risky leaders for that model.

which structural constraints dominated individual leaders and the power competition between the United States and the Soviet Union drove decision making. For us, the Cold War illustrates exactly why leaders are important and why adding our theory to existing explanations can help advance our understanding of international politics more generally. With the world on the brink of nuclear annihilation, the Cold War pushed individual leaders to the peak of their personal capacity to make decisions under stress.

While both Nikita Khrushchev and John F. Kennedy are known for their involvement in conflicts and the war they did not fight over Cuba, their personal histories provide useful information about the ways in which the backgrounds of leaders shape their conflict propensity. Both leaders are in the top 10 percent of our Risk Index, based on leader attributes, and in the top 10 percent of a risk index based on system-level factors. However, while Khrushchev initiated twenty-six militarized interstate disputes, including the brutal suppression of the Hungarian Uprising, Kennedy initiated only two. We argue that the inclusion of personal-level variables, in addition to traditional system and domestic political explanations, explains how these two men, in extremely dangerous situations, made different choices.

NIKITA KHRUSHCHEV

Nikita Khrushchev, like many of his generation, especially in Russia, straddled two very different eras, living from the end of the preindustrial era through the Space Age.[60] Khrushchev was born in a poor, nearly preindustrial village and was not marked for greatness. His rise from one living in the poorest segments of society to one of the most important leaders in the modern world, like Ronald Reagan in the United States and P. V. Narasimha Rao in India, is enormous.

It is remarkable that Khrushchev became a leader, given the tumultuous times in which he lived. Along the way, he barely survived several critical events

[60] Tompson 1995, 1.

that could have ended his life, most notably, the Russian Revolution in which he fought as a soldier; Stalin's purges of the 1930s that killed almost all of his colleagues; and World War II, during which, even as a political commissar, he became involved in some of the most deadly battles of the war.

Nikita Khrushchev grew up in extreme poverty. Even though he, along with his sister, enjoyed an intact family (meaning he avoided the kind of family fracture that can lead to more risky behavior later in life), his father left the family as a seasonal miner in order to support them. His parents were not just peasants but were at the lowest end of the lowest class, in a minority of households that did not even own a horse.[61] Khrushchev worked almost continuously from childhood, asking in a speech in Hollywood, "Would you like to know what I was once? I started work as soon as I could walk. Up to the age of 15 I looked after calves, then sheep and the landlord's cows."[62]

Khrushchev initially received a limited education of only two years of primary schooling. His teacher at this age, however, was an influential radical who introduced him to books banned under the tsarist regime. Later, as a metalworker, he received a few more years of secondary education equivalent to high school, but, due to the war, did not officially finish. His last education came in Moscow in 1929, at the Moscow Industrial Academy, where he was primarily involved in political battles against the "Rights," activity that brought him to the favorable attention of Stalin.

While Khrushchev participated in labor protests, he was not overtly political at first. After the Russian Revolution, he was unable to remain politically disengaged during the subsequent conflict. Taubman describes this time:

Sometime in late 1918 or early 1919, Khrushchev was mobilized into the Red Army. By this time the White forces, the Germans having left Ukraine when the armistice was signed in November 1918, were savaging Yuzovka ... Farther south, where Khrushchev was now stationed with the Reds' Ninth Army, the fighting was even more barbaric. Although Commissar of War Leon Trotsky had barred executing prisoners, "wounded or captured [White] officers were not only finished off and shot but tortured in every possible way."[63]

Because of his humble background, Khrushchev's experiences in the Russian Civil War were remarkably different from those of the intellectuals who would later be his comrades leading the communist hierarchy. "He still lived in a totally different world from Bolshevik leaders. His understanding of the Revolution and its direction was still very naïve ... This is the picture of a man for whom the Revolution was made, not of a man who in any real sense made it."[64]

---

[61] Taubman 2003.   [62] Medvedev 1982, 4.   [63] Taubman 2003, 49.
[64] Frankland 1966, 29.

Nikita Khrushchev (on left) at Stalingrad.
Source: RIA Novosti archive, image #882837 / Knorring / CC-BY-SA 3.0

After spending the interwar years working for the Communist Party, Khrushchev went on to participate in World War II as well. The large-scale intensity of mechanized warfare in this war meant that he witnessed extraordinary brutality, including the Battle of Stalingrad in which he served as the Red Army's political commissar:

[World War II] changed Khrushchev. From June 22, 1941 on, he was in the thick of the fight, retreating with the Red Army from Kiev to Stalingrad, then tramping back to resume his duties as Ukrainian party leader. Thousands died before his eyes, from simple soldiers mowed down in ill-advised battles to a general who committed suicide in his presence, guilty of nothing except defending their country and indeed Stalin himself. That was why Khrushchev felt free not only to lament unnecessary losses but to try to prevent them.[65]

---

[65] Taubman 2003, 150. Khrushchev related a particularly disturbing event in his memoirs: "We encircled Paulus' army in the fall and finished it off in the winter. I saw a horrible scene when we moved into the city in the early spring. Of course, there are always horrors in time of war. Our troops were busy gathering up the corpses of German soldiers. We were afraid of what might happen if we left them lying around with spring coming on and a hot summer ahead. We gathered thousands of corpses and stacked them in layers alternating with layers of railway ties. Then we set these huge piles on fire. I once went to watch, but I didn't go back a second time" (Khrushchev 2004, 199).

Khrushchev was married three times. His first wife, the mother of his two oldest children, died during the famine that swept Ukraine in 1921.[66] On the advice of his mother, he abandoned his second wife, mentioned only by Taubman, because she was unwilling to care for his children.[67] His third wife, Nina Petrovna, bore him two more children and remained with him until his death.

The mixed image of Khrushchev that the camera caught – on the one hand, outgoing and exuberant, on the other, tense and insecure – emerges from what is known of his private life. As a rising Kremlin star, he was living the good life Soviet style. Yet he was also under incredible strain stemming not only from his visible public role but from domestic pressures hidden from public view.[68]

Descriptions of Khrushchev include "intense," "energetic," and "hands-on," but also "boorish," "obnoxious," and "tactless." Despite his almost complete lack of education, most observers described him as very intelligent. His common background gave him a common touch in his job as a political leader, but also led his colleagues to repeatedly underestimate him. General Yeremenko, with whom Khrushchev worked closely at the Battle of Stalingrad, related:

At first sight N.S. Khrushchev seemed to me weary and tired, but the preoccupation and agitation with which he carried on the conversation spoke of the fact that he was full of energy. His worker's simplicity and sincerity at once won over the person he was talking to. He gave the impression of a gifted man of great intelligence who knows something particularly important which gives him the ability to solve the most difficult problems.[69]

From a leader attribute perspective, Khruhschev's struggle to achieve power and military service, with combat, in an autocratic regime should have made him conflict prone. He is in the top 1 percent of leaders predicted to use military force according to our leader risk model.

From an institutional perspective, Khrushchev worked under a set of incredibly complex constraints with mortal consequences for missteps. This made him acutely aware of the tenuous nature of his position in power.

He had been mentored and encouraged from an early stage by Stalin himself, "a creature of Stalin's making," and was required to stay in Stalin's favor for his own self-preservation.[70] Particularly in the last year of Stalin's life, his closest associates were engaged in incessant intrigues, which took a physical and mental toll on Khrushchev:[71]

Every aspect of his life and work during this period (1949–1953) was overshadowed by the presence of Stalin. In Kiev, he had been the king; now he was merely a member of the court – not infrequently the jester ... On one famous occasion [Stalin] ordered Khrushchev to perform the *gopak*, a Ukrainian folk dance, in front of a group of high party

---

[66] His eldest son, Leonid, was a fighter pilot and was killed in World War II, when he had been sent on a particularly dangerous mission as punishment for accidentally killing another soldier.
[67] Taubman 2003.   [68] Ibid., 108.   [69] Frankland 1966, 64–5.   [70] Ibid., 55.
[71] Taubman 2003.

officials. This was both embarrassing and physically uncomfortable for Khrushchev, but he pretended to enjoy it. As he later remarked to Miokan, "When Stalin says dance, a wise man danced."[72]

Eventually, most of Khrushchev's rivals were killed in Stalin's purges, and he was one of a handful of top party officials left standing after Stalin's death.[73] His unique background was actually an asset that helped differentiate him from the intellectuals that Stalin viewed as a threat.[74]

Post Stalin, Khrushchev began consolidating power. In 1953, he fronted an elaborate conspiracy to destroy his rival, Beria, whom the authorities arrested in June.[75] By 1956, Khrushchev was confident enough in his power base to reconstruct the institutions that Stalin, in his paranoia, had undermined. That year, he denounced Stalin's cult of personality and began the "mass liberation of almost all political prisoners and the rapid review of the cases of those who had died between 1935 and 1955 in Stalin's camps and prisons and their rehabilitation."[76] Millions of former political prisoners were returned to society.[77] By July 1957, however, adversaries in the Central Committee attempted to unseat him. In response, Khrushchev defeated and later expelled them.[78]

Ideologically, Khrushchev seemed driven to defend and promote the honor of the Soviet Union because he truly believed in the ideals of communism and had worked hard for many years to put them into practice for Russian peasants. He was deeply sensitive to the frequent attacks in the West in which Soviet critics portrayed the USSR as backward and uncivilized.[79]

At the system level, Khrushchev was in power during an extended period of repeated crises. The dramatic increase in the numbers and lethality of nuclear weapons during the 1950s was a danger that threatened the entire world, and the Cold War stage required careful maneuvering by its most important players. Khrushchev was arguably operating under even greater constraints than his counterparts in America and Europe. He had as much to learn about his adversaries as they did about him, because, as Taubman relates, "for the first fifty years of his life he had little exposure to the outside world and almost none to the great powers."[80] In these circumstances, his visits with foreign leaders took on greater significance.

---

[72] Tompson 1995, 105.
[73] "Khrushchev assisted in the arrest and liquidation of his own colleagues and friends. Of 38 top officials of Moscow city and province party organizations, only three survived. Of 146 party secretaries of other cities and districts in the Moscow region, 136 were, to use the post-Stalin euphemism, 'repressed.' Of 63 people elected to the Moscow city party committee in May 1937, 45 presumably perished. Of 64 on the province committee, 46 disappeared ... According to a historian who interviewed survivors, Khrushchev did little or nothing to help save his friends and colleagues ... But Khrushchev could not or would not prevent even his closest and most trusted associates from being arrested and shot" (Taubman 2003, 99–100).
[74] Tompson 1995, 63.   [75] Medvedev 1982.   [76] Ibid., 97.   [77] Ibid., 92.
[78] Frankland 1966.   [79] Taubman 2003.   [80] Ibid., 326.

Before coming to power, Khrushchev attended the 1955 Geneva Summit, a critical meeting including the leaders of the United States, Britain, France, and the Soviet Union. The purpose of the Geneva Summit was ostensibly to hammer out conditions for peaceful coexistence, but instead, "Khrushchev left Geneva, 'encouraged, realizing now that our enemies probably feared us as much as we feared them.' That prompted him to practice nuclear bluster so as to play on American fears."[81]

According to our system and institutional risk model, as with the leader risk model, Khrushchev is predicted to be a conflict-prone leader. One thing neither model incorporates, but which seems to have been an important influence on Khrushchev, is learning. In September 1959, Khrushchev was the first Soviet leader to visit the United States. He left with a very positive impression of fellow World War II veteran Dwight Eisenhower, believing he could be trusted. This made the U-2 spy plane incident the next year, when the Soviets discovered U.S. spy plane overflights were occurring and shot down one plane flown by U.S. pilot Gary Powers, even more troubling for Khrushchev. According to one biographer, "Khrushchev was 'horrified' to learn the president [Eisenhower] had approved the spy flights."[82]

While Khrushchev briefly met Eisenhower's successor, John F. Kennedy, during that initial visit in 1959, he became better acquainted with him at a summit in Vienna in 1961. The summit was a significant opportunity for each leader to learn about the other, which ultimately benefited Khrushchev more than Kennedy:

> The summit's principal significance turned out to be the effect it had in shaping the two leaders' impressions of one another ... Kennedy erred badly by joining a casual debate with Khrushchev on the merits of Marxism. Kennedy, his Harvard education notwithstanding, was ill prepared to rebut the claims made by the former Red Army Commissar. Khrushchev easily got the best of Kennedy during that go-round. When Kennedy warned of the dangers of "miscalculation" setting off a nuclear war, Khrushchev exploded, enraged by the President's apparent condescension. Khrushchev's harsh tone was the product of Kennedy's refusal to accept any negotiations over Berlin, which Khrushchev saw as a retreat from Eisenhower's acceptance speech in 1959 of the need for talks.[83]

Sensing weakness in his opponent, Khrushchev felt emboldened to, among other actions, build the Berlin Wall and send nuclear missiles to Cuba. They did not seem to know each other well, however. It was not until the Berlin crisis of 1961 and the Cuban Missile Crisis in 1962 that they gained greater understanding of their adversary.[84]

The combination of these personal experiences and an understanding of his responsibility as the leader of the Soviet Union made Khrushchev comfortable with the use of force and making the first move in a conflict but also keenly

---

[81] Ibid., 352.   [82] Ibid., 459.   [83] Tompson 1995, 234.   [84] Medvedev 1982, 180.

aware of the risks of escalation. For example, in a discussion with U.S. newspaper editors in 1962, Khrushchev stated:

> If some unintelligent statesman of some small state goes mad, this harms no one. But if lack of intelligence is shown on the part of leaders of such states as the United States of America and the Soviet Union, then it would not only be a calamity for the people of our countries, but for the people of the whole world. A great deal depends on the mutual understanding between our two states.[85]

Khrushchev's concern over Mao's "cavalier" attitude toward the risk of nuclear war, after Mao seemed unconcerned about the prospects of nuclear escalation, also could have derived in part from his own wartime experiences.[86]

Khrushchev's militarized behavior in office illustrates the pattern of behavior predicted by both our Leader Risk Index and a more traditional, system and institutional approach. Khrushchev initiated the use of force twenty-six times while in office, including the infamous 1956 suppression of the Hungarian Revolution.[87] That conflict alone, in which the Soviet Union enjoyed a significant advantage in relative power over its opponent, resulted in more than 20,000 Hungarian and 15,000 Soviet casualties.[88]

Both our theory and a more traditional, system-based theory accurately predict Khrushchev's militarized behavior. Both also can arguably explain why Khrushchev was willing to back down at higher levels of the escalation ladder. For traditional theories, the consequences of nuclear war for the Soviet Union made Khrushchev cautious when the Cuban Missile Crisis threatened to spin out of control. In 1955, the USSR detonated the first transportable hydrogen bomb.[89] This solidified the Cold War and the terrifying potential of the use of force, for which Khrushchev felt the heavy weight of responsibility, balanced with the need for credible deterrence. According to Taubman:

> This was vintage Khrushchev. The missiles were meant to frighten, not to be fired. Eisenhower's thinking hadn't been all that different, but Kennedy's was: Worried about how to make deterrence credible, he sought a nuclear superiority great enough to convince Moscow that he would actually risk nuclear war. Khrushchev's notion was simpler: As long as he had (or seemed to have) a minimum number of missiles and sounded prepared to use them, the Americans would be intimidated.[90]

These numerous threats, provocations, even murderous decisions notwithstanding, Khrushchev repeatedly went to the brink of nuclear Armageddon without stepping over the cliff. Khrushchev himself, however, provides additional evidence about how his personal experiences also shaped his willingness to avoid escalation when confronted. In the Cuban Missile Crisis, his letter to

---

[85] Frankland 1966, 156.   [86] Tompson 1995, 194.

[87] Under his watch, there were 7 attacks, 14 seizures, 1 territorial occupation, and 7 border violations.

[88] Taubman 2003.   [89] Medvedev 1982.   [90] Taubman 2003, 535.

President Kennedy drew on his experiences to explain his desire to find a peaceful solution. The letter reads, in part:

I have participated in two wars and know that war ends when it has rolled through cities and villages, everywhere sowing death and destruction. For such is the logic of war. If people do not display wisdom, they will clash like blind moles and mutual annihilation will commence.[91]

Like many other combat-experienced leaders in highly autocratic regimes such as the Soviet Union, Khrushchev reacted to his combat experience and the need to fight – sometimes literally – to reach a leadership position by developing strong instincts in favor of aggression and the use of military force. However, our theory does not necessarily speak to the willingness to escalate in a situation such as the Cuban Missile Crisis. In this case, despite an external security environment that made the worst case more likely, Khrushchev reached back into his personal history and derived empathy about the consequences of a conflict.

While our theory does not diverge from system and structural level theories in observed outcomes – both correctly predict militarized behavior and incentives to back down at higher levels on the escalation ladder – it does provide additional insight into how risk-acceptant leaders come to be. When we consider individuals who are not yet world leaders but are currently living through similarly dangerous situations, we may have greater insight into the risk-acceptant tendencies of heads of state in future dangerous settings.

JOHN F. KENNEDY

We conclude with an overview of another Cold War leader, John F. Kennedy, who, despite personal characteristics suggesting a risky profile, demonstrated restraint in dangerous circumstances, although he also engaged to some degree in risky adventurism. He is especially interesting because he initiated only two militarized disputes in his time in office, despite appearing as one of the top ten leaders predicted to engage in the use of military force by both our leader-based model and a traditional approach. So, was Kennedy's lack of military adventurism the result of something that all of these models miss or was he aggressive in ways that our models do not capture, because they focus on the explicit use of military force?

Unlike Khrushchev, John F. Kennedy was born into a life of privilege and wealth. He father, Joe, raised his sons with an eye to future political leadership; Joe Kennedy promoted intense mental and physical competitiveness in all his children. Despite frequent, often near-fatal illnesses from a young age, Kennedy strove to live up to these expectations. Intense sibling competition

---

[91] JFK Presidential Library and Museum 1962.

with his older brother, Joe Jr., who was expected to be the standard bearer for the family, served only to magnify these challenges.

Growing up in the Kennedy family was a high-pressure experience. Kennedy's father was an energetic, competitive, and driven entrepreneur with extremely high expectations for all of his children. His mother was often absent, not affectionate, and ran the household very strictly.[92]

Jack, as the second son, lived in the shadow of his preferred elder brother until Joe Jr.'s death in World War II. As Ambassador to England, Joe Kennedy, Sr., brought his family with him to Europe, where they witnessed firsthand the escalating tensions prior to World War II. In 1937 and 1939, Jack went with his friends on tours of Europe, including Germany, and encountered Nazism for himself. According to Renehan, Jack and Joe Jr. were in Berlin on August 21, 1939, the date the Molotov-Ribbentrop Pact became known.[93] Jack returned to London two days later and took on an unofficial role as representative of the United States for the American survivors of the *Athenia*, a passenger ship accidentally torpedoed by the Germans.[94]

Jack received an elite education at Choate and Harvard, although he was far from a model student. Despite his severe health problems, Kennedy joined the U.S. Navy and became the commander of PT boat *109* in World War II. It was his actions as captain of *PT-109* that brought him into the national eye. On August 2, 1943, near the Solomon Islands in the Pacific, a Japanese destroyer ran over *PT-109*, cutting it in two and sinking it. Kennedy and the remaining ten survivors, some badly injured, swam or were dragged to the nearest tiny island where they were stranded for two days without supplies before being forced to swim to another distant island for water. Kennedy famously pulled the most severely injured crewmember, Pop McMahon, by holding the straps of his life jacket in his teeth and swimming for five hours. In total, Kennedy and his crew spent five days stranded on the island, during which time the Navy presumed them dead, never sending a search party. Rescuers located Kennedy and his men after Kennedy met two locals and used them to send a message he carved onto a coconut shell back to American commanders. The experience embittered Kennedy toward both the Navy and the Japanese. However, as Renehan notes, his military experience was personally important to Kennedy:

It would be a mistake to believe Kennedy looked back on his experience of the war cynically, or viewed it as little more than a useful PR tool. Quite the contrary. He considered World War II to have been the seminal, defining event of his life. "I firmly believe," he once wrote, "that as much as I was shaped by anything, so I was shaped by the hand of fate moving in World War II . . . The war made us. It was and is our single

---

[92] Meagher and Gregg 2011, 7.   [93] Renehan 2002.

[94] About this incident, one reporter commented, "His boyish charm and natural kindliness persuaded those who he had come to comfort that America was indeed keeping a benevolent and watchful eye on them . . . Mr. Kennedy displayed a wisdom and sympathy of a man twice his age" (ibid., 112).

greatest moment. The memory of the war is key to our characters ... We were much shrewder and sadder when that long battle finally finished. The war made us get serious for the first time in our lives. We've been serious ever since, and we show no signs of stopping."[95]

Health reasons, in particular damage to his back suffered during his PT boat incident, forced Kennedy to retire from the Navy in 1943, and he returned home in 1944. Kennedy won a seat in the U.S. House of Representatives in 1946, a seat in the Senate in 1952, and the presidency in 1960. He entered office at a critical time in American history, and neither his extensive intellectual understanding of foreign affairs nor his war experiences adequately prepared him for the task.

Joe Jr.'s death, the death of Jack's sister Kathleen in 1948, and the lobotomization of his sister Rosemary were all profoundly painful experiences for Kennedy that made him question his own longevity and strive to make a difference as quickly as possible.[96] Throughout his life, Kennedy suffered from numerous severe illnesses that often threatened to end his life, likely giving him shorter time horizons about his future (a characteristic, as explained in Chapter 1, that is also generally associated with risky behavior). He became acutely ill when he was seventeen years old and spent most of June 1934 at the Mayo Clinic undergoing a series of invasive tests.[97] He received the last rites of the Catholic Church at least four times as an adult.[98] In 1947, he was first diagnosed with Addison's disease and given only a few years to live.[99]

As described in Chapter 1, significant health issues often drive leaders to have shorter time horizons, making risky behavior more likely as an individual seeks to make his or her mark before passing away. Kennedy seems somewhat unusual in this respect. His health deteriorated throughout his time as president, and he was medicated daily to help him cope with constant physical pain. His medical condition, however, became a critical part of his personality. According to Pitts, "it fortified his spirit and became and indelible part of his character."[100]

When Oswald assassinated Kennedy in 1963, JFK had already outlived his doctor's expectations for the maximum life expectancy for someone with his condition.

Thus, Kennedy had a set of background experiences, especially health issues, that should have led him to feel that he had only a short amount of time to make his mark. From the perspective of the LEAD dataset, that shorter shadow of the future should have inclined him toward a medium level of aggressiveness. What about the institutional constraints that might have shaped Kennedy's behavior? Kennedy's institutional constraints should have been few, with the Democrats controlling both the House of Representatives and the Senate.

---

[95] Ibid., 2.   [96] Mahoney 2011, 37.   [97] O'Brien 2005.   [98] Reeves 1994.
[99] Mahoney 2011, 7.   [100] Pitts 2007, 18.

Theoretically, he therefore had significant leeway to implement his preferred policies. However, Kennedy suffered from a lack of experience that made him vulnerable to actors from the established bureaucracy. As Mahoney explains:

The president feared that the "total victory" patriotism of General LeMay and Senator Goldwater exaggerated the evil of the other side and miscast the capacity of the United States to alter human destiny. It created a psychosis of siege and suspicion. The cruel invective of anticommunism, Kennedy felt, made nuclear Armageddon a "moral imperative" and excused America in the name of national emergency from addressing the scarred and inhuman corners of its own society.[101]

The mid–Cold War period in which Kennedy led the United States was also one of the most dangerous periods in American history. According to the model based on international system attributes presented earlier in Table 2.2, Kennedy is predicted to be one of the most conflict-prone leaders in the dataset. Kennedy acutely felt the pressure of leading the United States in the early nuclear age, a period when people regularly discussed the possibility of a thermonuclear war between the United States and the Soviet Union that might wipe out humanity. When he met Eisenhower, for example, he told his brother, Robert Kennedy, that Eisenhower seemed amazingly calm when discussing the potential end of the world.[102]

Despite strong systemic pressures and personal risk acceptance, presented with few opportunities not posing the risk of nuclear escalation, John F. Kennedy initiated only a few militarized conflicts, including his authorization of the Bay of Pigs invasion of Cuba and the blockade that launched the militarized portion of the Cuban Missile Crisis.[103] He also strongly supported building up U.S. military forces to help ensure success against the Soviet Union if war did occur. The interaction of his personal attributes with domestic political institutions and the security environment produced aggressive policies tempered at higher levels of the escalation ladder.

CONCLUSION

The geopolitical world is not nearly as deterministic as traditional international relations theories suggest, and human agency is more important than many scholars would have us believe.[104] World leaders have personal agency that matters in what we observe as outcomes of war and peace. In some cases, structural factors do swamp and overwhelm individual leaders' freedom of independent action. When this happens, theories based on system- or institutional-level factors are sufficient to understand world politics outcomes.

---

[101] Mahoney 2011, 256.   [102] Reeves 1994.
[103] Kennedy was also responsible for MID #1801, which from May to November 1961 involved a show of force, by use of warships off the coast of the Dominican Republic.
[104] Waltz 1979; Wendt 1999.

In the absence of a real-world counterfactual, we can only imagine how leaders with different personal characteristics would react to similar exogenous pressures.

However, in world politics, things do not always go according to plan. Instead of discounting unexpected cases of war and peace as outliers to structural theories, we argue that they require closer examination at a different level, that of the state leader. Our data and the cases in this chapter powerfully illustrate the ability of individual executives to impose their will on the rest of the world.

In Chapter 3, we dive further into a comparison between the benefits and drawbacks of focusing solely on the international system and domestic political institutions versus focusing on leaders. The chapter explores how leader and system risk work across space and time, as well as how bringing all of these factors together could produce an even more accurate understanding of international conflict than we can gain from just one perspective. Chapter 3 also explains how leaders are selected and why we have to take that into consideration to fully flesh out how and why leaders matter in international politics.

3

Leader Risk across Geography and Time

How important are leader attributes, compared with the predictions of system-level theories, when it comes to the outbreak of international conflict? The previous chapter began the process of systematically examining the importance of leaders by describing the creation of an index of leader risk that measures, based on the background experiences of leaders, their propensity to start international conflicts.

This chapter compares the Leader Risk Index to more traditional explanations for warfare. It maps conflict across the world, as well as across specific regions, from 1875 to 2001, to highlight the importance of understanding leader risk. Using advanced statistical models, the results in this chapter show that while the effects of leaders are almost certainly influenced by the relative power of their countries and the domestic political contexts in which they operate, leaders still exercise independent influence over international politics.

MAPPING LEADER RISK

The empirical literature on war outbreak and escalation provides strong evidence for the importance of analysis at the regional level.[1] International relations theory acknowledges the fundamental importance of geography as a risk factor either mitigating or exacerbating the risks of interstate war. John Mearsheimer notes the "stopping power of water," for example, that makes it difficult to project power across oceans even for the most powerful countries in the world.[2] Mountains, rivers, and swamps make for relatively stable national borders because they greatly increase the difficulty of projecting military power. States such as Poland, with borders lacking natural defenses, have

---

[1] Vasquez and Henehan 2001; Senese and Vasquez 2003.   [2] Mearsheimer 2001, 114.

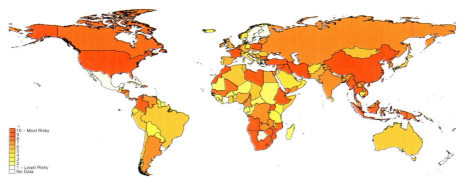

FIGURE 3.1. Leader risk map, 1989.

been among the most frequently conquered. One of the strongest findings from empirical research on international conflict, not surprisingly, is that contiguous neighbors are more likely to fight, whether the disputes are related to territory, revenge for past grievances, or ethnic conflict.[3]

In attempting to understand the role of leaders in shaping the distribution of international conflict more generally, one approach is to look at particular regions and the distribution, or lack thereof, of conflict-prone leaders. Figure 3.1 shows a global risk map for leaders in office in 1989, at the end of the Cold War.

In this map and the ones that follow, the color corresponds to the risk level associated with each country's leader. Compare the leader-risk data in Figure 3.1 with the same map based solely on the same "system" level models of international conflict used in Chapter 2, in Figure 3.2.

While there are many similarities between these maps, as one might expect, note one important difference: while the system-risk map from 1989 paints a bright red, meaning extremely conflict-prone, Soviet Union, the leader-risk map more correctly identifies that the trend in Soviet behavior, due to the leadership of Mikhail Gorbachev, was away from conflict.

One disadvantage of the map approach is that we can view leader risk only over a single year. Creating estimates of the "system" level of leader risk over time helps create an estimate that is more comparable with system-level models of international conflict. Figure 3.3 shows variation in leader risk, at the global level, over the time period covered by the LEAD dataset, 1875–2001.[4]

---

[3] Vasquez and Henehan 2001a; Rasler and Thompson 2006; Huth 2009. Such territorial issues are particularly salient for publics (Hutchison and Gibler 2007). Seemingly indivisible territorial disputes can be driven by the need for legitimacy on the part of the disputing leaders (Goddard 2006). Significantly, internal civil conflicts can spill across borders, triggering international disputes (Salehyan 2008) and fostering less democratic regimes (Rasler and Thompson 2011).

[4] George and Bennett 2005.

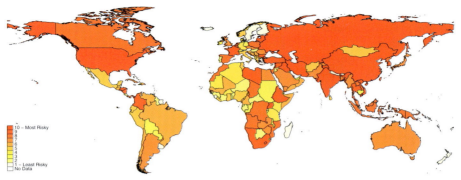

FIGURE 3.2. System risk map, 1989.

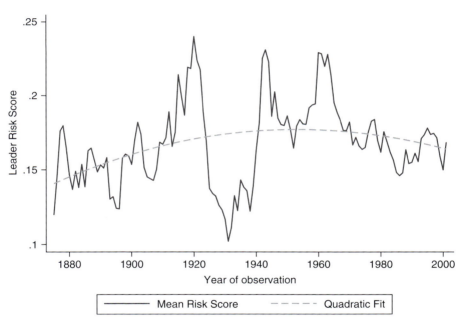

FIGURE 3.3. The annual mean of global leader risk, 1875–2001.

Figure 3.3 illustrates the system-average risk level for all leaders over time. If we compare theories of international politics, some, such as structural realism, are unable to predict any single instance of war or conflict because the factors that theorists argue as being most influential rarely change. For example, structural realists maintain that polarity, or the number of major powers in the international system, is the key indicator of international stability and risk of great power war. While we agree that the structure of the system can both inhibit and foment conflict, we cannot look to the system structure as an explanation for variations in the number of conflicts that occur year to year because this polarity is so stable. During the Cold War, which by most definitions lasted from 1945 to 1989, there was no change in the system structure. However, during that time there were several periods of relative peace and occasional periods of large-scale warfare between states. Structural realism, because its key explanatory factor did not vary at all during that period, cannot provide an explanation for the outbreak of the Vietnam War, the Cuban Missile Crisis, or any of the host of deadly Cold War quarrels.

As Figure 3.3 illustrates, this period featured a shift in the relative risk of leaders in the system. During the period leading up to the Cuban Missile Crisis, for example, we can see that the level of risk in the system was on the rise. Following this event and the beginning of the large-scale decolonization movement, we see a long-term reduction in system risk, although it is a decline punctuated by occasional high-risk leaders replacing low-risk leaders, resulting in an increased risk for some regions. If we smooth out all the local and annual variations, the dashed line in Figure 3.3 suggests that there has been, on average, a general increase in risk over time. This suggests that, in contrast to the views of scholars such as Steven Pinker, violent international conflict may not become increasingly rare.[5]

Moving from the global to the regional, Figure 3.4 shows the leader-years in each region around the world that fall into different categories of leader risk. For example, the size of the Europe bubble for the 100th percentile shows that there are over 350 leaders in LEAD dataset that fall between the 90th and 100th percentile when it comes to leader risk. A key initial takeaway from this chart is that no region has a monopoly on conflict-prone leaders.

Even regions featuring countries with relatively low levels of relative power, such as much of Africa, have produced extremely risk acceptant leaders according to our Leader Risk Index, a judgment that matches up with historical reality. Closer inspection on shifting from the global to the local reveals important differences in leader risk across regions and over time. In what follows, we look at each region in the world and show how the general distribution of leader risk has shaped conflict.

One initial question to consider is what happens when conflict-prone leaders emerge side by side. Considering earlier empirical and theoretical work on territorial aggression, we expect, on balance, that regions featuring conflict-prone leaders in close proximity should, on average, be more dangerous.[6]

---

[5] Pinker 2011.
[6] This is, of course, a probabilistic prediction. There are a number of observations in which this is not the case, of course. However, on balance, we should expect that the clustering of more risk-prone leaders should lead to more conflict.

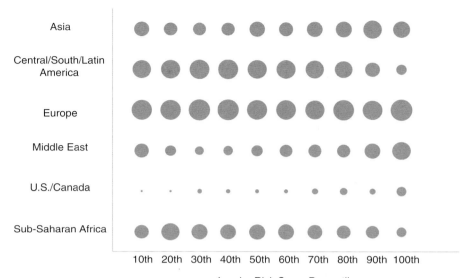

FIGURE 3.4. Global leader risk by region, 1875–2001.

Europe

In the last quarter of the nineteenth century, as the map of 1875 Europe in Figure 3.5 indicates, leader risk attitudes in Europe were quite homogenous, with central Europe and Great Britain having the higher risk leaders on the continent. As the twentieth century arrived, leaders in central Europe became increasingly willing to take on greater military risks. Just before World War I, we can see the aggressor leaders' countries highlighted in bright red. Looking, for example, at Europe in 1913, we see that Germany and the Austro-Hungarian Empire had the most dangerous leaders. Carol I, king of Romania, was similarly risky. Meanwhile, the leaders of France, Italy, Belgium, and the Netherlands were relatively risk-averse. In other words, from a leader perspective, they were sitting ducks.

By 1938 – strictly from the point of view of leader characteristics – Europe was blinking red. Highly conflict-prone leaders headed Spain, France, Italy, Greece, Germany, and others. Germany and its Axis partner, Italy, were run by two of the most risk-acceptant leaders in our dataset, Hitler and Mussolini. In Great Britain, Neville Chamberlain faced a problematic power distribution: Germany's open window of opportunity in 1938, due to its militarization, coincided with relative British weakness (because British militarization had not yet begun in force).[7] Europe in 1938 was full of leaders ready to fight

---

[7] Chamberlain's risk "score," according to our Risk Index, is in the top 25% of leaders, but far below Hitler's, Mussolini's, and that of Great Britain's other opponents in 1938.

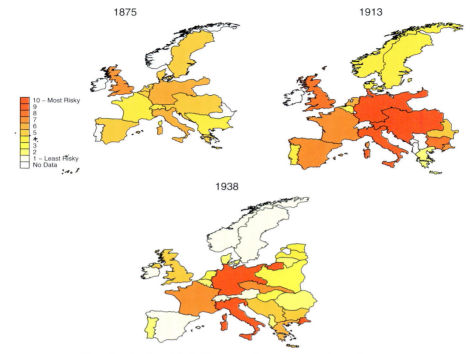

FIGURE 3.5. Mapping leader risk in Europe, 1875, 1913, and 1938.

and willing to take significant risks. The former balancer, Britain, was saddled with a leader unwilling to take risks to deter a general war. By the time Churchill, a leader cut from a different bolt of cloth and one with quite different formative experiences, arrived in 1940, Europe was far along the path to another large-scale war.[8]

Meanwhile, in the prewar years, France was led by Camille Chautemps (in the lower 50 percent of leader risk according to our leader attribute model) and then Édouard Daladier (slightly above average in risk propensity). In 1938, Hitler, correctly believing he faced leaders in Britain and France with less interest in conflict than he, forced the issue and precipitated the largest war the world has seen. Figure 3.5 shows this change over time in leader risk in Europe.

North America

The United States consistently elects some of the most risk-acceptant leaders in the LEAD dataset. The general trend for the United States has been upward

---

[8] Lucas 1996.

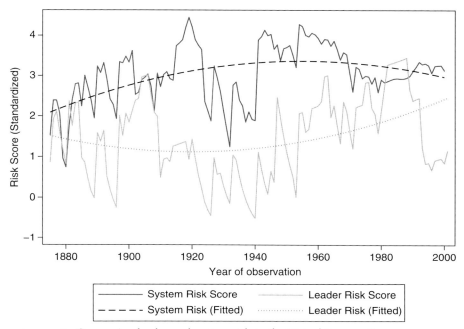

FIGURE 3.6. Comparing leader and system risk in the United States, 1875–2001.

since the nineteenth century. The personal stories of American presidents such as John F. Kennedy and Ronald Reagan indicate why. As Figure 3.6 shows, however, these leaders are less risky than systemic factors would predict. This indicates that, in most periods, Americans elect leaders who can act to restrain the power of the nation. One interesting case of this is Woodrow Wilson.

During the presidency of Woodrow Wilson, according to traditional explanations, the international system appears dangerous, and the background attributes identified in the LEAD dataset, in the aggregate, suggest the leader would not be aggressive, yet the leader engages in large-scale interstate war. The Wilson case demonstrates that incorporating leader attributes into existing models of international conflict is only a first step toward a more complete understanding of why and how wars occur. More is necessary, and much of that appears driven by the personal attributes of Wilson, although in ways not entirely captured by our Leader Risk Index.

Wilson, as a reluctant, late entrant to World War I, illustrates an executive with less risk-acceptant personal attributes who could still lead his country into war due to forces beyond his control. Thomas Woodrow Wilson was born on December 28, 1856, to the Rev. Dr. Joseph Wilson and Janet Woodrow in Staunton, Virginia. He was the third child, following two daughters, and later had a younger brother. His father was a well-educated reverend from Ohio, while his mother, Janet "Jessie" Woodrow, was from a family of first-generation English immigrants. Before attending Princeton University, Wilson spent a year at Davidson College in North Carolina.

Wilson excelled at college academically, but also fit into the social environment. One biographer writes:

Robert (Bob) Bridges, who became his closest friend at Princeton, remembered that "what he called 'the play of the mind' was as exhilarating to him as the play of the body to an athlete."[9]

Wilson next attended law school at the University of Virginia, passed the bar, and started his own practice, but, "[a]s the end of his first year as a lawyer approached, Wilson decided to leave the profession and the South in order to approach politics from a different direction, as a teacher and writer."[10] He remained interested in public affairs, thinking that he could influence public policy from his position as a professor, but later decided that the only way to bring about change in the political system was to be a part of it.

As Wilson became more interested in politics, he decided to run for office in New Jersey, leaving Princeton University in 1910 to run for governor. He spent less than two years as governor before running for president as a Democrat, defeating Theodore Roosevelt in 1912 and assuming the presidency in 1913. While Wilson entered office without much experience in foreign policy, he did have some views, drawn from his career at Princeton, about the United States and its role in the world. Lacking the sort of background generally associated with military expertise, Wilson's "approach was a mixture particularly his own, a combination of idealism, national interests, and ideas carried forward from his early studies of democratic development. Contrary to what has been generally assumed, he did not enter public life without having given considerable thought to this field."[11]

This lack of experience with foreign policy might have made Wilson cautious and less likely to use force. However, while in office, Wilson initiated the use of military force ten times (eight more times than John F. Kennedy), culminating in his decision to take the United States into World War I. What characteristics of Wilson and/or the environment in which he led the United States can explain this outcome?

The institutional environment that Wilson faced in office, especially in his early years as president, gave him relatively larger latitude in making policy than many leaders in democracies. Wilson, as a Democratic president, worked with a same-party Congress for the first six years of his time in office. Therefore, while he faced the institutional restraints that all democratic leaders face, he led in a more permissive environment, providing more flexibility to successfully carry out his preferred policies.[12] Bolstered by

---

[9] Cooper 2009, 26.   [10] Clements 1987, 10.   [11] Heckscher 1991, 129.
[12] Bar-Joseph and McDermott 2008; Cooper 2009. In his first term, Wilson achieved a great deal; he was particularly successful in pushing through his progressive domestic policy agenda.

Woodrow Wilson.
Source: Library of Congress Prints and Photographs Division.

a compliant Congress and buoyed by an American public largely uninterested in foreign entanglements and open to considering domestic changes previously considered radical, Wilson could implement an agenda of his choosing.[13]

---

[13] Brands 2003, 23.

How is it that Wilson, a leader with personal characteristics that did not predispose him to the use of military force and with domestic institutions likely to favor his preferences, became involved in so many militarized disputes? One explanation is simply that systemic forces, over time, overwhelmed Wilson's general desire to avoid war.

Woodrow Wilson became president in 1913. The next year, Europe began its descent into World War I. While he supported several smaller uses of force in the Western hemisphere during his first term, he regarded the war in Europe as someone else's responsibility. Supported by a Democratic majority in Congress, which was also skeptical of intervention, Wilson kept the United States out of World War I throughout his first term. At the outset of World War I, for example, Wilson embarked on a number of peace initiatives between 1915 and April 1917. He first appealed to the publics of the belligerent nations; however, "[w]hen, notwithstanding this public appeal, the Allies showed no interest in activating the House-Grey memorandum and indeed seemed to be committed to a total victory in pursuit of extreme war aims, Wilson abandoned the attempt to collaborate with them."[14] He ran for reelection in part on the slogan, "He kept us out of war."

However, after the Germans began unrestricted submarine warfare on February 1, 1917, and with the publication of the Zimmermann Telegram, a ham-handed German attempt to encourage Mexico to declare war against the United States, Wilson had no choice but to ask for a congressional declaration of war. By that point, it was clear that the Great War was inflicting severe casualties on all sides, and Germany's U-boat campaign was a direct threat to American interests. Neutrality was no longer an option; events in Europe forced Wilson's hand, pressing him into service as a war president.

The question Wilson faced was how to bring the American public along to share his view that it was no longer in American interests to stay out of the European Great War. Wilson's War Message to Congress on April 2, 1917, was intended as much to turn public support in favor of what he now believed was a necessary war as it was a message for Congress itself. Wilson decided it was necessary for the United States to intervene on its own behalf. His far greater difficulty was in framing the U.S. entry into the war as being on the world's behalf, as well as on behalf of the United States. This was not just a case of a leader taking sole responsibility for a decision. Wilson, as many presidents would have as well, feared the consequences of a German victory and sought to prevent any country from dominating Europe.

While Wilson's decision to bring the United States into World War I was probably overdetermined, in that there were systemic, domestic political, and personal reasons to act, he used military force several times beyond World War I as well. Wilson first used force as president when he refused to recognize the

---

[14] Thompson 1985, 336.

dictatorship of Victoriano Huerta in Mexico in 1913, sending U.S. forces to occupy the Mexican seaport at Veracruz.[15] Wilson's initial concerns with Huerta were consistent with his ideological views that, in order for governments to be recognized, they must be legitimate:

In short, Wilson believed that all mankind was capable of self government and democracy, and that it was the duty of the United States to help those who were unable to achieve these aims unassisted. Wilson felt the right to revolution was synonymous with establishing liberty and self-government. Consequently, revolutions against constitutional governments were, in the Wilsonian scheme, intolerable evils.[16]

Because Huerta had his predecessor, Francisco Madero, killed, his government was illegitimate in Wilson's eyes. McDermott argues that this use of force was "uncharacteristically aggressive" and related to Wilson's grief over the concurrent illness and death of his wife, Ellen.[17] He reconsidered his decision in light of U.S. casualties and eventually reversed his position.[18] Later, Wilson ordered Marines to occupy Haiti in 1915 and then the Dominican Republic in 1916. The same year, he authorized the American response to Pancho Villa's deadly attack on Columbus, New Mexico, in March 1916, the so-called Punitive Expedition.[19] Here, Wilson commanded General John J. Pershing to pursue Villa until his band was "known to be broken up."[20] Ostensibly to protect Americans in the region who were suffering reprisal attacks, Wilson kept U.S. forces at hand.[21]

The presence of U.S. soldiers resulted in additional skirmishes, however, with the president of Mexico beginning preparations for war. This was enough to make Wilson back down and withdraw Pershing in 1917 to seek a peaceful settlement to the ongoing concerns of border security.[22] In the end, "Wilson's bitter Mexican experience had taught him that military intervention to install 'good government' could not resolve deeply rooted economic, social, and political problems in the country concerned."[23]

An additional factor, ideology, which is not captured by either the background characteristics in the LEAD dataset or systemic accounts of international conflict, may help explain Wilson's behavior. Dispositionally, Wilson viewed foreign policy as an opportunity to help build a safe and just world. One biographer explains that "Wilson was neither a starry eyed idealist nor a Machiavellian realist but rather a statesman attempting to reconcile power politics and liberal ideals so as to underwrite a structure of international security that would be both stable and just."[24] Ideologically, Wilson's progressive views on both foreign and domestic policy trace to a combination of his innate personality and in part to his religious upbringing:

---

[15] Henderson 1984.   [16] Ibid., 163.   [17] McDermott 2008, 60.   [18] McDermott 2008.
[19] Katz 1978.   [20] Sandos 1981, 293.   [21] Ibid., 304.   [22] Ibid.   [23] Lynch 2002, 433.
[24] Ibid., 422.

The notion of a national mission that would both bring Americans together and at the same time make for a more peaceful world by offering the same freedoms Americans enjoyed to others captivated Wilson. Variations on this theme dominate his speeches. His sense of divine calling has generally been attributed to his Puritan and Calvinist upbringing, rich sources indeed for the idea of a chosen people and a national covenant.[25]

The combination of his ideology and desire to reshape the world, as historian Walter McDougall argues, meant that in the case of World War I, for example, when his efforts to mediate the conflict failed, Wilson felt compelled to pick up "the flaming sword of democracy promotion"[26] and lead the United States into war.

Thus, while Wilson's background characteristics, on the surface, suggest that he would have a low tolerance for risk, he became an extremely conflict-prone president. His individual background factors – specifically, his lack of military and rebel experience – indicate risk aversion. His public statements about refraining from war further demonstrate his reluctance to engage in military activities unless absolutely necessary, but he was willing to discard that reluctance when events challenged his core principles. His almost messianic belief in the ideology that we have come to call Wilsonianism, combined with structural and institutional pressures, overcame his reluctance to engage in military action. Ultimately, his most important contribution was his ideology. As one biographer states:

Adherents, opponents, and agnostics agree that Woodrow Wilson's liberal internationalism has decisively shaped the theory and practice of foreign policy and international politics throughout the twentieth century. No less a critic than Henry Kissinger has ruefully observed that "Wilsonianism has survived while history has bypassed the reservations of his contemporaries."[27]

Figure 3.6 above shows, based on variation in the predicted risk from our international system and leader models, how the risk of conflict has changed over time in the United States. The chart reveals a few interesting things about the Leader Risk Index that help explain U.S. leaders' behaviors over time. In the 1980s, for example, Ronald Reagan's leader risk score exceeded the inherent level of risk in the system, explaining what many regard as provocative American military behavior in the 1980s. That provocative military behavior was often successful, and Reagan may have been better calibrated than some observers realized at the time. Our model, which focuses on the risk of a leader starting conflicts, categorizes Reagan as a leader more prone to conflict than the average. The figure also indicates that Reagan's personal level of risk did not have an effect on the systemic level of risk in subsequent years.

---

[25] Gamble 2001, 6.   [26] McDougall 1997, 138–9.   [27] Lynch 2002, 419.

FIGURE 3.7. Mapping leader risk in the Middle East and North Africa, 1960 and 2001.

The plot also shows that George H.W. Bush and Bill Clinton possessed leader risk scores lower than that of Reagan. This squares with the cases of those leaders as well. As a democratic leader with prior combat experience, our model predicts that George H.W. Bush would be more moderate in thinking about the use of force than Reagan. Similarly, with no prior military experience or other significant risk factors predicting a propensity toward conflict, Clinton also demonstrated relatively low risk propensity (for an American president, that is; both George H.W. Bush and Bill Clinton have risk scores well above that of the average leader in the world).

Middle East and North Africa

In popular perception, the Middle East and Africa are regions of the world prone to endemic conflict. Figure 3.7 suggests that that image is consistent with reality; the Middle East and North Africa have long been regions with volatile leaders. As in Europe in 1938, when we look at the level of risk in the Middle East over all of the time periods, based on personal characteristics alone, we see a highly dangerous environment. To what extent are the findings the result of a strategic selection process? Knowing that dangerous neighbors surround them, do citizens in these countries select more aggressive leaders, believing that they will be better able to aggressively negotiate with their neighbors? Even though most of the states in this region are not democracies, a combination of leader and institutional forces could help ensure that aggressive leaders come to power and stay in power.[28]

What does the view from leader-background variables tell us about possible trends in the Middle East? Figure 3.8 shows the general rise, which peaks in the late 1980s, in the average risk score of Middle East leaders over time. This peak in the 1980s makes sense given that the 1980s saw the rise of leaders such as Saddam Hussein of Iraq and Ayatollah Khomeini of Iran, the latter of whom started more than sixty small-scale military conflicts while in office, including a war with Iraq.[29] Also during the 1980s, Muammar Qaddafi reigned in Libya.

---

[28] Bueno de Mesquita et al. 2003.   [29] According to the Militarized Interstate Dispute dataset.

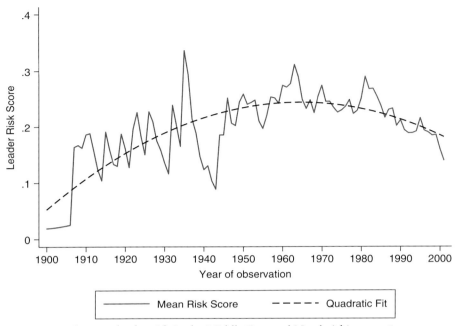

FIGURE 3.8. Average leader risk in the Middle East and North Africa, 1908–2001.

However, the 1980s were not the only risky period in the Middle East, according to the LEAD data. Risk scores increased throughout the post–World War II period, as decolonization occurred. Middle Eastern and North African countries fought a number of wars during this period: wars of independence, wars against Israel, and wars between Arab states. Many risk-prone leaders reigned in Middle Eastern and North African countries during this period, including Gamal Nasser, Egypt's leader in the 1950s and 1960s, who scores in the top 2 percent of riskiest leaders in the leader risk models presented in the previous chapter.

Explaining the changing risk of war over time in the Middle East also requires a separate understanding of Israel. Rather than having uniformity among its leadership, Israel has seen a fair amount of variation in the risk propensity of its leaders over time. For example, Golda Meir's rise to power reflects important aspects about the intersection between leader risk and system risk, including the factors that drive the selection of leaders in the first place. Meir came to power in 1969 after Levi Eshkol's death in February of that year. Meir was an ardent nationalist, willing to use measured force to achieve what she viewed as necessary for Israeli security. Her contemporaries, including Israel's first prime minister, David Ben-Gurion, understood her perspective. "[In explaining her appointment as foreign minister,] Ben-Gurion considered [Golda Meir], alone among his associates, tough enough to confront the [*Fedayeen* invasion] crisis. Like Ben-Gurion, she was an activist on security matters and totally approved his policy."[30]

Meir was an aggressive leader, repeatedly willing to take significant risks to advance Israel's interests. As a committed Zionist, she expressed a willingness to resort to violence in order to advance the cause of the new nation. As she relates in her memoirs, when discussing the possibility of confrontation with the British in post–World War II Palestine, she supported further immigration even if it risked violence with the British. She thought committing to conflict was necessary to preserve her people.[31]

She was acutely aware of the dangers of interstate war, and on several occasions expressed her fears for her own children and grandchildren, who were born and lived in Israel. However, that did not constrain her: because she feared war as a threat to Israel, she viewed hawkish policies as necessary to sustain the Israeli state.[32]

Once she entered office, Meir was highly conflict tolerant and led her cabinet with fixed ideas about right and wrong. She was clearly comfortable making difficult decisions, initiating three different militarized disputes when in office. First, she authorized the Israeli military to remove two Algerian military officers from a British Airways flight traveling from Hong Kong to Europe that had made a refueling stop in Lod. After questioning in detention, it became clear that one officer was apparently involved with the Algerian secret police. Claiming that Algeria was technically at war with Israel, the Israel Defense Forces (IDF) removed the Algerians from the plane to use them as bargaining chips for the release of two Israeli pilots being held by Syria and Egypt. After spending two months in custody, the pilots were able to return home on October 14, 1970.[33]

Next, Meir gave approval for an Israeli fighter jet to shoot down a civilian Libyan Arab Airlines Flight with 113 civilians aboard after it veered into Israeli airspace on February 21, 1973. Only five survived. Meir expressed publicly that the shooting had been a mistake,[34] but most nations, including the United States, rejected Israel's explanation and publicly condemned its action.[35]

Meir's best-known military decisions as a leader involve the 1973 Yom Kippur War, when Egypt and Syria simultaneously attacked Israel. Her decision not to attack preemptively despite multiple indications of the pending war led to significant Israeli losses. In her memoirs, Meir relates regret at her personal failure:

That Friday morning I should have listened to the warnings of my own heart and ordered a call-up … It doesn't matter what logic dictated. It matters only that I, who was so accustomed to making decisions – and who did make them throughout the war – failed to make that one decision.[36]

---

[30] Steinberg 2008, 128.   [31] Meir 1973, 161.   [32] Steinberg 2008.
[33] *Jerusalem Post* 1970. Militarized Interstate Dispute #1068.   [34] *Jerusalem Post* 1973.
[35] Phelps 1985. Militarized Interstate Dispute #1043.   [36] Meir 1973, 424.

Others, however, suggest that this was a predictable outcome of her decision-making style. Having come to power at an advanced age, Meir was very much set in her beliefs about right and wrong. She also limited the number of people around her from whom she was willing to take advice. A small group of trusted party members made almost all important decisions, in an informal arrangement known as "Golda's kitchen."[37] Steinberg explains how this dynamic influenced the development of the Yom Kippur War:

> Under Golda Meir, senior ministers were not privy to secret matters and were thus unable to participate effectively in foreign and security discussions. This was most evident on the eve of the Yom Kippur War ... On the evening of 5 October 1973, only a select few ministers in Meir's government understood definitively that the Egyptians and Syrians were prepared to attack. Early the next morning, Meir was told that an attack would take place at 6:00 P.M. that day. At a cabinet meeting called for 8:00 A.M., Meir, in conjunction with her military advisers and close cabinet ministers in Tel Aviv, decided not to launch a pre-emptive strike against either the Egyptians or the Syrians, lest Israel's allies argue that, since Israel had initiated the conflict, it was not entitled to military assistance.[38]

Like Margaret Thatcher, Meir was a hard-nosed leader willing to take risks in the name of national security. Moreover, like Thatcher, there does not seem to be direct evidence relating Meir's military decision making to gender issues. We discuss gender and family issues related to Meir in Chapter 5.

Meir was not an outlier in Israeli politics. She was both the product of and a contributor to a policy of reciprocated aggression that attracted risk-acceptant leaders and shut out those with more peaceful inclinations. The Middle East is an example of the diffusion of leader types in a certain area, of which a theory of individual risk propensity is an important component.

Africa

In Africa, regional levels of risk have echoed earlier periods of conflict in other parts of the world. Africa in 1989 looked dangerously similar to Europe in 1938, for example, with high areas of risk distributed throughout the continent. Numerous countries had highly risk-acceptant leaders who are in the top 10 percent of all leaders in our dataset for that year. Several areas featured a cluster of nations where dangerous leaders lived side by side, and the next decade did feature a wave of violence throughout the continent, including brutal civil wars and insurgencies. Figure 3.9 depicts leader risk in Africa in 1989.

Paul Kagame of Rwanda is representative of the more dramatically violence-prone leaders of the postcolonial era. The conflict in Rwanda and Burundi in 1989 created an ongoing cycle of violence that continues through the Congo

---

[37] Steinberg 2008, 184.   [38] Ibid., 187.

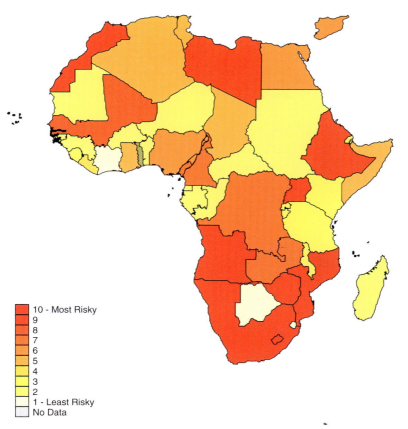

FIGURE 3.9. Mapping leader risk in Africa, 1989.

and central Africa. In 1994, Kagame, leading the Rwandan Patriot Front (RPF), set off a regional conflagration that persists to this day. The Great Lakes region is home to a number of geographically small nations with a significant history of conflict. Kagame received his military training in neighboring Uganda with the rebel leader Yoweri Museveni, who took power in 1986 and remains president as of this writing. As Waugh described, "Paul Kagame and Fred Rwigyema would draw strongly on the thought leadership of Yoweri Museveni, and when the time came for struggle in Rwanda, the National Resistance Movement (NRM) model provided the inspiration for a change of government through force in Uganda's southern neighbor."[39] Chapter 4, which discusses the prominence of former rebels among the riskiest leaders in the LEAD dataset, profiles Kagame in greater depth.

[39] Waugh 2004, 31.

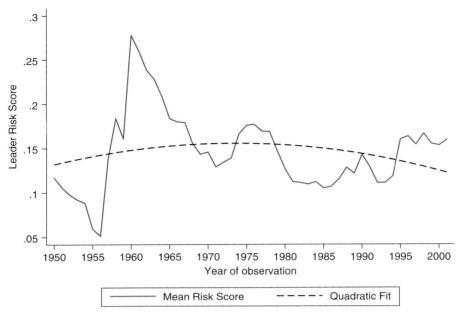

FIGURE 3.10. Average leader risk in Africa, 1950-2001.

To the extent that leaders with dangerous personal background characteristics, such as Museveni and Kagame are in power, it is also possible for a spillover effect to occur that encourages similar potential leaders in nearby locales. Figure 3.10 shows the trend of risk scores in Africa since the period of decolonization after World War II. While there was a large spike in disinhibited leaders in the early 1960s, from the ranks of rebels who fought colonial rule, this trend declined in the next decade and then again in the 1980s. Since the early 1990s, however, the trend has been upward.

A number of current presidents of African nations are in fact former rebel leaders, including Mohamed Ould Abdel Aziz of Mauritania, Yahya Jammeh of Gambia, Blaise Compaoré of Burkina Faso, Omar al-Bashir of Sudan, Joseph Kabila of the Democratic Republic of Congo, and Idriss Déby of Chad. While many of these men have been in power for long periods of time, it is unclear if they will be replaced by leaders with similar backgrounds. The individuals who comprise the selectorate of these nations may believe, if their neighbors are doing the same, that they have no other option than to retain aggressive leaders with military backgrounds.

Asia

China and its large land mass and population dominate Asia. In the 1960s, Chinese leaders were among the most volatile in the dataset. In most of China's

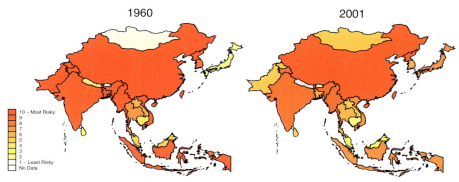

FIGURE 3.11. Mapping leader risk in Asia, 1960 and 2001.

neighbors, including contiguous states, leaders were also very aggressive. In fact, China was an aggressor in twenty-five out of the thirty-eight MIDs with which it was involved in the 1960s, including a number of border-related disputes with the Soviet Union. The most serious of these occurred in early 1969, when China attacked Soviet troops at the disputed Zhenbao Island post, killing dozens of soldiers and launching a series of fatal Sino-Soviet clashes that year. Figure 3.11 depicts changing risk, based on leader attributes, in Asia over time.

The rest of Asia's leaders in the 1960s remained somewhat more moderate, between the 50th and 70th percentile range of conflict-prone leaders. Few, if any, countries in the period between the 1960s and 1990s had leaders who were in the bottom quartile. Instead, leaders who could be described as moderately risky either came to power or were elected. Notable, however, is the persistence of conflict-prone leaders in Asia throughout the period. In contrast to the Middle East in the 1990s, for example, where leader-based risk declines somewhat, leader risk remained fairly stable in Asia. One interesting example of the intersection of leader and system risk in Asia is the Indian leader P.V. Narasimha Rao.

Under Rao's leadership, traditional theories predict there would be peace, and that is what occurs, even though Rao has background characteristics that would lead our model to predict conflict. For example, Rao was an active supporter of the movement for Indian independence. Our theory predicts that, as a former rebel, he would be more likely to engage in militarized behaviour once in office. His advanced age and poor health also suggested, based on our theory, an inclination toward riskier behavior.

However, Rao initiated no military conflicts and was responsible for only one clash that had begun, in fact, during the term of his predecessor. In this case, the characteristics of the system and domestic institutions overwhelmed any potentially aggressive preferences of the man. This case helps demonstrate that, while leaders themselves are important, they are also often constrained, especially when they operate within democratic systems or their country lacks sufficient power, giving the leader less flexibility to act. Alternatively, if one thinks of the situation in which leaders matter as the situation once a potential dispute presents itself, the lack of opportunities during the Rao period may have made conflict less likely.

Rao took power in 1991 during a highly turbulent time in Indian political history. Sri Lankan terrorists had just assassinated the young and popular Rajiv Gandhi, and Indian National Congress Party leaders were looking for an experienced leader to take the reins. Rao's long-time demonstrated loyalty to party leader Indira Gandhi made him the top choice.[40] Writing the same year Rao took office, Attar Chand explained:

A scholar by inclination, there is little of an everyday, ordinary politician in the new Prime Minister P. V. Narasimha Rao's characteristics which one associates with a politician these days: party intrigue, factional manipulation, electoral manoeuvre. He has all along in his long 50 years career as an active politician been far removed from, even above and beyond such manoeuvres. And yet he is not lacking in those political talents and skills which a leader in his role is required to possess.[41]

Rao was born in 1921 to a poor agricultural family in Andhara Pradesh, in southern India. This region was, at that time and for many years afterward, a Naxalite stronghold, home to Communist rebels later branded as terrorists.[42] Separated from his parents while quite young because of his clear intellectual potential, he was adopted at age five and rarely saw his parents afterward, a fact that caused him sadness in his youth. Rao excelled in school, usually placing at the top of his class.[43]

He eventually completed his studies and became a practicing lawyer before entering local politics.[44] Chand explains: "A Nationalist to the core, he gave up legal practice in the pre-Independence days when the State was subjected to repression by the British. He also took active part in the 1942 'Quit India' [movement] for three years."[45] Rao served as a minister in his home state of Andhra Pradesh and captured a national parliament seat in 1972. There, he had several portfolios, the most important of which was Minister of External Affairs. When he became prime minister, he was the first Southern Indian, and the first outside the Nehru dynasty, to hold power for a significant length of time.

As a politician, Rao relied on being underestimated by his opponents. Rao's *New York Times* obituary states: "Not known for his charisma, and loath to give interviews, Mr. Rao was a wily, even ruthless politician capable of outfoxing rivals in a faction-riddled party."[46] Although an outsider, his quiet and deferential demeanor helped him last through decades of tumultuous Indian politics. Rao's thoughtful and deliberate approach to policy served him well

---

[40] Jai 1996.   [41] Chand 1991, 51.   [42] Ibid.   [43] Jai 1996.   [44] Ibid.
[45] Chand 1991, 2.   [46] Waldman 2004, C8.

through several internal crises that occurred during his administration. One biographer explains:

But one feature of the Rao hallmark now gradually emerging is that it is the situation of crisis and little else which is shaping his distinctive style. A keen consciousness of the dimensions of this crisis is the source of the confidence and decisiveness he has been able to display, qualities which are all the more impressive for never having been evident before in quite this way in the conduct of public affairs.[47]

As an active participant in India's civil disobedience movement that culminated in the end of the British Raj, Rao was comfortable upsetting the status quo. As an older leader, he had short time horizons. By the time he came to power, he had almost forty years of political experience at all levels with the party that nominated him. He certainly had the connections and bureaucratic knowledge necessary to advance any aggressive actions he may have had in mind. With a constantly provocative Pakistan as a neighbor, there was certainly opportunity for conflict.

What explains the lack of conflict? From an institutional perspective, Rao did face constraints on his behavior, perhaps helping to explain his lack of aggressive actions in office. Rao was a member of the India National Congress Party, a left-leaning party established by Nehru at the founding of an independent India. Although the India National Congress Party was a minority ruling party, in that it held fewer than 50 percent of the seats in parliament, Rao's major threat to his position as prime minister came from internal party dynamics. Shah explains: "He is neither overawed by his job nor daunted by it. His approach is low-key, serene, and calibrated, and he appears to take the onerous tasks in his stride. It is, so to speak, his political karma, and his attitude seems fashioned accordingly: he must do what he has to do."[48]

Rising to power after the traumatic assassination of Rajiv Gandhi, Rao handled the transition well. In this case, Rao's age and experience provided both the political connections that were a precondition of the post of prime minister and a level of trust that he would act in his usual tempered fashion, especially given his advanced age. Chand relates an interview with Rao:

I asked him why he was not projecting himself more forcefully in the Congress politics and the national scene and why he was continuing to adopt a low profile when there was such an enormous good will for him in the country and party, thanks to his non-controversial personality. "You are asking me to change my style at this late age? How is that possible? I am content to serve my country and party in my own humble way!" he replied.[49]

This also suggests other factors relevant to leaders, not captured by the LEAD dataset, that influence leader behavior: ideology and preferences. Party leaders selected Rao specifically because of his age, extensive experience, and tendency

---

[47] Shah 1992, 154.   [48] Ibid., 144.   [49] Chand 1991, 49.

not to rock the boat. This almost assured that he would be able to achieve his preferred policies, much in the same way that Lyndon Johnson was able to carry out his own domestic political agenda following the assassination of John F. Kennedy in the United States. Rao's overriding preference for peace and diplomacy in response to external provocations accounts in large part for the negligible number of military disputes in which India participated during his period of leadership.

Institutional level theories also suggest another reason Rao may not have engaged in external military activity: the many domestic challenges that required his attention on assuming office. India was in the midst of an economic crisis that required substantial focus and time. Radicals had just murdered the country's young and popular prime minister. The country was in turmoil for some time afterward. It is unlikely that any leader, no matter his or her qualities, would have had time or the political will to precipitate a military crisis with India's neighbors. There was certainly the opportunity, however, given India's tense relationship with Pakistan. The party leadership selected Rao in no small part because of his reputation, gained through decades of political life, that he would not be confrontational during this critical time.

This provides some evidence in favor of a more traditional view of the interaction of domestic and international politics, because he arguably lacked the flexibility or political capital to act abroad due to the political capital he spent at home. His military decisions, however, when expanded to include domestic activities, do demonstrate the more aggressive tendencies that our theory predicts. For example, Rao strongly promoted the development and testing of the Prithvi missile, which provided a new but potentially provocative capability for the Indian military.[50] Rao also favored muscular action against domestic threats such as the Sikh rebellion. When threatened, for example, he authorized a strong offensive against the Sikhs in their stronghold, Punjab.[51]

Rao's decision to invest in long-range missile development had broad public support and moved the military focus away from short-term conflicts to long-term defensive improvement. As Thakur explained:

[T]he Indian military establishment reportedly believes that if India can withstand diplomatic pinpricks by Pakistan for another four years until the production of indigenous missiles stabilizes, then the Kashmir problem will be solved without a war for the missiles will transform the traditional battlefield by their reach and firepower ... The destabilizing effects of India's nuclear option on relations with Pakistan are regarded by New Delhi as regrettable but acceptable "collateral damage."[52]

The intersection between the international military behavior that is the focal point of the Leader Risk Index and Rao's actions suggests the importance, in future research, of focusing on domestic conflicts as well as international conflict. Often, the two are substitutes for one another. For example, in the

---

[50] Thakur 1996.   [51] Haridas 1998, 78.   [52] Thakur 1996, 588–9.

1980s, the Argentine military junta, facing rising domestic unrest, chose to externalize the threat of violence and precipitated a war with Britain over the Falkland Islands, as we have seen in the Thatcher case. Rao stayed focused on domestic threats, in contrast.

In combination, what this suggests is that only a close reading of Rao's personal biography, in combination with the institutional constraints he faced, can explain his behavior in office. The fact that Rao was not at the head of a militarily aggressive India shows the importance of combining our new, leader-based explanation with more traditional theories.

Beyond India, it is striking how China, despite leadership changes, remained conflict prone, from a leader perspective, throughout the period. This squares with what happened in the real world, as China fought wars with the United States, the Soviet Union, Vietnam, India, and Taiwan in the thirty years after the end of the Chinese Civil War in 1949. One reason suggested by the LEAD model from the previous chapter is that China's leaders after World War II were generally former rebels. There was also a very small number of them.

In 1960, China's revolutionary leader, Mao Zedong, still ruled China. Mao was born in 1893 and began fighting as a rebel in his twenties. In 1989, Deng Xiaoping led China. Deng was born in 1904, participated in the Long March of 1934 and 1935 – noted by both participants and scholars as a particularly salient event in the lives of those who survived it – and saw less front-line combat than Mao. During the 1990s, China was involved as the aggressor in only thirteen MIDs, none of which involved fatalities. In 2004, Jiang Zemin came to power. Born in 1926, the first year of the Kuomintang's Northern Expedition, Jiang was from the next generation of Chinese leaders.

As leaders with rebel experience in China continue to age out and the bureaucracy continues to select middle-aged men as heads of state, we expect to see a continuing decrease in the risk acceptance of Chinese leaders. This trend runs counter to predictions based on classical realism, power-transition theory, and the domestic institutions literature, all of which suggest a more pessimistic future of relations with China, both in the region as well as across the Pacific.

By 1989, China was still led by high-risk leaders, but many of its continental neighbors were beginning to select more risk-averse leaders. Leaders in India, Vietnam, and Japan were less risk-acceptant than they had been in 1960. At the same time, perhaps offsetting this trend, the island nations of Southeast Asia began to choose increasingly risk-acceptant leaders. As new nations in Asia became independent, many of the leaders taking power had also been active in proindependence rebellion movements. This dynamic of rebel leaders coming to power is replicated in other former colonial regions, especially Africa, and is an overlooked part of the story for why these regions continue to experience interstate conflict.

However, by 2004, most Asian nations were again selecting leaders with backgrounds that made them less prone to military aggression. Leaders who were middle-aged in the early 2000s were, by and large, born around the time of World War II or the Korean War.

Note that this was not true across the board. In Southeast Asia, the process of decolonization occurred somewhat later and under the cloud of combat, due to regional fears of the spread of communism. Vietnam, Laos, and Cambodia continued to engage in interstate combat over the territory through the 1970s. The current prime minister of Vietnam, Nguyễn Tấn Dũng, was born in 1949 and fought with the Viet Cong during the Vietnam War. Nguyễn exemplifies the connection between individual leaders, institutional factors, and the historical record. The selection process for leaders in Vietnam favors those who have demonstrated competence and loyalty to the dominant party. Due to the historical legacy of the Vietnam War, the primary or only way to demonstrate both competence and loyalty was through military service. History – in the form of the way generational experiences drive perceived qualifications for the job of head of state – echoes until leaders exposed to large-scale violence age out of power.

Central/South/Latin America

Unlike many countries in Africa and Asia, most Latin American countries had already achieved independence by 1875, the beginning of the LEAD dataset. The charts in this section therefore tell a slightly different, but still interesting, story of variation over time. Latin America is a prime example of variance in conflict outcomes despite the presence of stable institutions and little change in the regional balance of power.

Is the changing face of leadership the source of this variance? From the perspective of autocratic institutions, we have unfortunately very little information. In 1875, Pedro II ruled as the last emperor of Brazil. The son of the first emperor, Pedro II took the throne as a child. His low risk score is largely due to the fact that he lived a fairly comfortable life, with no reason to serve in the military or fight in a war. Brazil was the initiator of seven military crises during his reign, including two wars that are not captured in our dataset. Because of its closeness with Portugal, however, Brazil was generally not acting in the interests of territorial expansion and conquest. Instead, these wars were intended to provide greater security by shoring up sympathetic factions in neighboring countries. Pedro II's neighbor in Paraguay, Francisco Solano López, provoked Brazil's largest military engagement in the continent's history, the War of the Triple Alliance.

What about the institutional story for the democracies? In this respect, Latin America poses more questions than it provides answers. Looking at the maps and Figure 3.12, there is no clear pattern in the leader data from period to period. In 1875, the most risk-acceptant leaders were in Venezuela, Chile, and Guatemala. By 1913, they were still in Venezuela, along with Colombia and Argentina. In 1938, Brazilian leadership was the most risk-acceptant, while

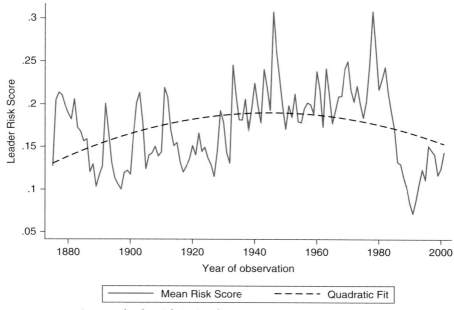

FIGURE 3.12. Average leader risk in South America, 1875–2001.

Colombia and Venezuela at this time had more risk-averse leaders. Not surprisingly, 1989 was also a time of disinhibited leaders in Colombia, Chile, Bolivia, and Paraguay. By the time of our most recent data, however, leaders are more homogeneous across states. Like Europe, South America seems to have achieved a kind of equilibrium, although the mean level of risk in South America exceeds that in Europe.

Another way to think about these issues is to consider which parts of the world have been most likely to feature the most conflict-prone leaders. While people do not generally think of Central America as a dangerous region, Figure 3.13 shows that Central America has featured some extremely risky leaders. The turn of the century and the 1920s through the 1950s show both dramatic spikes as well as a strong rising trend of risk-acceptant leadership in the region.

José Figueres Ferrer came to power in Costa Rica in 1948, leading a group of irregular forces in the Costa Rican Civil War.[53] Figueres was acutely aware of the dangers of the region; at the time he led his small rebel army to victory, military rulers governed most of his Central American neighbors. Anastasio Somoza Garcia had established a brutal dictatorship in Nicaragua that he and his sons would retain for another twenty years. While Costa Rica's other

[53] Guerra 1997.

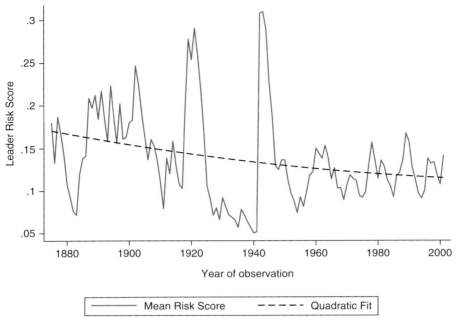

FIGURE 3.13. Average leader risk in Central America, 1875–2001.

contiguous neighbor, Panama, was somewhat less oppressive, the governments of Honduras (Tiburcio Carías Andino) and El Salvador (Salvador Castaneda Castro) were also controlled by military *jefes*. In other words, it was not an opportune time for the few conciliatory leaders; in fact, structural-level theories seeking to explain arms races would expect that Costa Rica would increase the power of its military. Instead, Figueres did exactly the opposite, abolishing the standing army and reverting to a police force for domestic protection. This was an incredibly bold and risk-acceptant move that had the potential to put his country in serious danger if Somoza decided to invade and capture territory. Given what he had seen of the power wielded by the military in his neighbors, he decided that the risk was worth it.

EVALUATING THE RELATIVE IMPORTANCE OF LEADERS

The results presented here and in Chapter 2 evaluate the importance of leaders themselves, in comparison with material and domestic institutional factors that influence national and international behavior. A relevant limitation to these results is that they do not put everything together and attempt to simultaneously evaluate the importance of leaders, material power, and domestic institutions. This is an extremely difficult test of the theory presented in this book about the importance of leaders. It would be problematic to be sure if bringing all of these factors together caused the relative importance of leaders to fade into the background.

An ideal experimental condition would place leaders with different sets of background characteristics in power in different situations. For example, if Saddam Hussein were in charge of the United States in 1990 or Franklin Roosevelt in charge of Germany in 1935, would we see different foreign policies than what we observed in the real world? Probably, but it is impossible to know exactly how this would turn out because the data we are using are gathered from the real world, not the laboratory.

Bringing together the analysis of leaders with other factors therefore requires estimating a statistical model called a "dyadic" model, in which there is one observation per pair or "dyad" of leaders in a given year. For example, Clinton (United States)–Hussein (Iraq) in 1999 constitutes one observation, whereas Hussein (Iraq)–Clinton (United States) in 1999 constitutes a second observation. Side A is the leader of the first state in the dyad, and Side B is the leader of the second state in the dyad. Setting up the data this way allows us to measure whether the United States, led by Clinton, would initiate a military dispute against Saddam Hussein's Iraq in a given year, but also whether Saddam Hussein's Iraq would initiate a dispute against Clinton and the United States.

Shifting to a dyadic approach makes it possible to account for other relational drivers of disputes such as power imbalances, concentration of power in the international system, the dyadic democratic peace, and the willingness of states to fight over territorial issues. We therefore estimate a dyadic model to account for the interactions of states from 1875 to 2001.[54]

Another modeling challenge to overcome is that the Risk Index is built by assessing whether leaders are likely to start military conflicts. Comparing the importance of the Leader Risk Index with the importance of system-level or domestic institutional factors would become circular if we test the model on the same data we used to build the model. Testing the comparative relevance of leaders, therefore, requires splitting the leaders' data in two. By randomly splitting the data in two, we can build a model on half of the data and then test the model on the other half of the data.[55] This avoids the problem of designing the model and testing it on the same data.

---

[54] The move to dyadic analysis represents an increase in sophistication and allows us to account for factors such as relative power. It remains a simplification, however. Recent work is beginning to move toward what is referred to as "K-adic" analysis where the unit of analysis is the K-ad, or some arbitrary number of states of two or more. Here, for the sake of simplicity, we focus on the similar unit, the state pair. We also assume away strategic behavior in the context of how leaders' risk attributes interact.

[55] We start by randomly splitting a dyadic sample in half by leader year, meaning each observation that involves a given leader in a given year is either placed in sample A or sample B. We also tried sampling based on the leader or the country code. Neither changed the results.

This technique, called cross-validation, is especially useful in a situation such as this when we are not certain of the exact combination of variables that might significantly influence an outcome of interest but when we do not want to test our index using the same data that we used to generate the index in the first place. This is the closest we can come to an independent test of the predictive value of our model.

It is also possible that, due to the large number of leader attributes, the inclusion of irrelevant factors biases these results. Given the concern that the sheer number of leader background variables in our dataset could bias the results in our favor, we also generated these results using a statistical technique called stepwise regression that helps reduce the number of variables to the ones that are consistently significant.[56] This approach lets the model identify the variables most likely to be significant across hundreds of potential specifications, keeping only the most robust variables.

One disadvantage of this strategy is that it might eliminate combinations of background attributes that might make a difference. For example, it might be the case that leaders with a certain educational background are less risk-prone, but only when the leader is an orphan and serves in the military. Thus, while the main results presented here derive from a risk index generated with all of the LEAD variables, in the Technical Appendix, we show that the findings in this chapter are consistent when we employ stepwise regression.

Running a model that includes only leader background characteristics, just on sample A, allows for the creation of a new Risk Index on the first half of the data.[57] This step is necessary because importing the values from the monadic Risk Index created in the last chapter would bias the results. Predicted values generated from that Risk Index constructed on half of the data are then used to estimate a Leader Risk Index for the other half of the data, sample B.

We generate predicted probabilities from that data, the newly generated Risk Index, and use those numbers to estimate a Leader Risk Index for the other half of the data, sample B. We then look at the relative probability of militarized dispute initiation across several different conditions, including variables measuring the importance of geography, material power, and political regimes on state behavior.[58]

As Table 3.1 demonstrates, even in a much more realistic dyadic setup, the relative effect of leader attributes on national military behavior is clear.

---

[56] Running a stepwise regression both forward and backward reduces the number of variations in our regression model that we use to build the index. We do this with a bootstrapped model with 100 bootstrapped samples (Efron 1983; Achen 1986; Shao 1996).

[57] We even remove the peace-year splines to make sure that we are not giving the leader variables too much analytical leverage. While unconventional, this choice actually reduces the relative weight of our leader attribute variables, meaning that this is a conservative assumption designed to understate, rather than overstate, the effect of leader attributes.

[58] The regression table is available in the Technical Appendix.

TABLE 3.1. *Relative Effect of Leader Risk Compared with Other Key Drivers of Conflict*

	Probability Relative to Baseline Probability of Military Conflict
Low system concentration of power	–10%
High system concentration of power	13%
Joint democracy	–25%
Low dyadic satisfaction	30%
High dyadic satisfaction	–10%
Low number of great powers	–14%
High number of great powers	30%
Low Side A relative material capabilities	–17%
High Side A relative material capabilities	20%
Low Side A leader risk	–22%
High Side A leader risk	31%

Holding other variables such as domestic political institutions and material power equal, a leader in the 10th percentile of the Risk Index is 22 percent *less* likely to start a military conflict than the average leader, while a leader in the 90th percentile is 31 percent *more* likely to start a conflict. One factor bolstering the credibility of the results is their consistency with prior research on material power and the democratic peace. For example, consistent with prior research, multiple indicators related to power at the system and state level, including the balance of power, dyadic satisfaction, and system concentration, influence the probability of conflict. Results in the Technical Appendix also show that contiguous states are also more likely to engage in military conflicts, similar to previous research.[59]

Moreover, consistent with the proposed link between leader risk and domestic politics, the results support democratic peace research showing that democracies are unlikely to fight each other. Even though this model focuses on low-level conflict initiation, the effect remains as the severity of conflict increases. Variations including both a joint democracy dummy variable and including the Polity score of the least democratic state in a dyad both support traditional democratic peace findings.[60]

However, a critical limit to even the dyadic analysis presented here is that it does not necessarily show that our model of leader attributes is predicting the militarized behavior of actual leaders in high-stakes crises. Perhaps, for example, these results are just artifacts of U.S.–Canada fishing disputes. A substantial proportion of the "crises" in our dispute dataset consists of very

---

[59] Bennett and Stam 2005.   [60] Oneal and Russett 2000; Dafoe 2011.

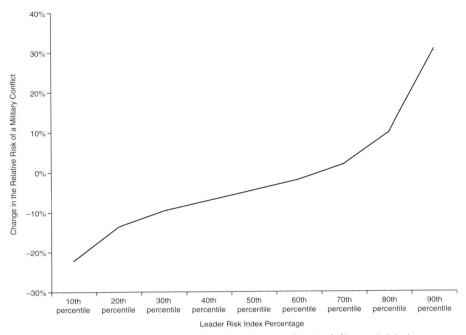

FIGURE 3.14. Comparative impact of leader risk on militarized dispute initiation.

small-scale diplomatic crises in which military forces were present, but the chance of a large-scale war occurring seemed highly unlikely. To control for that, other available results in the Technical Appendix show that these results are consistent both for disputes in which military fatalities occurred and for war initiation.

These results also show the importance of a small number of leaders in driving international conflict. Figure 3.14 focuses on the leader-risk portion of the results presented earlier in Table 3.1. The figure shows the change in the relative risk of a military conflict between two states as the leader-risk score of the leader of Side A increases from the 10th percentile of the Leader Risk Index to the 90th percentile. The total effect is a more than 50 percent swing in the probability of a military conflict as a leader moves from being less risky (–22 percent) to more risky (+31 percent).

The shift from the 90th percentile to the 98th percentile of the leader risk score, however, increases the probability of a military conflict to over 100 percent above the baseline. Essentially, as leader risk increases above the 90th percentile, the relative impact of leaders increases. This makes sense, since those leaders at the high end of the risk spectrum should be more willing to use force.

At the highest extremes of leader risk, the relative importance of leaders grows. Relative to the baseline, a leader in the 99th risk percentile is over

160 percent more likely to start a military conflict. That percentage then grows by more than 60 times for the most dangerous leaders. Moreover, even when focusing on countries with significant material power, for example, the countries most likely to get involved in military conflict according to many traditional accounts, a shift from an average leader risk score to the maximum leader risk score increases the probability of a militarized dispute by over 160 percent.[61] This demonstrates how, even though institutions and material resources significantly influence whether most leaders will start conflicts, at the extremes, risk-prone leaders are more likely to start conflicts regardless of their circumstances.

HOW LEADERS MATTER DEPENDING ON THE BALANCE OF POWER

One question about these results is: How does the relative importance of leaders change when countries are more or less powerful? It might be, for example, that even risky leaders are much less likely to start conflicts when they do not have stronger armies than their adversaries. On the other hand, history is full of examples of risk-acceptant leaders who start or join conflicts even when the balance of forces is not necessarily in their favor. Mao's decision to bring China into the Korean War was a huge gamble; he was still in the process of consolidating control over China after the Chinese Civil War, and the United States possessed the strongest military in the world. A few missteps and his regime stability would have been at risk. Yet he pushed for Chinese entrance into the war anyway.

To begin testing the relationship between the balance of power and leader risk, Figure 3.15 imports the monadic Leader Risk Index and plots it against the balance of forces in a given dyad for all cases in which a leader started a military conflict. The balance of forces is the degree to which one side or another controls the actual and potential military capabilities of the dyad. If the effect of leader risk depends almost entirely on the balance of power, the chart should be heavily weighted to the right; leaders facing an unfavorable balance of power (less than .5 on the horizontal axis) should not initiate military conflicts. However, that is not what the chart shows. Instead, the almost random distribution shows that the relationship between leader risk and conflict does not entirely depend on the balance of power. Looking closely, the distribution shifts slightly up as the balance of power shifts toward favoring the potentially initiating state, meaning that more powerful states are more likely to start military conflicts. This is what one would expect from a traditional material power explanation, so it is not surprising that risk-prone leaders take advantage of those circumstances to start military conflicts.

---

[61] The confidence interval is quite large, however, suggesting a necessary degree of modesty concerning these results.

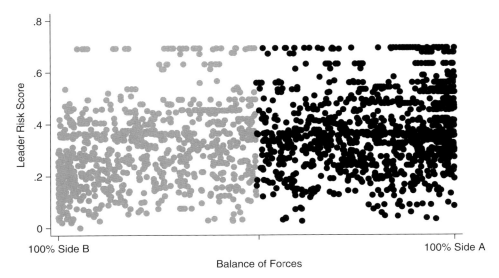

FIGURE 3.15. The effect of leader risk as the balance of power changes.

HOW LEADERS MATTER ACROSS DIFFERENT
POLITICAL REGIMES

Next, we return to one of the core questions raised when thinking about the importance of individual leaders: How does the effect of leader risk propensity interact with and vary across different types of political regimes? This is a central question because it gets to the heart of the flexibility that leaders have, despite domestic political constraints. To test this, we reestimated the model used to generate the Risk Index with a few changes. We estimated our regression model including a continuous measure of the regime type and created an interaction between the domestic political regime and the Leader Risk Index.[62] The statistical results, shown in the Technical Appendix, show that the interaction is negative and significant. As leader risk propensity increases, the probability of a militarized dispute increases in an autocracy, but the effect decreases as the regime becomes more democratic. Given the complexities in estimating the substantive effect of interaction terms, we turn to a graphic representation of this contingent relationship.[63] Here, we generate the predicted probability of a militarized dispute across the range of regime types in two

---

[62] We use the Polity IV variable *Polity*, which runs from –10 (highly autocratic) to 10 (highly democratic).

[63] We use Clarify (King et al. 2000) to generate the subsequent totals.

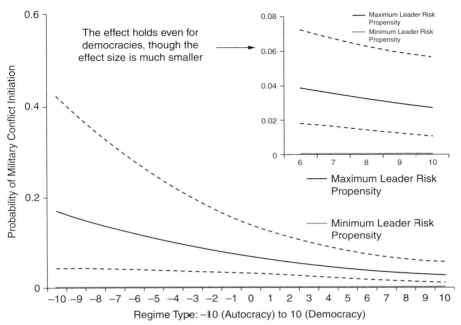

FIGURE 3.16. Substantive impact of leader risk propensity across regime type.

circumstances: first, when the Leader Risk Index is at its minimum, and then when the Leader Risk Index is at its maximum.

Figure 3.16 shows the results, demonstrating the interactive effect between leader risk propensity and regime type. When the Leader Risk Index is at its minimum (the solid gray line), as regime type moves from heavily autocratic to stable democracy, the predicted probability of a militarized dispute barely moves. It even increases slightly as the country becomes more democratic. Essentially, the effect of having a leader with an extremely low risk propensity swamps the shift in regime type. Note the enormous difference, however, across regime types when the Leader Risk Index is at its maximum (the solid black line). Put another way, the predicted probability of a militarized dispute jumps to almost .20, an extremely large substantive probability, when the Leader Risk Index is at its maximum in an autocratic regime. The predicted probability of a militarized dispute in an autocratic regime is more than 100 times larger as the Leader Risk Index shifts from its minimum to its maximum. This enormous substantive finding demonstrates the way less-constrained leaders in autocracies, such as Saddam Hussein or Pol Pot, have the propensity to engage in more militarized behavior. Figure 3.16 demonstrates the importance of incorporating leader backgrounds into our understanding of the factors that explain militarized disputes.

Moreover, these results highlight the way focusing on leaders complements, rather than replaces, existing research on domestic institutions. For example, if the effect of leaders overwhelmed that of domestic institutions, then at the extreme, one might expect incorporation of leader risk to destabilize the statistical significance, in a regression model, of one of the most stable results in all of international relations research: the democratic peace. However, the effect of the democratic peace is relatively stable across different levels of leader risk, reducing the probability of a military conflict between two states by about 40 percent whether the leader on Side A is a low-risk leader or a high-risk leader.

CONTROLLING FOR LEADER SELECTION

Defenders of conventional wisdom may not find our statistical results persuasive because the attributes that countries consider when selecting leaders are some of the very attributes that make up our Risk Index. As described in the Introduction and in Chapter 1, while this is a valid theoretical question, in practice, leaders tend not to be selected into office because they are particularly risky (potentially excluding rebel leaders and others who rise to power through violence, which is part of our theory and explained in Chapter 4). We believe this is more of a theoretical issue than a substantive concern, as Chapter 1 details. To be as thorough as possible, however, we also estimate a statistical model in which we look at those leaders selected into office through a random process and compare their behavior with that of those who came into office through normal selection procedures.

To generate the set of randomly selected leaders, we identify those leaders by looking at the leaders who, according to Archigos, died in office of natural causes.[64] The leaders who replace them through a "regular" entry process (e.g., a vice president of the United States who replaces a president who dies of natural causes while in office) are subject to selection criteria different from that of a head of state. Harry Truman, for example, was not voted in by the American people, nor is there any evidence suggesting that Roosevelt chose Truman as a running mate with the notion that Truman would be a particularly effective and bellicose commander in chief. It is the person at top of the ticket, in democratic regimes, whose experiences generally matter most for selection purposes. Therefore, we can isolate those leaders who entered office through a regular process after the prior leader died of natural causes and test our theory on that set of leaders.[65] This significantly reduces any remaining concern that leaders are being selected because of our key variables of interest.

---

[64] Jones and Olken 2005; Goemans et al. 2009; Besley et al. 2011.
[65] As opposed to regular or foreign-imposed transitions. See Goemans et al. 2009.

We then regenerated Table 2.3, focusing only on the leader risk and system risk scores of these leaders. The results show that, just as in the broader population of leaders, our Leader Risk Index is as good at predicting the leaders likely to start conflicts as system-based models. The Technical Appendix also includes much greater detail on this question of selection and the steps we have taken to increase our confidence that the results presented here are really due to the backgrounds of leaders.[66]

CONCLUSION

Behavior within the system of states is a function of structural, institutional, and individual leader attributes. This was Kenneth Waltz's key insight,[67] which is often overlooked in academic analytical practice but not in the real world. The levels of risk associated with individual leaders can either moderate or exacerbate institutional constraints, but leaders are rarely neutral. The systematic variance in leader behavior can be captured using the same tools of objective analysis as are used in other international security research. Focusing on regional variation demonstrates the importance of understanding how leaders interact with each other and their exogenous environment to drive the war outcomes we observe.

Moreover, as we have seen, states' leaders are the most important determinants of state action. While leaders operate within varying levels of institutional constraints and in the context of an interstate power distribution, the world's leaders exercise more independent human agency than generations of scholars have given them credit for. The background experiences of leaders and our tests from our dataset present a new way for students of international relations to think about leaders and leadership. Our data allow us to move beyond looking at the effect of domestic institutions on leaders to see how leaders themselves may have an independent role in shaping national policy, especially militarized policy. In doing so, it becomes clear that we should be considering the personalities of current and prospective leaders in a systematic manner, rather than treating each leader and his or her experiences in isolation.

Describing, in systematic and predictable ways, how leaders matter does not imply that structural and unit-level variables do not matter. Our results show they matter a great deal. However, our research demonstrates an important link between the background experiences of leaders and the probability that they will engage in militarized behavior when they get into office. The findings are especially strong in autocracies and show that leaders' background experiences

---

[66] Our results are also consistent when we use coarsened exact matching to reduce imbalance in our data across our leader- and/or national-level variables. See the Technical Appendix.

[67] Waltz 1959.

have a substantive importance on par with many domestic institutional and material variables. Put another way, while the American media's screening of every detail of the backgrounds of American presidential candidates may overstate the relevant information for voters in terms of the likely behavior of their candidates, leader backgrounds do communicate important information about basic behavioral tendencies and, *ceteris paribus,* beliefs.

4

The Experiences That Matter I: Military/Rebel Status, Age, and Education

In contrast to the leader index presented and tested over the last two chapters, this chapter focuses on individual background characteristics that our theory of leader attributes suggests should make these men and women more or less prone to engage in armed conflict.[1] Of course, in the real world, many different experiences shape leaders' characters. That is why we start with the broader leader index. Focusing on specific background experiences can help us isolate which characteristics shape leaders' attitudes, making them more or less inclined to use force as an active part of their states' foreign policies.

In this chapter, we focus on four areas of experience. First, we explore the role of military service, emphasizing the way participation in combat, or the lack thereof, shapes how leaders think about the use of military force later in life. Second, focusing on rebel experience in violent movements or coups against status quo governments, we find that leaders such as Mao Zedong and Muammar Qaddafi are more disinhibited not just because of the circumstances that put them in power, but also because of their different personal beliefs about the efficacy of violence. Third, building on earlier work about leaders' ages and their propensity to initiate military actions, this chapter explores whether younger or older leaders are more prone to conflict. Finally, while some might expect to see a significant relationship between education and conflict, as there is between education and economic policies, with more educated leaders being more likely to seek peaceful resolution to disputes, the evidence suggests there is no relationship.

---

[1] Statistically, what this means is that the models available in the Technical Appendix generally feature just one background experience, except where we note differently, along with traditional control variables such as the balance of power and whether or not the country is a democracy. This helps us isolate the effect of individual leader attributes or packages of attributes.

MILITARY AND REBEL EXPERIENCE

As discussed in Chapter 1, the single leader background experience most plausibly relevant to the initiation of military conflict is whether a leader has had prior military service. Evidence of the potential importance of military service comes from a variety of sources. In addition to the U.S. presidential examples discussed in the Introduction, our overall findings for three categories of leaders (those with national military service but no combat experience, those with national military service and combat experience, and those with prior rebel experience, e.g., military experience with a nonstate actor) show that some of the most conflict prone leaders around the world are those with military experience but no combat experience. These leaders, such as Kaiser Wilhelm II, Saddam Hussein, and Muammar Qaddafi, have the familiarity with military service that makes them more likely to support use of the military when they reach office, but they lack the combat experience that might make them more knowledgeable about the risks and consequences of combat.

Domestic political institutions clearly matter, however. In highly autocratic countries or regimes that lack strong civilian control of the military, even controlling for other characteristics of those regimes, leaders with combat experience appear significantly more likely to engage in militarized behavior than the average leader. This results from both socialization and a selection process that, in authoritarian regimes such as Saddam Hussein's Iraq, rewards individuals with an unusually high willingness to engage in violence and aggression.

Military Experience Without Combat

As described in Chapter 1, previous work on how military background shapes the later behavior of a leader often fails to differentiate peacetime military service from participation in combat. Many world leaders have come to power wearing a military uniform but without directly experiencing violent warfare. One of the strongest findings in our research concerning individual background experiences is that leaders with national military service but no combat experience are among the most likely to start conflicts in the world.[2] They are familiar with military culture, structure, and capability, but lack the visceral experience to understand the risks associated with military action. While the set of leaders with national military experience but no combat experience never rises above 15 percent of the total leaders in a given decade, many of the most notorious late nineteenth- and twentieth-century leaders appear in this category: Francisco Solano López of Paraguay,[3] Mobutu Seko of the Democratic Republic

---

[2] Horowitz and Stam 2014.
[3] López exited office before 1875, so does not officially appear in the LEAD dataset.

of the Congo, Saddam Hussein of Iraq, Muammar Qaddafi of Libya, and Hafez al-Assad of Syria.

Francisco Solano López, as discussed in the Introduction, was a leader who admired the accoutrements of military life – the oaths, the traditions, the weapons, and the uniforms – but who had no actual combat experience, as the Paraguay of his youth was sheltered and peaceful. He is an example of the ways in which limited military experiences, especially in the absence of combat, can reinforce tendencies to favor the use of military force. López's fascination with military pageantry and his lack of firsthand experience with the viciousness of war resulted in the literal annihilation of his country. According to Bray, "[a]n immense pride, not to mention a certain dramatic vanity, constituted the dominant feature of his haughty and arrogant character."[4] López was a man whose lifelong occupation had been in the military, with brief excursions into diplomatic service at the behest of his father. Yet he had never fought in a war or seen combat when he took power in 1862. His father promoted López to general when he was only eighteen years old.[5] He received little real training in the military arts, as Paraguay lacked military academies and, due to its long spell of peace, any native teachers with actual military experience. His trips to Europe focused on the pageantry of peacetime military service, not on the violence and destruction of war.

"Long live the Republic of Paraguay! Independence or Death!" This phrase begins almost every letter written by López and his closest associates. We should not underestimate its literal meaning. Most of the letters written by López himself, available in the National Archive in Asunción, Paraguay, are from his time as a young military officer. His military journals, kept during uneventful expeditions between 1845 and 1851 (ages nineteen through twenty-five), and the letters written to his father during the same period reveal careful prose, filled with detailed descriptions of mundane events and often expressing feelings of deep boredom.[6] López desired a military career from a young age, and, having spent so much time with the military, he was eager to see some action.[7]

There is no doubt that López was preoccupied with honor and prestige, not only for himself, but for his nation as well. Leuchars describes him as "not an irresponsible young man but one who was filled with an overwhelming sense of duty, and it was this that gave him that profound sense of self-importance and destiny."[8] This became apparent in his desire to pursue war as a means of raising the national standing of his country:

He had an idea that only by having a war could Paraguay become known, and his own personal ambition drove him on, as he knew he could assemble every man in the country immediately and raise a large army.[9]

---

[4] Bray 1957, 66.   [5] López 1845.   [6] López 1849a, 1849b, 1850.   [7] Bray 1957.
[8] Leuchars 2002, 11.   [9] Thompson 1869, 25.

Indeed, from a young age, he seemed convinced, unlike his father, that war with Paraguay's neighbors would prove important to the modernization and development of his country. López's intuitions would prove to be prescient, but not in the way he believed – quite the opposite. Feeling threatened by Argentina and Brazil and, from his brief visit to the continent in 1855, inspired by European balance of power theories, he returned seeking to advance Paraguay's interests through a preemptive attack against his neighbors. At least in his own mind, and in the minds of his closest advisors who survived to the end, López kept his promise to defend his country even to the point when there was nothing left to defend.

Another example comes from Kaiser Wilhelm II, who led Germany into World War I. While our leader risk model places him in the top 5 percent of leaders overall, this may actually underestimate his risk profile. Raised as royalty, he received a military education and attended the University of Bonn. He joined the German army in the late 1870s, but left military service soon after, in 1881, when he married and became more involved in German politics. After his father, Emperor Frederick III, passed away in 1888 after only a short period of rule, Wilhelm II assumed the throne at the age of twenty-nine. This likely exaggerated the effect of his military service on his later behavior, because he lacked other life experiences, especially as an adult, from which to draw when evaluating the costs and benefits of war. In his first public statement to the German people after rising to the position of Kaiser, he explicitly referenced his relationship to the military, stating, "Thus we belong to each other – I and the Army – we were born for each other and will cleave indissolubly to each other whether it be the Will of God to send us calm or storm."[10] A biographer of Wilhelm II, John Van der Kiste, notes that "[b]ehind these words stood a determination to compensate for his lack of military experience."[11]

Throughout his reign, Wilhelm II pursued a series of militaristic policies, from a naval arms race designed to counter British naval supremacy to a series of diplomatic moves, including the Moroccan Crisis in 1911, which demonstrated his desire to push for German expansion. Based on his military background but lack of combat experience, it is not surprising that he glorified the military and did not fully consider the potential downsides of the use of force. Throughout his reign, he cloaked himself in uniform and encouraged military pageantry, demonstrating a fascination with the martial world. "Field service exercises, parades and inspections followed one another in seemingly endless sequence."[12]

His lack of battlefield experience exacerbated rather than tempered his aggressive tendencies, as he sought to demonstrate that, despite his lack of combat experience, he was a worthy leader of Germany. "Almost every other

---

[10] Van der Kiste 1999, 89.   [11] Ibid., 89.   [12] Fiebig-von Hase 2003, 74.

king, grand duke, or sovereign prince in the German empire had had more experience of war. Insecurity drove him on to strut and swagger, assuming a theatrical pose that the martial atmosphere of Berlin demanded he should personify."[13] As his military aide, Captain Adolf Von Bülow, stated, "Wilhelm had adopted the external trappings but not the values and mental habits of a Prussian officer."[14] When it came time to make important decisions, Wilhelm's knowledge of the military trailed far behind his ambition. Wilhelm II was a "military dilettante,"[15] and when he began to realize, at the dawn of World War I, the potential consequences of this aggressive outlook, it was too late to stop the German war machine from swinging into action, as Germany played its part in plunging the European continent into four years of brutal conflict.

This type of aggressive behavior among leaders without combat experience appears consistently to the present day. Franjo Tudjman of Croatia drew lessons about war from his partisan newspaper; Ronald Reagan experienced World War II as an interpreter and film actor instead of as a soldier. During their wars, both Tudjman and Reagan were responsible for boosting morale of the troops and the public and putting the best possible spin on setbacks. They were wartime propagandists who believed their press clippings perhaps a bit too much. In this role, they were dedicated believers in the righteousness of their work. Both were successful at this and learned how to express themselves in ways that motivated their followers to action. Yager describes how this affected Reagan, noting:

Another distinguishing element in Reagan's intellect was its proclivity to rely less on analysis and more on narration in comprehending reality ... Reagan often relied on stories and anecdotes to interpret reality. This is uncommon in American presidents, largely because so many have had legal or military backgrounds that place a premium on analysis.[16]

At the same time, Tudjman and Reagan saw the best side of the military, the public face put forward to spur patriotic feelings and public support despite wartime casualties. Without witnessing firsthand the most direct results of military violence, they were uniquely risk-acceptant, creating an overly optimistic view of the results of military action without adequate consideration of the risks and consequences. This is, in part, why Reagan and Tudjman are both predicted by our leader-based model to be likely to initiate militarized disputes, and they actually did initiate many disputes while in office.

Figure 4.1 shows the substantive importance of different types of military background experiences over time. These results draw from a regression model in which the dependent variable is whether a leader started a military conflict in a given year. The independent variables include military service variables drawn from the LEAD dataset and other variables, such as the balance of power and regime type that other scholars argue are important factors

---

[13] Van der Kiste 1999, 89.   [14] Clark 2000, 6.   [15] Ibid., 6.   [16] Yager 2006, 91.

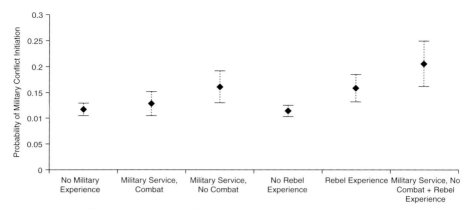

FIGURE 4.1. Military and rebel backgrounds and international conflict.

influencing national behavior.[17] Note the large increase in the risk of a military conflict for leaders with military service but no combat experience, compared with those with no military service at all.[18] A shift from no military experience to having military experience but no combat experience increases the probability of a militarized dispute by 66 percent.[19] As with all of our statistical findings, we want to dig into the data to see if these results actually reflect patterns in the real world. Here the pattern is quite clear.

Regular Military Experience with Combat

Recall from Chapter 2 the two contrasting theories about the relationship between combat and later behavior. Some argue that experiencing combat makes people less risk-acceptant, because they are more likely to recognize the costs of military conflict. Others maintain that surviving combat biases people toward favoring the use of military force. Experimental psychological research on risk propensity shows that exposure to fear-triggering events generally has a restraining influence on future risk-seeking behavior. As a risky experience likely to trigger fear in most individuals, direct exposure to combat most commonly generates more sensitivity to risk in the future, although not for everyone. Military experience during wartime can make leaders more conservative by increasing their understanding of the actual workings of the military. This relationship, however, depends a great deal on the type of

---

[17] We look at military experience in combination with a battery of traditional control variables used in social science models of international conflict such as the balance of power and whether or not a state is a democracy or an autocracy. See the Technical Appendix for more details.

[18] The result is also significantly different from those leaders with prior service but also combat experience.

[19] Substantive effects generated using Clarify (King et al. 2000).

country someone grows up in, that is, whether it is a democracy or an autocracy, as well as an individual's genetic makeup. Although there are exceptions to every rule, in general, leaders with combat experience who rise to power in democracies tend to react to that experience dispassionately, not in a way that biases them toward aggression. In contrast, those with combat experience who come to power in autocracies are especially prone to aggression because that is how they gained power in the first place.

As we noted earlier, John F. Kennedy experienced combat in the regular military, as a Navy PT boat captain in World War II. Although he could have avoided active combat for health and family reasons, Kennedy was attracted to the PT boat service because it provided a rare opportunity to captain his own vessel, a situation of potential high risk and high reward.[20] A Japanese ship destroyed his boat in August 1943, killing or severely injuring several of his men. Because his crew was on its own in dangerous waters, Kennedy made the quick decision to swim for land.[21] Kennedy and his men survived for five days on abandoned islands with minimal resources before he was finally able to get word out of his safety by carving a message on a coconut shell and giving it to friendly locals. As a perpetual reminder of this event, Kennedy had the coconut shell encased in plastic and made into a paperweight, which he kept on his desk in the Oval Office.

The trauma of the event, witnessing the deaths of men under his command and feeling that the Navy had left him for dead, had a profound impact on Kennedy. After receiving treatment for his injuries, he returned to service as a gunboat captain for several more months until his discharge from service. According to Renehan, "November 2 saw him rescuing marines trapped by Japanese ground forces on the island of Choiseul. After he'd gotten the men off the beach, Jack watched several severely wounded soldiers struggle and die in the main cabin of the gunboat, one of them in his very bunk."[22]

These experiences gave Kennedy a unique insight into the realities of war, in line with the military conservatism hypothesis. Such experiences reduce soldiers' later aggression, as compared with that of members of the military who do not see combat directly. Writing to his parents after his rescue, Kennedy stated:

I can now believe – which I never would have before – the stories of Bataan and Wake. For an American it's got to be awfully easy or awfully tough. When it's in the middle, then there's trouble. It was a terrible thing though, losing those two men ... It certainly brought home how real the war is – and when I read the papers from home, how superficial is most of the talking and thinking about it![23]

These experiences influenced his interaction with others who had avoided World War II combat, due to age or other reasons. Kennedy also learned directly about the functioning of the military bureaucracy in wartime, which

[20] Dean 1998.   [21] Renehan 2002, 264.   [22] Ibid., 271.   [23] Fussell 1991, 470.

further underlined his caution in dealing with them in the midst of international crisis: "He was particularly surprised by the incompetence and indifference of many of the 'top brass,' whom he denounced in scathing but funny letters home ... God save this country of ours from those patriots whose war cry is 'what this country needs to be run with is military efficiency.'"[24]

Kennedy's observations indicate that the trauma of combat does not necessarily drive military conservatism among veteran leaders, particularly in democratic states. As described in Chapter 2, our Leader Risk Index ranks Kennedy as very likely to start conflicts, but a detailed look at his behavior in office demonstrates the importance of domestic political institutions in shaping his behavior. Moreover, Kennedy's combat experience could also have exercised a restraining influence, despite the rest of his profile.

This does not mean, however, that veterans are pacifists. Coll writes that "[f]or Eisenhower, who had witnessed the carnage of the Normandy landings and the Battle of the Bulge, and later claimed to 'hate war as only a soldier who has lived it can,' political assassinations represented an alluring alternative to conventional military action."[25]

Personal experience with the bureaucracy of the armed forces, during the critical period of wartime, inevitably influences leaders' later beliefs about their level of understanding once they come to power. Knowing what the military is and is not capable of provides a more balanced context for evaluating the potential outcomes of military activity.

Nikita Khrushchev lived through some of the most brutal, high-intensity warfare of World War II. This was a learning experience for him. As Khrushchev biographer Mark Frankland wrote, "[H]e had experienced modern warfare with an intensity that few professional politicians outside the Soviet Union could match. In years to come, and in a way then quite unforeseeable, this experience was to mean a great deal to the world."[26] Despite the drama of the Cuban Missile Crisis, Khrushchev was generally more cautious about the dangers of nuclear war than his fellow Communist leaders, Fidel Castro and Mao Zedong.[27] Although all three experienced war first-hand, Khrushchev uniquely had experience with the terrifying power of modern weapons and their potential for large-scale destruction. In Cuba, Castro had not faced down tanks and heavy bombers, and it is difficult to know if this would have changed his perception of the fallout from such extraordinary killing.

Statistical models that include an interaction between the domestic political regime of a state (e.g., whether it is an autocracy or democracy) and whether a leader has experienced combat show a strong and positive interactive relationship between combat experience, military or more autocratic regimes, and the probability that a leader initiates a militarized dispute in a given year. In an extremely autocratic regime such as Saddam Hussein's Iraq or Joseph

---

[24] Wills 2009, 52.   [25] Coll 2013, 76.   [26] Frankland 1966, 66–7.   [27] Tompson 1995.

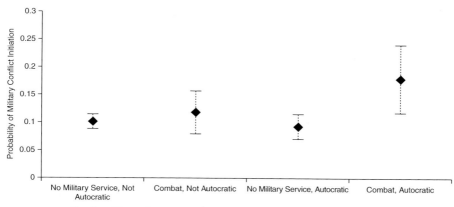

FIGURE 4.2. Regime Type, Prior Combat Experience, and Conflict.

Stalin's Soviet Union, the probability of a militarized dispute roughly doubles if the leader has had prior combat experience compared with a leader in the same circumstances with no prior military service.[28] Figure 4.2 depicts this relationship.

The set of extremely autocratic leaders with prior combat experience includes infamous examples such as Germany's Adolf Hitler. The leaders with prior combat experience who rule explicitly military regimes include South Korean leaders such as Park Chung-hee and Chun Doo Hwan, as well as Sarit Thanarat of Thailand. This relationship between prior combat experience in a uniformed military and regime type demonstrates again a point made in Chapter 3: it is critical to take into account the relationship between regime type and leader risk, because different types of regimes, to some extent, select different types of leaders.

Rebel Experience

Consistent with the arguments we laid out in Chapter 1, as shown in Figure 4.1, we also find a strong and consistent relationship between prior rebel experience and the initiation of martial actions. In fact, our statistical models show that the probability that a country gets into a military conflict, roughly doubles when the leader has prior rebel experience compared with when the leader does not have that kind of experience.[29] This finding is not simply a statistical artifact; Mao Zedong, Fidel Castro, and Mobutu Sese Seko are just a few former rebel leaders who later came to power. Moreover, while we tend to think of rebels as

---

[28] The difference is also statistically significant.
[29] These findings are consistent with Horowitz and Stam 2014.

those who fought in revolutions, rebels actually comprise a much broader category, such as those willing to fight against the ruling state. The category includes democratic leaders such as Charles de Gaulle of France, who fought as a partisan against Vichy France, and David Ben-Gurion of Israel. Both are former rebels who engaged in militarized behavior as the head of democratic states.

Our findings regarding former rebels are among the clearest examples of a background attribute with a significant link to later behavior. Figure 4.1 clearly depicts this relationship between prior rebel experience and the probability that a leader will start military conflicts. One example of a former rebel who demonstrates a strong belief in his ability to use force to achieve national ends is Mao Zedong of China. Mao's beliefs evolved over decades participating in and then leading the Communist opposition to the Nationalist regime. After experiencing enormous setbacks, including the Long March retreat and an invasion by Japan, Mao's Communists finally took control of mainland China in 1949. One might think that, given this enormous accomplishment and the challenges of governing a country the size of China, Mao might have sought to consolidate power and avoid provoking international unrest. However, just two years later, Mao led his new nation into an extremely costly war on the Korean Peninsula with the strongest country in the world, the United States.

To illustrate this point, consider Paul Kagame, the current president of Rwanda, whose case shows in greater depth how prior rebel experience can shape the later militarized behavior of leaders. Kagame joined Yoweri Museveni's National Resistance Army (NRA) in 1979 and fought as a guerrilla for six years, receiving training in military intelligence in Tanzania and eventually becoming the NRA's military intelligence chief. To strengthen these skills, Museveni sent Kagame to train with the U.S. military at Fort Leavenworth, Kansas.[30]

Despite his success in the NRA, anti-Rwandan sentiments in Uganda in the late 1980s profoundly affected Kagame.[31] Kagame and other refugees began to develop plans to start a guerrilla war in Rwanda. Tito Rutaremara founded the Rwandan Alliance for National Unity (RANU) diaspora group and provided early fundraising support for the Rwandan Patriotic Front (RPF). Kagame, the RPF leader during the height of the civil war and subsequently president of Rwanda, explained:

It was for us a very important formative stage. For me and many others, it was a good education. It followed what we went through as refugees, when conditions were bad, but that was a blessing in disguise. It was an example. It showed us we had to live like that if we wanted to win. We saw the difficulties that characterized the struggle we were to face. It was very important, certainly. The lesson was that if you have to wait for a long time, then you do it.[32]

---

[30] Waugh 2004.   [31] Gourevitch 1999.   [32] Kinzer 2008, 41.

Kagame's frustration with living in the refugee camps of Uganda, away from his homeland, encouraged him to join the rebel military there, to overthrow the government in power. Kagame explained:

I had already decided [to fight]. Even as a kid, when I was in primary school, we would discuss the future of the Rwandese. We were refugees in a refugee camp in a grass-thatched house for all this period. So this was always eating up our minds, even as kids. The political consciousness was there. We had ideas of our rights. Fred and I used to read stories about how people fought to liberate themselves. This was on our minds all the time.[33]

In an interview with journalist Philip Gourevitch, who asked him, "Did you like fighting?" Kagame replied: "Oh, yes. I was very annoyed. I was very angry. I will still fight, if I have reason to. I will always fight. I have no problem with that."[34] Kagame is highly aggressive and risk-acceptant, as demonstrated throughout his training and the military invasions he has led. This example supports the statistical conclusions laid out previously. In military regimes and extreme autocracies, a path to leadership through irregular activities, including coups, is more likely. Rather than being screened out as in democracies, those who react combat by becoming exceptionally aggressive and risk-acceptant are more likely to come to power in autocracies and military regimes.

When Former Rebels Lead Democracies

Rebel group participation indicates a high level of risk tolerance associated with greater willingness to resolve conflicts violently once a leader comes to office. However, some former rebels, who do not appear prone to conflict, come to power in democracies. Prior rebel experience is not deterministic.

José Mujica, the current president of Uruguay, was, in his youth, a leader of the Tupamaro terrorist group. In the 1960s and early 1970s, the Tupamaros used urban terrorist tactics such as car bombings, kidnappings, and robberies in the hopes of indirectly fomenting revolution. The Tupamaros actively targeted the populace of Uruguay, almost ensuring alienation and resistance.[35] A brutal counterinsurgency campaign eventually crushed the group, and many leaders, including Mujica, were put in prison. The man who eventually became president spent fourteen years imprisoned, ten of which were in solitary confinement. Yet, as he told a *New York Times* reporter in 2013, "I learned that one can always start again."[36] Instead of using his power to exact revenge or start martial spats with his neighbors, Mujica eschewed the presidential palace to live in his own modest home, continued to donate 90 percent of his salary to the poor, and spearheaded an ambitious domestic agenda of progressive reform.[37]

---

[33] Gourevitch and Kagame 1996, 171.   [34] Ibid., 171.   [35] Joes 2007.
[36] Romero 2013, A1.   [37] Romero 2013.

Another example from Latin America is Figueres Ferrer, referenced above, who led an armed insurrection against the government of Costa Rica in 1948, but disbanded his country's military when he took office. Figueres Ferrer's action is unique and deserves further consideration. Why did such a clearly risk-acceptant individual champion pacifism in a very dangerous region? Figueres Ferrer's non-violent approach demonstrates an alternative form of risk acceptance, one built around disarmament, not deterrence. Ronald Reagan arguably tried to take a similar path with his proposal for nuclear disarmament in negotiations with Gorbachev in Reykjavik, Iceland, although there are doubts that the proposal was meant as anything more than a stalking horse to demonstrate the lack of interest in disarmament on the part of the Soviet Union.

One reason for Figueres Ferrer's initial military successes lies in the lack of preparation by the Costa Rican government. Although he had been planning guerrilla operations for some time, no one took him seriously because he seemed "foolhardy."[38] In response to electoral fraud by the oligarchic ruling party, Figueres Ferrer launched his forty-day War of National Liberation on March 11, 1948. Navarro Bolandi[39] relates that:

Figueres applied to the art of war the same sense of organization that gave rise to his commercial enterprises, and with the faith of his convictions, that is always the necessary first line of war. The rest of his support came through national sympathy, moral support and indirect contribution.[40]

The conflict led to approximately 2,000 casualties on both sides. Figueres Ferrer took control of a junta government and dissolved or suspended many of the country's existing laws. This is usually an opportunity for leaders to consolidate control as a dictator, amassing wealth and protected by a loyal selectorate. However, Figueres Ferrer was a true believer in peace, not ongoing war. Following his victory, one historian[41] states that:

Their goal, Figueres proclaimed, was the Second Republic, but he reminded his soldiers, "Arms bring victory; only laws can bring freedom" ... They needed something more, he affirmed: a philosophy, a fundamental concept "to illustrate their path," which, although he apologized for its lack of lyrical quality, he suggested should be "the greatest good for the greatest number."[42]

Figueres Ferrer used the subsequent eighteen-month junta government to dissolve the Costa Rican military, replacing them with police forces. This was an extremely risky move, as it left Costa Rica vulnerable to regional threats "in the midst of a region virtually occupied by the armed forces."[43] Just over a week later, Figueres Ferrer faced his first test in response to Nicaraguan aggression at the border, but decided against military action, instead appealing to the Council of the Organization of American States (OAS) for arbitration. Why did Figueres

---

[38] Ameringer 1978, 50.   [39] Navarro Bolandi 1953, 96.   [40] Ibid., 96.
[41] Ameringer 1978, 65.   [42] Ibid., 65.   [43] Guerra 1997, 31. See also Navarro Bolandi 1953.

Ferrer take such a bold and potentially dangerous move? One reason is that he decided that keeping a standing army in the barracks was a greater danger to the democracy he sought to create than dissolving the army.[44]

Like Franjo Tudjman of Croatia, Figueres Ferrer was powerfully committed to an idealistic vision for the future of Costa Rica. Unlike Tudjman, however, his idea was one of peace. Figueres Ferrer devoted the remainder of his time in office as head of the junta to drafting and garnering support for Costa Rica's progressive new constitution. In his second term, in response to an invasion from Nicaragua, he temporarily recruited a volunteer army and again sought help from the Council of the OAS and the United States to defuse the situation. However, he never reinstitutionalized the army, and Costa Rica remains without a standing military to this day.[45]

In the universe of leaders, Paul Kagame is more typical of a former rebel leader than José Figueres Ferrer. Both had grievances with the government against which they rebelled, grievances they did not believe could be resolved by means other than force. While in power, both continued to engage in extraordinary risk-taking behavior, which in both cases proved successful for their respective states. While Kagame continued to take martial risks with his neighbors, Figueres Ferrer maintained his commitment to the intellectual ideals that formed the basis of his rebellion. Figueres Ferrer built his vision for a new Costa Rica on political risks instead.

This highlights the interactive complexity of the variables in the LEAD dataset; being a rebel fighter interacts with different personal factors to produce different outcomes. It also reinforces the importance of understanding personal-level variables in conjunction with institutional variables. Rebel leaders, if successful, are in the unique position of being able to shape the institutions of their new governments. Rebels with militaristic and aggressive backgrounds typically choose to set up new institutions that are more autocratic in nature. This is what Paul Kagame did in Rwanda after his successful rebellion. However, rebels with other kinds of personal-level background factors sometimes make different choices. José Figueres Ferrer was a self-taught intellectual who developed his ideas for a better Costa Rica from reading philosophy and history. Only by closely examining and expanding on the personal-level variables in the dataset can we begin to explain these divergent political outcomes for leaders who otherwise appear similarly risk-acceptant.

LEADER AGE

As Chapter 1 explains, the conventional wisdom about the relationship between age and military conflict suggests that young, brash leaders are more likely to start wars. Think of Alexander the Great or Julius Caesar. Both had

---

[44] Guerra 1997, 31. See also Ameringer 1978.   [45] Ameringer 1978, 279.

the experience to know their military capabilities, coupled with an intense drive for personal glory. Thus, the risks taken by leaders such as these were bold but calculated. Alexander and Caesar knew that, if they succeeded, they would reap the great rewards of personal fame for the rest of their lives. Of course, they could not foresee that they would both die unexpectedly at relatively young ages. They *believed* their time horizons were longer.

However, when we isolate the effects of age, we find that older leaders, on average, are more likely to start military conflicts. Why might that be? The answer likely has to do with time horizons. Older leaders fear that they may lose office due to poor health and generally discount the present much more. To put it in the context of American politics, they enter office already in legacy mode, seeking to establish their place in history and make the world safe for their country. Additionally, older leaders potentially have more institutional credibility because they have had more time to build up a political power base, giving them more freedom of action in office.[46] Therefore, in situations where a domestic political institution is not necessarily in favor of a conflict, a younger leader is less likely to get his or her way and start the conflict than an older leader.

Since 1875, the Alexander the Great model does not hold up when studying who starts wars. Instead, it is older men who are much more dangerous. Leaders in their forties and fifties, of course, would still be expected to have some fight in them. However, highly motivated people tend to become CEOs and political elites rather than career military officers. The height of one's career usually occurs in middle age, when driven individuals have the gravitas, wisdom, and energy to develop and execute complex projects as the leaders of teams of young followers, such as campaign volunteers, newly minted MBAs, or eager young scientists with fresh ideas. The average age of the 2,500 leaders we cover in the LEAD dataset is fifty-seven.

In fact, our statistical models show that, for military initiators, the relative risk increases more rapidly after age seventy than before. While we find that the likelihood of starting conflict is higher as one ages, this increase is even greater for the oldest leaders. Some of the most dangerous people in our dataset are geriatric. By the normal physical and psychological standards for people of this age, they ought to be weak and getting weaker as their faculties fail. Instead, we find examples of leaders who took on incredible tasks, including provoking major wars. The surprising question, therefore, is why are older leaders so much more dangerous than younger leaders?

Leaders are the product not only of their personal experiences, but also of what happens around them in the broader world. For example, the American experience in the Vietnam War arguably shaped how the United States weighed the costs and benefits of conflict for a generation, even for those who were not

---

[46] Horowitz et al. 2005.

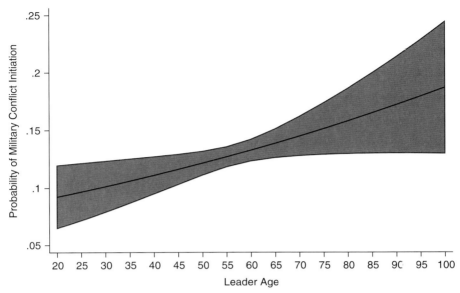

FIGURE 4.3. Leader age and international conflict.

in the military and did not have family in the military. Franjo Tudjman lived almost his entire life underneath the umbrella of what he viewed as the artificial state of Yugoslavia. Like many of his generation, he never accepted Yugoslavia, instead holding out hope for an independent Croatian state.[47]

Entering leadership office at an older age means that, inevitably, a leader has had more experiences that provide greater confidence and certainty about the outcomes of their actions. At the same time, older leaders have shorter perceived time horizons and a desire to leave a legacy through successful interstate conflict. Figure 4.3 shows that the risk of military conflict almost doubles as leaders reach an advanced age.

Another leader whose age seems to have had a large effect on his behavior is Ronald Reagan. Entering office at the age of sixty-nine, Reagan was also aware of the short period he had in which to accomplish his policy objectives.[48] Reagan also faced an assassination attempt in 1981. Multiple authors and Reagan himself report that the 1981 assassination attempt triggered a sense of his need to fulfill his "mission" as president and prevent nuclear war. Kengor relates:

[47] Sadkovich 2006c.
[48] Democratically elected leaders should have shorter time horizons, on average, than leaders in other regimes, because they have a limited amount of time in office. Age works somewhat differently, however. Older leaders discount the present more because they want to make their mark and secure the future, making them more likely to gamble, in general. On Reagan in general, see also Nau 2013.

While recovering in the hospital, Reagan told his daughter Maureen that he felt God had spared him for a reason, and that he would devote the rest of his time on earth to whatever it was God intended him to do ... As he sat in the White House solarium in robe and pajamas one morning, awaiting his doctors' go-ahead to resume a full work schedule, he pondered how to start the negotiating process with the Soviet Union. Reagan figured: "Perhaps having come so close to death made me feel I should do whatever I could in the years God had given me to reduce the threat of nuclear war; perhaps there was a reason I had been spared." It was a conviction that had a slow but certain ripple effect on Reagan's Cold War strategy.[49]

While Reagan was certainly aggressive in office, he does not fit a simple model of an older, more aggressive leader. Reagan also pursued groundbreaking arms control measures. In some ways, this contradicts the image of older leaders more prone to conflict. However, this behavior is consistent with the notion that risk-acceptant older leaders are more likely to go for broke in the policy realm in an effort to establish a legacy.

For Reagan, in addition to supporting a massive military buildup to make the United States safe against the Soviet Union, it meant pursuing radical agreements with the Soviet Union designed to ensure that nuclear war would not occur. He wanted the legacy of winning the Cold War and protecting the United States, which helped drive him, even at an advanced age.[50]

Besides the assassination attempt, Reagan's advanced age led to inevitable health problems while in office. Physically, as it would be for any older person, recovery from the assassination attempt was difficult for him. Reagan took a number of powerful pain medications during and after surgery and recovery known to interfere with mental clarity and decision making.[51] He underwent further successful surgeries for colon and skin cancer. Critics often also wondered about his mental health, especially when he exhibited typical senior forgetfulness. However, doctors who observed him closely reported no signs of dementia while Reagan was still in office.[52]

Consistent with our findings for military service, evaluating the relationship between autocracies and age shows how different types of leaders are important in different types of domestic political circumstances. Figure 4.4 shows how the effects of age look very different across different types of domestic political regimes. In fact, the positive relationship between advancing age and the probability that a leader initiates a militarized dispute disappears in dictatorships.

Given the lack of domestic political constraints in more extreme autocracies such as Saddam Hussein's Iraq, one would expect younger leaders in more autocratic regimes to be more disinhibited than older leaders. Essentially, while in most types of countries, it is older leaders, due to their shorter time horizons, who are more likely to start conflicts, in dictatorships, it is younger leaders whose impetuous instincts are less constrained by domestic political institutions.

---

[49] Kengor 2004, 199.   [50] Nau 2013.   [51] McDermott 2008.   [52] Altman 2004.

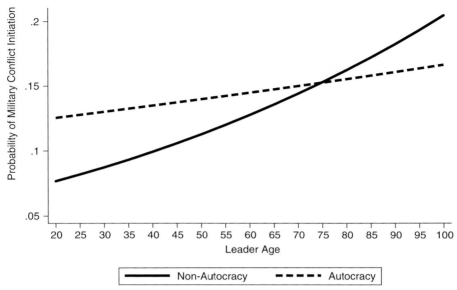

FIGURE 4.4. The effect of age in autocratic regimes.

EDUCATION

Formal education is one background characteristic that one might think, based on popular media, is truly important in shaping the future behavior of leaders. Some have argued, for example, that more educated leaders better understand the nuances of behavior and international politics, making it easier for them to avoid potential conflict.

In contrast, results drawn from the LEAD dataset show little if any systematic relationship between the educational level of a world leader and the probability that that leader starts a military conflict. If anything, the data suggest, albeit very weakly, that more educated leaders are more likely to engage in militarized disputes. One reason has to do with the relationship between education and the selection of leaders. Often, even in countries where most people do not receive an advanced education, those in the "pool" of potential leaders are those who *are* educated, rebel leaders being on average a conspicuous exception. More than eighty percent of the leaders in the LEAD dataset had at least some college education and almost fifty percent had at least some graduate education (defined broadly). Additionally, we are concerned, of course, that education itself might be a proxy for other factors such as wealth or social status that we have trouble measuring directly. The case studies here, however, attempt to tease out the relationship.

Woodrow Wilson is one of the most educated of all of the leaders in the LEAD dataset. Wilson received his Ph.D. in history and political science from

Johns Hopkins University in 1886, the only American president to earn a doctorate. Although he had started a career in law, Wilson was much more interested in an intellectual life.[53] Wilson was a popular and well-respected educator and author, writing several influential books on American government.[54] Before becoming president of the United States, he was president of Princeton University and later, in 1910, became president of the American Political Science Association.

Some of Wilson's biographers noted that when he was in office, he applied some of the same skills and theories he employed as a professor. His use of the bully pulpit to try to mobilize public opinion, for example, flowed from his view of the ability of the president to shape the national agenda. His academic background also led to one of his most ambitious efforts during World War I: the creation of the Committee on Public Information to conduct "psychological warfare" by influencing public opinion in Germany and elsewhere abroad toward ending the war.[55]

The upbringing of Israeli leader Golda Meir, discussed in Chapter 3, presents a contrast to Wilson and is another example of how the educational background of a leader can shape his or her behavior later in life. Even as a small child, Golda Meir was an eager immigrant to the United States. Once she realized the opportunities provided by an American education, Meir loved school and learning. She consistently ranked at or near the top of her class, and, as a young girl, was upset when family responsibilities made her late for school.[56] Her eventual goal was to become a teacher, a desire she put aside once she committed to emigrating to Palestine. Although she completed primary and secondary school (despite initial family objections), she completed only one year of teacher's college before her activist responsibilities completely took over all of her time. Throughout the rest of her career, Meir remained sensitive about her lack of formal education, making her suspicious of intellectuals:

She considered the diplomatic professionals to be too polished, excessively inclined to understand diverse points of view, and afflicted with analytical and intellectual traits that made communication and understanding between them difficult. In contrast, Meir's own talent lay in the simplification of issues; the very word "analysis" provoked her to irritability. When officials analyzed the contradictory waves of influence that flowed into decision making, she tended to interrupt them with an abrupt request for the main point.[57]

Her decision making style, developed later in her career, was limited by sharing information with a few key advisors in a close-knit group called "Golda's kitchen."[58] Some have argued that this influenced the way she made decisions during the Yom Kippur War of 1973, which resulted in an official inquiry and

---

[53] Clements 1987.   [54] Brands 2003.   [55] Turner 1957.   [56] Steinberg 2008.
[57] Ibid., 124, 128.   [58] Ibid., 184.

Meir's resignation. In that way, her educational background directly shaped the way that she made decisions while in office.

These examples show that, even though education does not appear to have a general relationship with military conflict, there are particular leaders whose educational backgrounds have played a critical role in shaping their attitudes concerning the use of force.

CONCLUSION

Why do some leaders use their power to exert martial force against their neighbors, while others look for peaceful solutions to conflicts? Neither history nor pure statistical correlations can give us clear-cut affirmative answers. However, in combination, a picture begins to form showing that leaders are not always buffeted by the forces of history, are not always overwhelmed by the constraints of material power, and are not automatons carrying out the desires of their selectorate.

Sometimes – as did Franjo Tudjman – they fight back. Incorporating leader attributes into the study of politics improves our ability to understand his decision to start and escalate conflicts in the former Yugoslavia. At other times, some individuals, such as Nikita Khrushchev, step back. Khrushchev led a superpower under incredible institutional constraints, but he was still a leader whose independent influence shaped the course of the twentieth century. Unlike Castro, Khrushchev's first-hand experience with the violence of large-scale modern warfare gave him pause when his finger was on the button. It is difficult to imagine that he could not still viscerally envision the slaughter he had witnessed during the Russian Revolution in 1917 and during the Battle of Stalingrad during World War II.

Still other leaders – such as Figueres Ferrer – give back. What current political science theory would foresee an armed insurrection resulting in the dismantling of a small nation's military in the midst of a very dangerous region? Nothing from system- or institutional-level theories can explain this. Figueres Ferrer was not balancing, bandwagoning, or even acting rationally, given the danger around his nation.

We do not claim that this analysis at the personal level provides all the answers, but rather that it stands alongside other explanations of international relations. This chapter helps provide another layer of evidence demonstrating when and how particular backgrounds of leaders shape the international security environment. In the next chapter, we move on from experiences such as military service or attributes such as age and discuss the way childhood, family, and gender can affect leader behavior.

5

The Experiences That Matter II: Childhood, Family, and Gender

Looking only at his early life circumstances and experiences, it does not appear that President Ronald Reagan was destined for greatness. Raised by a father who was down on his luck more times than not, Reagan's childhood was marked by instability as the family moved from town to town whenever his father lost a job.[1] Aspiring to do more, Reagan worked every summer to save enough money for college, and after his graduation from Eureka College, he began work as a radio announcer at station WOC in Davenport, Iowa.[2] In 1937, after a successful screen test on a trip to California, Reagan landed a job as a contract actor for Warner Brothers.[3]

He eventually became the first actor in Hollywood history to sign a million-dollar contract. He spent World War II in a U.S. Army film unit run by his studio boss, Jack Warner, and testified before the House Un-American Activities Committee during the Red Scare, all before even beginning his political career and switching parties from Democrat to Republican in 1962.[4] According to Eliot, Reagan's most formative years occurred during his time in Hollywood when he perfected the art of storytelling and the craft of negotiation, while developing a deep-seated enmity toward communism.[5]

Reagan was the oldest person ever elected to the American presidency, beginning his term just a few weeks shy of seventy years old. He was also the only president who had ever served as a union president. Finally, he was the only president to ever survive a wound from an assassination attempt, a near-death experience from which he developed a spiritual sense of mission about the remainder of his presidency.[6]

---

[1] Noonan 2001; Diggins 2007.   [2] Cannon 1982.   [3] Eliot 2008.   [4] Ibid.   [5] Ibid.
[6] Brinkley 2005; Evans 2006.

Psychologist Albert Bandura argues that if we are ever to truly understand how people develop the way they do, researchers should take the importance of chance encounters seriously. He notes that "[f]ortuitous influences may be unforeseen, but having occurred, they enter as evident factors in causal chains in the same way as prearranged ones do."[7] Ronald Reagan did not plan to become president. Instead, throughout his life, he capitalized on a series of events that eventually propelled him to become the leader of the Free World. In addition, as president of the United States, his background came with him, informing his outlook, ideology, and policy positions.

Does variation in childhood experiences incline some leaders to be more aggressive later in life? Do leaders with difficult childhoods and unstable families become more likely to act aggressively in office? The personality characteristics that make leaders who they are can be traced to their early life experiences. In the United States, we see greater levels of interpersonal violence among those who have grown up in poverty, those without an intact family, and those with lower levels of education. Does this apply to leaders from other countries and across periods? This chapter explores those questions, focusing on the experiences of leaders as children and in families, as well as on the effect of gender.

FAMILY BACKGROUND

The experiences of childhood provide fundamental emotional and mental memories that most of us carry throughout our lives. When children grow up in stable, loving environments, psychological research suggests that they are more likely to evolve into stable adults. Yet many world leaders grow up in less than ideal circumstances, ranging from variations on the "perfect" childhood to truly dire circumstances.

As the eldest son of a dictator, Francisco Solano López came of age in an affluent, comfortable environment. López's first studies were with the Argentina maestro Juan Pedro Escalada and, later, with the Jesuit Bernardo Parés.[8] He read a great deal and learned English and French. Whigham describes López's father, Carlos Antonio López, as "gluttonous," permitting his wife and children to partake in corrupt practices.[9] Arturo Bray gives insight into what the unusual childhood of López must have been like:

Accustomed from an early age to the flatteries of command and fortune, made by courtesans in honeyed flattery and homage, heir presumptive to the supreme repository of power, the climate was certainly not conducive to growing up humble and docile, although he was not naturally inclined to be prone to these virtues, he was even less so.[10]

---

[7] Bandura 1982, 747.　　[8] Zubizarreta 1961.　　[9] Whigham 2002.　　[10] Bray 1957, 66.

In contrast, John F. Kennedy's family was supportive, but extremely competitive. Eunice Kennedy Shriver recalls that "the family motto was 'Finish First.'"[11] Led by the powerful patriarch, Joe Kennedy, Sr., relentless intellectual and physical pressure marked JFK's early family life. The Kennedys were wealthy, and Jack was never left wanting. Despite its dysfunction, the presence of a strong and close-knit extended family provided crucial support to Kennedy throughout his life.

While very different in many ways, both Kennedy and López grew up wealthy. By contrast, Ronald Reagan's father, Jack, was an in-and-out-of-work alcoholic. Because his father could not hold a steady job, Reagan moved with his impoverished family all over Illinois before settling in Dixon in 1920.[12] As a child, Reagan and his family sometimes ate oatmeal hamburgers when their father's drinking depleted the family budget for meat.[13] Nonetheless, he had a strong relationship with his mother, Nelle, and his older brother, Neil, who provided a supportive base on which Reagan could develop a sense of independence and resilience.

These are just three examples, but they are illustrative of how leaders across time, space, and regime types can have very different upbringings. In this chapter, we use the same statistical tests that we used in the previous chapter to evaluate the way an individual background characteristic or set of related characteristics influences the probability of military conflict. While our results for the upbringing of leaders are less decisive than child psychologists might predict, some of the individual stories we lay out here show that learning about the early lives of leaders is an important part of understanding the total package of who they eventually become. Moreover, while these do not comprise the totality of the experiences captured in the LEAD dataset, they represent a large segment of those experiences, selected to help illustrate the ways that childhood and family backgrounds can shape how leaders behave later in life.

Parental Stability

The loss of a parent, either due to death or due to family abandonment, can be an especially acute trauma for children. Child development research indicates that the path to lifetime resilience for trauma-affected children comes from strong parental attachment, which is one of the key mediators of childhood trauma that help individuals develop resilience as adults.[14]

However, our overall statistical results generally show what all of us have likely observed in our own lives as well: while emerging from a broken home may make success in life less likely, it is far from determinative. For example, as we describe in later in this chapter, despite losing his parents, future U.S.

---

[11] Renehan 2002, 3.   [12] Kengor 2004.   [13] Noonan 2001.   [14] Werner and Yuen 2005.

President Herbert Hoover emerged from that trauma with an independent personality that served him well in his future educational and business ventures. When we conduct statistical tests on whether having divorced or otherwise unstable parents influences leader behavior, we find very little in the way of significant results. Of course, in becoming world leaders, by definition, these individuals are resilient.

An example of a leader whose early childhood did seem to influence his behavior is U.S. President Calvin Coolidge, who lost his mother when he was only twelve years old.[15] Her death removed a critical base of support during an important formative time. With an emotionally distant and busy father, Coolidge relied on his only sibling, Abbie, for consolation and support. A few years later, Abbie also died, and Coolidge became depressed and despondent. Nonetheless, he eventually found professional success in politics and personal joy in his own family and children. Tragically, his sixteen-year-old son died during Coolidge's first year in office, which led to an extended period of clinical depression from which he never recovered. His overwhelming and untreated grief interfered with his ability to carry out his preferred policies. Robert Gilbert[16] relates:

In a very real sense, Coolidge's presidency died when his son died, and he served out his remaining years in office as a mere shadow of his former self. Always industrious, he now became lethargic; always conscientious, he now became lackadaisical; always astute, he now became inane; always successful, he now became a failure. Psychological illness ravaged his presidency and his life.[17]

The loss of his mother at a young age not only had an immediate effect on Coolidge; it also made him less able to cope when his son passed away. Ultimately, Coolidge was not able to fully engage with the demands of his presidency, including with foreign and military policies, as he led the United States into a form of isolation after World War I. To test this idea more systematically, we also looked at whether other leaders who had children who passed away were more likely to engage in militarized behavior when in office. Our models suggested there was not a significant relationship between losing a child and becoming more risk-acceptant.

It was during this stage in his life that Franjo Tudjman suffered the deaths of both parents. In April 1946, his father and stepmother were both found shot to death in their home. The police attributed the deaths to a murder-suicide,[18] although Tudjman himself believed it was a revenge killing by the Communist Party. Steve Coll wrote in 1993:

At 70, Tudjman is also an aging orphan who has spent years investigating the deaths of his father and stepmother – and the conclusions he has reached shape his outlook in today's conflict hardening his view of his present enemies. "The tragedy itself is his

[15] Gilbert 2003. [16] Ibid., 3. [17] Ibid., 3. [18] Sadkovich 2006a; Husic 2007.

personal obsession," said Slavan Letica, a former Tudjman adviser. The context for this obsession, Letica added, "is the rebirth of history."[19]

Sead Husic noted, "In his subsequent political activity he tried to realize the unfulfilled wishes of his father in order to overcome his own perceived guilt in the death of his father."[20] Tudjman's personal trauma interacted with his work as a revisionist historian, his occupation before entering politics, to provide an internal and external justification for his increasingly nationalist views. Under these circumstances, it was easier to defend his ethnic cleansing policies. Tudjman provides a stark example of the role of emotion in the decision-making process leading to war.

Parental loss interacts with other individual and contextual factors in a leader's background. As the histories of Coolidge, Hoover, and Tudjman indicate, this specific trauma does not necessarily result in risk-acceptant behavior that leads to military aggression. Coolidge's loss of his parents as a child compounded with so much other tragedy that he became incapacitated from depression while in office. Hoover's parents died of natural causes, and the members of his pacifist Quaker faith provided a strong basis of emotional support during a critical time. Hoover was risk-acceptant but only in domains other than military aggression, specifically business. On the other hand, Tudjman's unique dual trauma focused his risk-acceptant personality on specific targets, whom he carefully planned to remove from a new Croatia. These cases illustrate the mediating factors that can change the outcome of a traumatic childhood. Even though these variables are not significant in a systematic way, as with some of the factors we examined in the last chapter such as education, they can play a significant role for particular leaders.

A more direct relationship might exist between those children who face more extreme challenges in childhood, such as being an "illegitimate" child or being an orphan. Both of these could lead to feelings of abandonment, which psychologists argue can trigger aggression in children. Do these characteristics carry over later in life? The results are not entirely clear. Of all of the upbringing variables, the most consistently significant factor is a relationship between being an illegitimate child and future militarized behavior. After all, leaders such as Fidel Castro and Mobuto Seko both were born illegitimate. However, the result seems to be the opposite of what basic psychological theories would predict. Instead of making leaders more likely to use force when they get into office, because the leader is more aggressive in general, illegitimate children who rise to leadership of their country are actually *less* likely to use military force. It is possible that this result simply represents statistical noise. Only forty-four leaders in the dataset were known to be illegitimate children, meaning there is potentially not sufficient variation to generalize about the way this type of background experience influences the future behavior of leaders.

[19] Coll 1993, B1.   [20] Husic 2007, 112.

Childhood Wealth

Another significant source of stress and potential trauma in children comes from growing up in poverty. An impoverished environment places stress on children because of the potential for physical danger and deprivation.[21] This can be mediated by social supportive factors, however. We focus here on two leaders who were born into poverty, but whose lives took very different paths.

Unlike many American presidents, including his immediate successor, Franklin D. Roosevelt, Herbert Hoover was not born into wealth but rather into humble circumstances on a frontier farm in Iowa in 1874. His family were Quakers, and his father worked as an enterprising blacksmith.

Hoover noted in his memoirs, "Sickness was greater and death came sooner."[22] Before modern medicine, the plains were a place where it was easier to fall deathly ill. Hoover's father died of "rheumatism of the heart" in 1880, when Herbert was six years old.[23] His mother, left to raise three children alone, died of typhoid fever with complications from pneumonia four years later. Although Hoover had extended family who helped raise him afterward, there is no doubt that the loss of his parents at such a young age had an effect on his thinking and worldview. George Nash relates:

Yes, life was tolerable, but it was not the same. Sometimes during the night, the boy would lie awake yearning for his mother who was gone. While his uncle and aunt were decent and understanding, no one could replace his parents ... Perhaps unconsciously, Hoover began to develop a certain detachment from his surroundings, a protective reserve that masked the loneliness of one who was, inevitably, an outsider.[24]

Orphaned as a young child, living with relatives in Oregon, Hoover worked from the time he was a teenager, first in manual labor and later as an "officeboy."[25] After an unsatisfying year at a local business college, Hoover petitioned a well-known Quaker and became among the first students to enroll at the new Stanford University. At Stanford, he took engineering classes while working summers to support himself as a geological surveyor in Arkansas, California, and Nevada.[26]

While Hoover managed to change his circumstances, as do nearly all who rise to become leaders, early life experiences with deprivation can have longer-term effects. Material deprivation, such as hunger, affects children in multiple ways and can have lifetime negative consequences on physical and cognitive development.[27] Insufficient nutrition can contribute to decreased

---

[21] Cicero et al. 2011.   [22] Hoover 1951, 7.   [23] Nash 1983.   [24] Ibid., 11.
[25] Hoover 1951.   [26] Ibid.
[27] Dupuy and Peters 2010. While we reference a few types of material deprivation in particular, the list is not meant to be exclusive. Contrast material deprivation here with deprivation from other sources, such as an unstable family situation. While it is certainly possible to overcome significant material deprivation, it can create large-scale mental, emotional, and developmental challenges.

social functioning and negative mental-health outcomes.[28] Deprivation of life's necessities, especially food and clothing, correlates with avoidant and hyper-vigilant behaviors in children and with neurobiological changes that can have long-term effects.[29] Hoover carried not only his cognitive memories of his youth, but also visceral and emotional memories that are observable in his later decision making behavior as the leader of one of the most powerful nations in the world.

Golda Meir, in contrast to Hoover, spent her impoverished youth in Ukraine (ironically, around the same time as Nikita Khrushchev). As a Jew in the Pale of Settlement, she witnessed violence and trauma at a very young age. She came from a home that was intact but marred by tragedy and poverty. Golda and her two sisters were the only surviving children of a total of eight, the rest having died in infancy. According to Ralph Martin, "Goldie had two sharp memories of her first five years in Kiev: hunger and fear."[30] Meir's young life in Pinsk, Ukraine, was difficult, marked by poverty and encounters with violent anti-Semitism, which she referred to throughout her career. Martin recounts one of her most terrifying memories, that of her family preparing for a pogrom:

"I remember how scared I was, and how angry." The pogrom never happened, but Goldie never forgot her fear and her anger. It was a fear and an anger that helped shape her life. Later she would say, "If there is any logical explanation ... for the direction my life has taken ... [it is] the desire and determination to save Jewish children ... from a similar experience."[31]

Anti-Semitism during this time and in this place was rampant. Although her father was a skilled carpenter, he was frequently unable to find work, and the family often had barely enough food to survive.[32] Even as a young child, Golda experienced traumatic anti-Semitism at the hands of Cossacks and peasants that helped motivate the development of her later beliefs.[33]

These experiences indicate the kind of trauma that children are more likely to experience when they grow up in conditions of poverty. Living in a danger-ous area such as the Pale of Settlement not only puts children at risk, but also makes it more likely that they will witness violence against others in their community.[34] Age and length of exposure to violent trauma can have differen-tial effects on later mental health. Young children may manifest immediate symptoms such as aggressive behavior, poor performance in school, bed-wetting, and nightmares.[35] Even children who have not directly experienced the most acute violence of war often suffer emotional trauma associated with being present during war. Children, in particular, can suffer post-traumatic stress disorder (PTSD) from a variety of experiences, including witnessing

[28] Cardozo et al. 2004b.   [29] Husain et al. 1998; Anda et al. 2006.   [30] Martin 1998, 5.
[31] Ibid., 7.   [32] Ibid.   [33] Opfell 1993, 34.   [34] Pynoos et al. 1995.
[35] Mousa and Madi 2003.

funerals, witnessing shootings or rapes, seeing injured or dead strangers, seeing family members injured or killed, experiencing family separation, and even having lack of access to adequate food and water.[36]

Despite her early trauma, Golda was lucky. She left with her family at age eight for Milwaukee, where she was a happy child, quickly assimilating into her new country and excelling in school and social life. Both Khrushchev and Meir exhibited resilience, a psychological construct that explains how children who experience trauma are able to recover. Both had intact families, a factor contributing importantly to the development of resilience.[37] They were able to emotionally and cognitively process their experiences and develop their own understandings, overcoming feelings of helplessness and developing an important locus of control as they aged This is important to understanding them as leaders, as Linda Luecken and Genna Gress point out:

The importance of secure attachment and positive parent-child relationships early in life is a recurring theme among studies of long-term resilience. Children exhibiting early signs of competence are also more likely to continue on a path of resilience during adolescence and the transition to adulthood.[38]

Childhood War Trauma

Exposure to wartime violence at a young age can also have a normalization effect manifesting in a desire for violent revenge. Some suggest that the motivation for revenge comes from the combination of initial trauma, PTSD symptoms, and individual attributes.[39] As one study suggests, "The psychological wounds of civilians who have suffered war-related traumatic events do not resolve spontaneously, but may linger for many years, and may even have multigenerational effects."[40] This may be particularly acute when a child has witnessed family members being injured or killed, which some studies have shown to be the most predictive of severe trauma.[41] According to other research, the revenge motive may also explain variations in the intensity of civil war violence in subsequent periods, while war survivors with PTSD are less likely to support "belief in nonviolence, belief in community, and interdependence with other ethnic groups."[42] Taken together, this implies that leaders who experienced war as children may be more willing to start military interventions and less willing to seek peaceful alternatives to disputes.

The number of leaders with childhood exposure to war has been steadily increasing over time. Figure 5.1 shows a general increase in the number of

---

[36] Pynoos et al. 1995, 78; Ramadan and Qouta 2000; Morgos et al. 2007; Roberts et al. 2008.
[37] Masten and Wright 2010.   [38] Luecken and Gress 2010, 246.
[39] Gabler and Maercker 2011.   [40] Cardozo et al. 2003.   [41] Morgos et al. 2007.
[42] Pham et al. 2004; Balcells 2010.

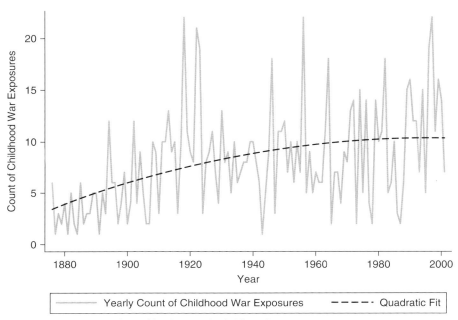

FIGURE 5.1. The number of leaders with childhood war exposures, 1875–2001.

leaders in power who experienced war of some kind as a child or young person. This chart indicates the total number of childhood war exposures by all leaders in power at a given time.

Results from statistical analysis available in the Technical Appendix show that the childhood experience of having lived through any war correlates positively with the propensity to initiate militarized interstate disputes, even when controlling for the influence of adult military experiences. Leaders with war experience tend to be more aggressive, when compared with those without such experiences. This is an example of a generational effect. In democracies, leaders' backgrounds can be particularly important when a country is choosing between leaders of different generations. The choice between Bill Clinton, of the Vietnam generation, and George H.W. Bush, of the World War II generation, in the 1992 U.S. presidential election, is one such example. However, when the plausible slate of leaders all come from the same generation, it is statistically more likely that cohort effects may exist. Common national-level experiences during childhood could shape the way the leaders of an entire time period behave.

As with many leader attributes, the effect is far from uniform. Take, for example, the case of French leader Raymond Poincaré. Poincaré, the French prime minister and president during World War I, who was ten years old during the Franco-Prussian War, saw his family's home in Lorraine occupied by and ultimately lost to Prussian soldiers in 1870.[43] Poincaré's experiences with war illustrate the direct effect of war on children. One biographer notes:

Certainly as a ten-year-old boy in Western Lorraine, he experienced first hand the invading Prussian armies during the 1870 Franco-Prussian War. He was forced to flee his family home to a series of hotels in Dieppe and then Belgium with his mother and brother for two and a half months, leaving his father in the family home in Bar-de-Duc. When he returned, he had to live under German occupation for three years until France had paid to Berlin the 5 billion gold francs imposed at the Frankfurt peace settlement.[44]

However, for Poincaré, rather than fueling a general tendency for revenge, the experience led to further fear of German military expansion. This is interesting because the general reaction of many who experienced the Franco-Prussian War on the French side was to funnel "a pathological desire for *revanche*"[45] into support for war. In contrast, fearful of the consequences of a conflict and aware that Lorraine would be a key battleground once again, Poincaré was more cautious.

BIRTH ORDER

Most leaders in the dataset had siblings, although the degree of closeness with their siblings varied. Francisco Solano López, the oldest son of a dictator, imprisoned one brother and executed the other. He had his mother and sisters beaten, on his orders, when they defied him. Kennedy was the second son of a powerfully competitive family, always playing second string to his older brother, Joe Jr., until Joe's service death in World War II. Hoover and Reagan both had an older brother with whom they remained close throughout their lifetimes. In contrast, Benazir Bhutto was the oldest child in her family, and, despite her being female, was selected by her father early on to be his intellectual and political heir. Franjo Tudjman was also the oldest son in his family and, like Bhutto, enjoyed a close personal and intellectual relationship with his father.

Does this matter for shaping the future behavior of leaders in a systematic way? Our research, like most other work on the topic, fails to find a conclusive link between birth order and later adult behavior, in this case, along the dimension of violent interstate conflict. Given that birth order theories, even if true, are not specifically about aggression per se, it is not surprising that we would fail to find a link. Moreover, in most cases, lack of data limits our ability to test birth order arguments. As we describe in detail in the Technical Appendix, it is extremely difficult to operationalize birth order theories in a systematic way for the purposes of statistically testing leader behavior. Even for well-known leaders, it can be difficult to find enough evidence about their family background. For example, because birth order theories focus on cohort effects,

[43] Kavanagh 1998.   [44] Keiger 2008.   [45] Ibid.

precise data are needed not only on whether a leader had an older brother or sister (for example), but also on the specific age gaps. Moreover, it is difficult to code for the way gender influences family dynamics. A son in one part of the world in one period of time who has an older sister may be treated as a first-born child, while in another might be treated as a second-born child.

GENDER

Other than monarchs who ascended to power by birthright, the first woman to independently lead her country was Khertek Anchimaa, the chairwoman of the Little Khural (parliament) of the Tuvan People's Republic in 1940. Little known in the West due to the small scale of the Tuvan People's Republic and as the emergent war in Europe overshadowed her ascendency, she nonetheless ushered in a new era of governance. In her four years, she pushed forward bold policies culminating in an agreement to end Tuva's independence and accept nonviolent, formal annexation by the Soviet Union. Another communist leader, Sükhbaataryn Yanjmaa of Mongolia, starting in 1953 served as president of Mongolia for a year, following the death of her husband. In the 1960s, two women took control of their governments in India and Israel. Indira Gandhi took office for the first time in 1966, while Golda Meir became the first woman in power in the Middle East in 1969.

While there were no female heads of state in our dataset before World War II, in each decade since, their numbers have increased to the point where today, a small but substantial number of world leaders are women. In the years since they first began to hold office, at times they have played an outsized role in their regions' politics and policies. At other times, they have played mostly symbolic roles, something not much different from their male counterparts.

As Figure 5.2 illustrates, coinciding with the world women's movement, female leaders have proliferated since the 1950s. In states where political leadership passes by birthright, as in monarchies, female leaders appear uncommonly but regularly throughout history. Beginning in the nineteenth century as more democratic or popular authoritarian forms of government proliferated at the expense of monarchic systems, women all but disappeared from the leadership roles. World War II seems to have provided the opening, and the expanding recognition of women's equality and rights coincides with an increasing number of women at the highest levels of political power.

The first elected women leaders came to power in authoritarian systems. Women appear in more liberal, democratic systems in the 1960s in South Asia and in the 1970s in the West. Although they make up much less than 50 percent of leaders, they have led some of the more powerful states and in these roles have guided their nations in times of war and strife. Moreover, we know from research by Valerie Hudson and others that states featuring higher levels of gender inequality are more prone to violence and suffer negative economic consequences (which is not surprising when you consider that states that fail

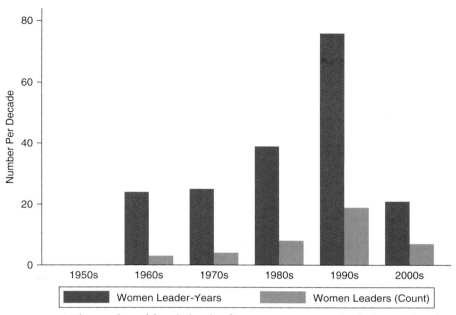

FIGURE 5.2. The number of female heads of state or government in the international system, 1950–2004.

to integrate women into the workplace are excluding, by rule, nearly half of the possible "talent" from contributing to the economy).[46]

In 2007, Argentine voters elected Cristina Fernández de Kirchner as president of Argentina. She was not the first female president of that nation. Isabel Perón, widow of populist former President Juan Perón, was the first female political executive in the Western Hemisphere, a titular head of a state controlled by a military junta. As was the case with many Latin American male leaders during that period, "Isabelita's" time as president looked little different from the years immediately before or after. She gave the military a free hand to conduct their Dirty War, in which thousands of Argentines died or disappeared on suspicion of leftist tendencies. Without popular or military support and isolated from her late husband's power base within the bureaucracy, Perón soon retreated from office and in 2007 was indicted for war crimes. Her time in office reflected a rather ignominious time in Argentine politics but ushered in the opening of executive politics in the West to women.

When Isabel Perón came to power in 1974, Cristina Fernández was just twenty-one years old. Cristina and her husband, Nestor Kirchner, were sympathetic to the left and knew victims of the Dirty War. They managed to avoid

[46] Hudson et al. 2012.

being caught up in its aftermath by moving from Buenos Aires to Patagonia, a region at the south end of South America shared by Argentina and Chile, to begin their legal careers. As a political "dream team," Nestor and Cristina supported each other's rise through parliamentary elections to Argentine national power.

Like Perón, Fernández took office following the end of her husband's presidency. She won election on her own after he was term-limited out, promising to continue the same policies. When Kirchner died suddenly of a heart attack in 2010, his base immediately rallied behind her. The next day, posters went up all over Buenos Aires proclaiming, "¡Fuerza Cristina!" Despite Argentina's ongoing economic setbacks, Cristina was reelected in 2011 and remains president to this day.

While Fernández has promoted relatively left-wing economic policies that have proven controversial in international financial circles, she has not proven to be an aggressive military leader. To be fair, Argentina faces a relatively unthreatening international security environment at present. Fernández's tenure raises an important question central to our project, however. Does the selection process for women leaders differ, and do women leaders behave fundamentally differently from men in similar situations? In this section, we explore the lives of several women leaders and what we can learn, more broadly, from the LEAD dataset about the relationship between gender and militarized behavior.

Women as Leaders

Commonly for men, from a young age, testosterone and an individual's socialization combine to encourage (or, at least, not discourage) violence as a means of resolving conflicts between males. If true, we would expect that women in office would be systematically less likely to engage in militarized behavior. Alternatively, the selection process for leaders could make it difficult to disentangle the specific effects of gender when women are perceived to be acting sufficiently like men to rise through the ranks into political office. In that case, we would expect very little in the way of variation based on gender when it comes to militarized behavior in office.

Women's entry into political leadership is a relatively new phenomenon, with over half of female world leaders having come to power only since 1990.[47] Since our dataset ends in 2001, the number of cases of women leaders covered is small, representative of their relative rarity; only twenty-nine women leaders are included in the analysis. The relative paucity of female heads of state makes it impossible to statistically test for effects of gender, making the use of case studies crucial for understanding the motivations of these individuals.

---

[47] Jalalzai and Krook 2010.

While these case studies point to some individual attributes that seem important and provide ground for future research, they also face inherent limits in terms of generalizability.

In general, women leaders have risen both in countries facing very dangerous security environments, such as Golda Meir in Israel, as well as in countries facing very pacific environments, such as Kim Campbell in Canada. Women have proven more likely to rise to power in democratic and especially parliamentary regimes, although cause and effect is difficult to parse given the small sample size. Most women leaders have been part of political families or dynasties. This enables them to bring the political capital of their families to bear on their careers.[48] In the United States, Hillary Clinton, the spouse of former President Bill Clinton, announced that she will run for president in 2016, while Liz Cheney, the daughter of former Vice President Dick Cheney, ran for a Wyoming Senate seat in 2014. To be fair, plenty of men (for example, George W. Bush) come from political families as well, but the proportions are somewhat higher for female leaders. Corazon Aquino of the Philippines and Benazir Bhutto of Pakistan were heirs to powerful legacies that ensured a political base of support, regardless of gender.[49]

Beyond selection, assessing the role of gender as a factor driving the behavior of female leaders is challenging. For example, women are less likely to have served in the military or seen combat as soldiers, making it difficult to assess how these experiences might change their selection into office or their risk orientation. As Francis Fukuyama remarked, "Statistically speaking it is primarily men who enjoy the experience of aggression and the camaraderie it brings and who revel in the ritualization of war."[50]

Additionally, female leaders may be older than male leaders when they begin their political careers, as they usually bear and raise children during a period when males are nurturing their early political careers. Essentially, there are life experiences potentially correlated with gender that may lead to predictions about the relationship between gender and conflict that have more to do with those other experiences than gender per se.

This also counsels against thinking of women as necessarily pacifistic. Numerous observers accuse Park Geun-hye, the current and first woman president of South Korea, of being dangerously aggressive. The daughter of former dictator Park Chung-hee (whose wife, Park's mother, was killed by a North

---

[48] Liswood 1996.

[49] Although the earliest women leaders emerged in communist authoritarian systems, Jalalzai (2010) observes that women leaders are more likely to arise from parliamentary rather than presidential systems, possibly because they are more collaborative and sheltered from the political whims of a sexist public. For the same reason, they also benefit from coming into office through temporary appointments before formal elections.

[50] Fukuyama 1998, 33.

Korean assassin), Park has explicitly taken on her father's hard-line stance against communists in general and North Korea in particular:

Ms. Park and her military have parried the North's over-the-top threats of nuclear holocaust with vitriol of their own; the military recently threatened to wipe the Communist dynasty "off the face of the earth" if it dared to launch a nuclear attack. And, breaking with the tone of her archconservative predecessor, Ms. Park told her generals that if the North staged even a limited attack, they should strike back "without political consideration" and without waiting for her approval.[51]

We focus here on the experiences of five women leaders to illustrate how their gender helped to shape their worldviews and risk propensities. Our cases in this section are Kim Campbell of Canada, Golda Meir of Israel, Margaret Thatcher of Great Britain, Benazir Bhutto of Pakistan, and Corazon Aquino of the Philippines. While, as a group, they are not necessarily representative of all women leaders in the dataset, each has a relevant set of life experiences that illustrates different aspects of the experiences of women leaders. All were married and, except Campbell, were mothers. None had any direct experience with war, although both Thatcher and Aquino lived, as civilians, through World War II. Except for Aquino, each leader was part of a parliamentary system of government. Bhutto, at age thirty-five, was the youngest of these leaders to take power, while Meir was the oldest, at age seventy-two.

In what follows, we focus on areas of experience to see when and how women leaders may differ from male leaders. We then assess the actual militarized behavior of women leaders. The results, as we explain in detail below, suggest that simple answers about the relationship between gender and conflict are hard to identify. As more women leaders take office over the next decade, we will gain greater insight into whether some of the trends identified here are due to a selection process, are genuinely related to gender, or are merely "noise" rather than information indicating a systematic trend.

Women and Age in Power

Given the demands of childbearing and child-rearing, we might expect to see differences in the age at which women leaders enter office, with women perhaps taking longer to reach high office. Instead, the reverse is true, although by a small margin. The mean age of women in office is fifty-two, while the mean age of men is fifty-five. While the average ages may be similar, men and women are likely to have had different experiences in the times leading up to their rise to power. While many men spend their younger years focusing on their career, most women devote relatively more time during their early adult years to childbearing and child-rearing. As girls and daughters, women experience the socialization process of childhood differently from boys and sons.

[51] Sang-Hun 2013, A1.

Traditionally, most girls were expected to grow up to be wives ar
instead of intellectuals and world leaders, although Margaret Tl
Benazir Bhutto are examples of women whose intellectual promise anu pu.
sonal grit showed early. The small sample size suggests caution when drawing
conclusions from the women in our work; however, from the qualitative data,
the nature of experiences before taking office is substantively different for
(most) men and women. Our statistical findings about age in general may apply
to women, but we cannot say that with any great certainty.

For both men and women, institutional experiences interact with age to
drive risk preferences. Older men are more likely to engage in high-risk
foreign policies because they have spent years forming contacts and because
of institutional knowledge that both expands their power base and also potentially insulates them from the potential costs of failure. For most women,
human reproductive biology dictates that they spend at least a few years
focusing on the demands of young children, instead of the demands of politics.
This might change their outlook on military matters if they enter at an older
age, with many of these experiences behind them.

Corazon Aquino, leader of the Philippines, is a prime example of this. Her
children were out of the house when she entered office. She entered politics
somewhat older and most unexpectedly. As a result, Aquino had not developed
the broad base of support within the bureaucracy typically required for leaders
to take on risky adventures. Kim Campbell of Canada appears in these pages
because, even without children, she spent her twenties and thirties not involved
in politics and was at the time overshadowed by her famous and older husband.
Campbell was not politically engaged during this period of her life but rather
fell into politics where, as opposed to what many might have expected, she did
well despite beginning her career at an older age.

Because of social norms or family instability, girls – even those with substantial promise – may be left behind. Women who, despite this background, go
on to become world leaders are "late bloomers" who must develop on their
own as adults. Aquino and Campbell both fit into this category. In both cases,
the political development of these women leaders occurred in later adulthood,
and both appear to have been highly risk-acceptant.

Corazon Aquino

Corazon Aquino grew up in the completely sheltered environment of a wealthy
and piously religious family. Her family did not prepare her for a life of politics
but rather encouraged her to succeed in traditional female roles and to take her
place as an upper-class wife and mother.[52] Although she had been educated at
private schools in the United States, she returned to her homeland to pursue this
traditional path. She started law school in Manila, but in 1954 left after the first

---

[52] Crisostomo 1987.

year to marry her husband, journalist and activist Benigno Aquino, Jr., the son of another wealthy Filipino family that was prominent in politics. "Ninoy" began his own career in politics at a very young age, becoming the mayor of his hometown of Concepcion at twenty-two and eventually a governor and senator. Throughout her husband's political career until his imprisonment, the shy Cory avoided the spotlight and focused primarily on raising their five children.

The most intense experiences of Aquino's life before her election involved her husband. In 1972, President Ferdinand Marcos declared martial law and arrested Ninoy. He was sentenced to death and imprisoned for over seven years, a time she found depressing, lonely, and anxiety-provoking, as many who had previously been family friends abandoned them for fear of political reprisals. It helped her identify more with the poor and oppressed, in turn building her determination to succeed. As Komisar wrote:

> Cory had been in the background during Ninoy's political career. Now she became his political stand-in, the one person he could confide in and trust to carry out his confidential tasks, to take messages between him and his political allies, often smuggling them past guards in a thermos jug or in her young daughter Kris' clothes. She carried sensitive information that required explanations and responses. Ninoy was extremely inquisitive, and she had to be prepared with detailed answers. He helped train her for the role. He would pose a question and then tell her how to answer it. She said her thirty hours with him every weekend were a political "brainwashing."[53]

This critical period laid the foundation for Aquino's eventual political career. Although she had never expressed any interest in becoming a politician herself, the seven years of her husband's imprisonment gave her an important base of understanding for what such a role would entail. After Ninoy's release from prison for health reasons, the family emigrated and settled near Boston, Massachusetts.[54] Nevertheless, her husband remained engaged in Philippine opposition politics and planned to return to continue his earlier work.

Aquino's life changed in the blink of an eye the day Ninoy returned to the Philippines. Members of a military conspiracy shot him in the back of his head as he walked down the steps of the airplane after returning from the United States, where he had been living in exile for the previous three years. Ninoy died on the tarmac at Manila International Airport on August 21, 1983. Although distraught, Cory rallied within a few hours and showed a "steely stoicism" to the nation.[55] She was fifty years old, and it marked a critical turning point in her life. Aquino could have easily nurtured her sorrow in safety, remaining in the United States as a grieving widow while, thousands of miles away, the Philippines remained in a state of violence and oppression. Why did she return? Crisostomo explains that the social tension in country due to the assassination drove her into politics as she stepped out from his shadow.[56]

---

[53] Komisar 1987, 42.   [54] Bacani 2010.   [55] Opfell 1993.   [56] Crisostomo 1987, 39.

Aquino had become a true believer in the anti-Marcos movement because her husband had died for it; she had the political skill-set with which he inculcated her during his time in prison. She was also an intensely religious person. In combination, this led her to view what had happened as God's plan and to view her entry into politics as a "heavy cross" that she had to bear.[57] Elected with the dramatic popular support of the "People Power Revolution," Aquino's lack of experience on the political stage led to initial struggles as she attempted to gain functional control over the government:

Although she held the same dictatorial powers that Marcos had retained from the martial law years, she seemed incapable of exercising them, either vengefully or benevolently. Aquino, totally inexperienced as a leader and a decision maker, floundered ... many of those closest to her, including her appointed advisers and members of her family, dominated the new president's time with what they unabashedly acknowledged as political gamesmanship.[58]

To be fair, the government institutions of the Philippines were such that almost any leader, male or female, would have faced these challenges. In particular, Aquino struggled for power with a strong Philippine military bureaucracy, whose loyalties she could never fully trust.[59] At the time of her election, rebels controlled one-fifth of the country, and Aquino was eager to bring domestic peace to end "the seventeen years of guerrilla war that had divided the country, killed tens of thousands of Filipinos and threatened the reconstruction she sought to begin."[60] She clashed with the military over her fulfillment of a campaign promise to release insurgent rebel leaders and was subject to several coup attempts, including one by her own defense minister and vice president. Her late start in politics meant she lacked a stable political base and expertise with governance, which caused difficulties for her throughout her term in office. Bacani argues that being a woman made her especially vulnerable to these attempts, but that her experiences made her especially unafraid. Given that she had survived her husband's assassination attempt, even the shooting of her son, Benigno III, did not drive her away from politics. She was determined to help the Philippines become a real democracy.[61]

Intense trauma suffered by a child can have particularly intense effects on the child's mother.[62] Would-be assassins shot Aquino's son five times in one of several coup attempts. In the shooting, three of her five closest bodyguards died of gunshot wounds. This event seems to have served as something of a turning point in her presidency. Early on, she gave the impression of serving a role rather than being an active participant in the political process. Later, Aquino asserted herself extensively, going so far as to dissolve parliament and to lead the way toward a new constitution:

[57] Komisar 1987, 60.   [58] Simons 1987, 305.   [59] Opfell 1993.   [60] Komisar 1987, 139.
[61] Bacani 2010.   [62] de Vries et al. 1999.

And Cory, for all her personal incorruptibility and sincere desire to rule well, was a woman in the traditionally macho business of politics and government. At least in the beginning, the men she worked with saw her as a figurehead president who could be influenced to further their own agenda. With Enrile, says Cory, "I felt that he was always thinking it should be me sitting there and not you." Laurel may have felt the same. Says Cory: "When he agreed to run as my vice-president, maybe some people told him, 'you will, in fact, be the president because Cory Aquino doesn't know anything about running a government. You will be calling the shots.' In fairness to him, I did not promise that he would be prime minister. But I did not know that there would be a People Power Revolution and that I would be given the opportunity to abolish Parliament and to call for a Constitutional Commission."[63]

Kim Campbell

Kim Campbell was Canada's first female defense minister, the first and only female Canadian prime minister, and among the shortest serving prime ministers in Canadian history. Growing up in a difficult situation (when Campbell was twelve, her mother abandoned the family to live in Europe with a boyfriend, while her father was distant), Campbell and her sister effectively raised themselves. Demonstrating the effect of early family stability on behavior, in her memoirs, Campbell spoke directly about the effect of the loss of her mother on her long-term outlook:

Losing my mother at the age of twelve and a half meant losing my female role model and losing the person who did most to encourage and validate me in life. But ... my heart was not irrevocably broken, just squeezed and wrung dry for a time. I was strong and resilient as a child – a result perhaps of the survivors' genes that came my way from both sides of my family. I would survive the loss of my mother, wounded in some ways but strengthened in others. The knowledge that I could survive this pain formed part of the emotional armament that would make it possible for me as an adult to face down the fear of other losses.[64]

Unlike Aquino, who did not really consider entering politics until the assassination of her husband, Campbell – identified by party leaders as a rising star before she was forty years old – jumped quickly from local to national-level politics. In 1985, when Campbell was thirty-eight, she accepted the job of executive director for British Columbia Premier Bill Bennett. The next year, she was one of nine women elected to the British Columbia legislature, where she came to the attention of Canadian Prime Minister Brian Mulroney. In 1990, at age forty-one, Campbell became Canada's minister of justice, the first woman in Canada to serve in this capacity.

Two years later, a famous photo appeared of her holding up her judicial robes and wearing a strapless gown, making her appear naked. The photo endeared her to the public, who came to think of her as a different kind of politician.

---

[63] Bacani 2010.   [64] Campbell 1996, 13.

Fife relates:

In Britain's tabloids, Campbell was described as a "bubbly blond" and a "national pin-up" ... Campbell loved the attention. "I think it's a hoot," she said, shrugging off the comparison with sex goddess Madonna ... "Seriously, the notion that the bare shoulders of a 43-year-old woman are the source of prurient comment or titillation, I mean, I suppose I should be complimented."[65]

This situation and her response to it demonstrates her supreme self-confidence by this time in her life. Like many individuals in their mid-forties, she was more or less set in her ways and beliefs. As with some other female leaders, Campbell spent her twenties and early thirties in the primary role of wife to a famous and much older man. Campbell found out in 1978 that she was incapable of having children, thus she never gave birth or even adopted. When Conservative political opponents later attempted to use these facts against her, she skillfully turned the criticisms back on them. She noted in her memoirs:

Joe [Clark] said that it was important for the person chosen as leader to be "stable." I wasn't the only woman to react instantly to that comment with a visceral anger. Here was the old code word for undermining women. Since there was no basis on which to attack my stability, the remark was just offensive ... This comment was matched by [his wife's] claim that my lack of children meant I didn't have a sufficient stake in the future. Aside from being a slap in the face to every woman who had been unable to bear a child, the comment was incredibly sexist and ahistorical, given our country's long tradition of being governed by childless men.[66]

In fact, Campbell built her reputation on her work ethic and facility with words. Her strong, confident personal style was jarring to her male colleagues but gained her the respect critical to her political advancement.[67] Twice divorced, without children, Campbell poured her energies into her work.[68] Once headed on the path of a political career, she advanced rapidly, becoming prime minister at the relatively young age of forty-six. Her quick rise to the top office in the Canadian government may have prevented her from developing the deep personal ties to fellow-travelers who might have helped to guard her against political attacks once in office.

Campbell served only a few months as prime minister of Canada. During this brief time, circumstances never tested her willingness to take risks in military affairs. Her role as defense minister, however, gave her the opportunity to put her academic understanding of the Cold War world to the test. Campbell's knowledge of international affairs began with her political science education as an undergraduate, her doctoral work in Soviet studies at the London School of Economics, and her several years teaching as an adjunct lecturer from 1974 to 1978. She had not expected to become the minister of defense, but she

---

[65] Fife 1993, 156.   [66] Campbell 1996, 295.   [67] Fife 1993.
[68] Covizzi 2008, 347–61; Keizer 2010.

was a quick study and apparently enjoyed the opportunity to see in person what she had learned on paper. Her time at the Ministry of Defense gave her some preparation for the same issues during her time as prime minister. In her memoirs, Campbell relates one such event:

Perhaps nothing more [could] convince the Canadian press that I could be a serious player in the international stage than the success of my participation at the [1993] G-7 summit and, in particular, my meeting with President Clinton. When I objected to Canada's not receiving prior notice of the cruise missile attack on Baghdad two weeks earlier, Clinton apologized. A vigorous defense of Canadian "cultural protectionism," which the president asked me to repeat over lunch with his senior cabinet officials, also made the news.[69]

Campbell engaged deeply with military affairs, and her Defense portfolio gave her practical experience with military bureaucracy. She is one of several female leaders for whom it is difficult to separate the effects of structural variables from personal ones when analyzing observed conflict outcomes.

Experiences with War

Unlike men, women have traditionally not had the opportunity to serve in the military (and even less opportunity to serve in combat within the military), although this is no longer the case in many countries (and many countries have made exceptions during times of large wars, such as the Women Air Force Service Pilots program in the United States in World War II). Women are more likely to experience war as civilians at home, seeing it through the worried eyes of a wife, mother, sister, or daughter. How might this affect women leaders, on average? One possibility is that it might make women more risk-averse, experiencing the secondary effects of war on the homefront, as witnesses to a community grieving over lost husbands, sons, brothers, and fathers. Another possibility is that, lacking direct experience with the downsides of combat, they could become more likely to use force when in office. In this section, we examine the wartime experiences of two women leaders.

Corazon Aquino

Corazon Aquino, despite being from a wealthy family, experienced some hardship as a young girl during the World War II Japanese occupation of the Philippines. She was eight years old when Japan invaded; she lost her home to bombing and several civilian relatives to the Japanese military.[70] But, as Bacani relates, suffering during the Japanese occupation caused her to, in her own words, decide that "I'd really put my heart and soul into [my studies]."[71] The sixth of eight children and sheltered by her highly protective family, she and her siblings traveled to the United States for secondary school and college.

---

[69] Campbell 1996, 329–30.   [70] Opfell 1993.   [71] Bacani 2010.

Aquino is an example of a woman leader whose home front experiences with war do not necessarily correlate with later aggressive behavior. Despite seeing her home country occupied, she maintained a positive outlook and a deep religious faith that tempered her willingness to fight once she came to power.

On the other hand, the lack of direct exposure to war could make women less risk-averse in a leadership position when facing military crises. Without seeing the most viscerally direct effects of combat and the associated trauma of the experience, women could be more likely to see war in abstract terms. Appeals to patriotism that remind them of their earlier experiences with war often succeed in motivating women to support the use of force. Unless women leaders have children of military age who face a potential mortal threat, these tendencies toward abstraction could result in tendencies toward aggression greater than those of leaders who have experienced war directly and at first hand.

Margaret Thatcher

Margaret Thatcher provides an example of a female leader who led her nation through a war, as described in Chapter 2. She came of age during World War II, although she did not serve in the military or the women's auxiliary; unusually, she remained in college.[72] She nonetheless observed the effect of the war on Britain, particularly the material difficulties of the postwar years. Thatcher's experiences as a home front civilian in wartime, several biographers argue, influenced her later attitudes toward war, particularly as they related to saving declining postwar British prestige. Uniquely among her biographers, John Campbell points out another way in which Thatcher's lack of military experience altered her perception of international affairs:

Unlike those who served during or after the war in France, Germany, the Mediterranean or the Far East, Mrs. Thatcher never set foot out of England before her honeymoon in 1952, when she was twenty-six. Seen from Grantham, the peoples of the Continent were either odious enemies to be detested, or useless allies who had to be saved from the consequences of their own feebleness by the British and Americans.[73]

The experience of war brings exposure not only to violence, but also to people from other cultures as soldiers travel to battle fronts and experience leave in new countries. World War II made travel at a young age impossible for Thatcher, and by the time she was able to leave England, she had already developed a firm set of beliefs from which she rarely wavered. Campbell concludes:

Her sex was really beside the point. What made Mrs. Thatcher a successful war leader – apart from the quality of forces under her command and a large slice of luck – was the clarity of her purpose. She had an unblinking single-mindedness about achieving her

---

[72] Campbell 2001.   [73] Ibid., 40.

objective and an extraordinarily simple faith that because her cause was right it would prevail. In war, as in economics, it was this moralistic certainty, not her gender, which set her apart from her male colleagues, enabling her to grasp risks they would have baulked at.[74]

In Thatcher's case, her lack of direct experience with war, which was only as a result of her sex, apparently made her significantly more risky than most leaders would have been under similar circumstances.

Are There Effects from Motherhood?

Most leaders in the LEAD dataset were parents, but the vast majority are men. Does the experience of parenthood influence a leader's decisions if she is a woman and a mother?

Conventional wisdom would say that parenting would make people more risk-averse, even as leaders. Women may wish to avoid plunging their nations into war if there is a risk that their children could be harmed, especially if they are of age for military service. Even if one's children could be protected from actual combat, it could also be possible that knowing other young people who are the same age as soldiers on the front line could inspire a sense of protectiveness that extends beyond a leader's immediate biological family. On the other hand, women leaders perceiving a threat may be more likely to initiate conflict if they believe it will prevent a more threatening war. So there may not be a gender effect.

Of the women we examine closely, only Kim Campbell of Canada was childless. The rest of the women leaders profiled here had at least two children. The domestic political consequences of having children can go both ways. In some cases, it becomes a liability in the eyes of the opposition, but it can also serve as a political asset.

Margaret Thatcher

Margaret Thatcher famously gave birth to twins, a son and a daughter, just a few weeks before sitting for and passing the bar examination. The birth of twins was a lucky accident that allowed Thatcher to more quickly reenter political life after their birth and during their early years.[75] Campbell suggests that having a family and children provided Thatcher with an advantage. Having passed her barrister exams "while nursing twins" made her seem all the more competent professionally, especially given that "she relished showing the men that she expected no concessions."[76] Throughout her career, Thatcher took advantage of her gender difference in such ways to intimidate political opponents who had little professional experience dealing with women, broadsiding those who had low expectations of her abilities and resolve.

---

[74] Ibid., 140.   [75] Garnett 2007.   [76] Campbell 2001, 107.

Benazir Bhutto

Similarly, Benazir Bhutto's political opponents in Pakistan unsuccessfully attempted to use her gender and status as a mother to undermine her political career. Bhutto had three children, and opponents tried to use her pregnancies strategically to gain advantage during times when she was perceived to be weak.[77] Bhutto faced an obstacle unique to women running in political systems where politicians can strategically time elections. As she campaigned for her party while pregnant during Zia's reign, for example, Zia timed the elections to coincide with the birth of her child. She had spread misinformation about her daughter's conception date, but nonetheless had to give birth clandestinely. Bennett describes the political maneuvering:

> Zia used her unmarried status against her, placing her "under surveillance" to try to catch her in a compromising situation with a man. She responded by agreeing to an arranged marriage. When she became pregnant, Zia tried to find out the child's due date, calling local elections for that day, which he thought would handicap her campaign. Actually, she had "lied about the due date," resulting in one reporter commenting that this was "the first election to be timed for gynecological consideration."[78]

Once, when the opposition planned a general strike action to help remove the government, Bhutto chose to have a caesarean delivery and return to work the next day. After Zia's death, when Bhutto led her party in elections to become prime minister, she gave birth to her son, Bilawal, during the campaign, just three months before she took office.[79]

How does being pregnant and having young children influence a leader's perception of risk? The experiences of both Thatcher and Bhutto indicate that women in these positions often try to minimize the effects of pregnancy and young children on their careers.[80] Instead of taking the early stages of child rearing off, both Bhutto and Thatcher sought to work through these difficult periods at nearly full strength. This indicates a tolerance for risk – the willingness to risk one's own personal to achieve career objectives while under emotional and physical stress. Male leaders with young children could face related, but somewhat different, dilemmas.

Golda Meir

Even when having children is not considered a political liability for a woman leader, raising a family can be a source of significant stress, as it is for most working mothers. As Steinberg describes Golda Meir, "[t]here are virtually no examples of Meir's 'taking it easy' on the job. Her commitment was absolute and she pushed herself to the limit."[81] Meir had two children, daughter Sarah and son Menahim, while living on a kibbutz in Palestine. Meir was a fervent true believer in the cause of Israel and was committed to having and raising her

---

[77] Halpert et al. 1993, 649–63. [78] Bennett 2010, 70. [79] Bhutto 2008.
[80] Desai and Waite 1991, 551–66. [81] Steinberg 2008, 183.

children there. Nonetheless, "[s]he was continually torn between her obliga-
tions and responsibilities to her close loved ones, on the one hand, and her
responsibility to the Zionist movement and later the state of Israel, on the
other." While she at times put her family's interest first, far more commonly
Meir placed the interests of Israel above the interests of her family or herself.[82]

In her memoirs, Meir wrote eloquently of the emotional pain she felt while
torn between her children and her strong commitment to the state of Israel.[83]
However, Meir's constant belief in the rightness of her cause led her to feel that
Sarah, Menahim, and her grandchildren ought to remain in Israel, even during
the wars in which she was a major decision maker, first as foreign minister, then
as Israel's prime minister. Meir described her state of mind regarding her
children immediately after the proclamation of Israel, on the eve of the Arab-
Israeli War:

Both Sarah and her Zechariah were wireless operators in Revivim, and I had been able to
keep in touch with them up till then. But I hadn't heard about or from either of them for
several days, and I was extremely worried. It was on youngsters like them, their spirit
and their courage, that the future of the Negev and, therefore, of Israel depended, and
I shuddered at the thought of their having to face the invading troops of the Egyptian
army. I was so lost in my thoughts about the children that I can remember being
momentarily surprised when the phone rang in my room and I was told that a car was
waiting to take me to the museum.[84]

In all her writings and interviews, Meir frequently refers to her own children
and grandchildren as part of the larger community of Israel. Although Meir
describes her worry for their safety, unlike the general tendency among mothers
found by some researchers,[85] there is no indication that this concern reduced
her propensity for risk when considering interstate aggression. Meir, rather,
indicates that the opposite may have been true. Her ideological commitment to
Israel was a commitment to an idea and to a state she wanted for her generation
as well as for her own offspring. Her protectionist feelings toward her children
became fuel for interstate aggression untempered by other experiences, such as
combat. This lack of perspective eventually contributed to her removal from
power after the Yom Kippur War.

Given the small number of women leaders, we lack the ability to state
conclusively the effects of having children on behavior in office. In general,
we did not find any significant results for leaders with children, male or female.
While there are certainly biological and psychological implications to becoming
a mother, the case studies do not suggest there is any systematic effect on the
propensity of women leaders to initiate militarized disputes.

The far greater issue is the nature of the selection effect. The case studies
reveal that the women who secure chief executive positions generally behave

---

[82] Ibid., 159.   [83] Meir 1973, 130.   [84] Ibid., 225.
[85] Conover and Sapiro 1993, 1079–99.

similar to men. They are independent minded, assertive, and more inclined to place the interests of their states ahead of their families than people in the general population. As Bhutto and Thatcher show, however, when the political opposition counts on a woman in office to behave in a way that is consistent with most generally-held conceptions of women and mothers, female leaders can use these biased expectations to their strategic advantage.

The Militarized Behavior of Female Leaders

The results from the LEAD dataset paint a mixed picture when it comes to the role of women leaders and militarized behavior. How does this stack up with the evidence we have on women leaders? Although neither Kim Campbell nor Corazon Aquino was involved in interstate military disputes during their tenures, both faced internal military crises. Campbell took control of the Defense portfolio of Canada during one of its most trying episodes. In 1993, Canadian military forces in Somalia were involved in scandals including shooting unarmed civilians and participating in neo-Nazi activities.[86] However, Campbell never faced serious internal military strife.

Aquino, for her part, wanted to make peace with Communist rebels on Mindanao, a major island in the Philippines, when she was elected. Her initial sympathies and pardons of key insurgent leaders enraged the military, some of whom had been instrumental in helping her come to power.[87] Those military leaders had hoped that she could be manipulated and believed she was soft on communism – or at least made that argument to try and turn people against her. Members of the Filipino military were involved in numerous coup attempts against Aquino.[88] At the same time, she was unable to make peace with the domestic insurgents. As a result, Aquino never had the opportunity to demonstrate her conflict propensity in the situations that are the focus of the LEAD dataset. While she was in office, Aquino faced one low-level militarized challenge from Malaysia, over the contested Spratly Islands; however, it did not escalate.[89]

Our description of Corazon Aquino suggests that while she may have been highly risk-acceptant compared with other leaders without the same life experiences, domestic problems consumed her administration, leaving her with little time or energy for exercising force abroad. For the Philippines, an enormous island archipelago, domestic threats are far more common than international ones. Furthermore, Aquino was personally committed to ideals of peace and did not express any desire to use martial power against her neighbors. She, therefore, represents a leader for whom structural and unit-level variables overwhelm internal personal characteristics in determining observed outcomes.

---

[86] Fife 1993.   [87] Aquino 1995.   [88] Opfell 1993; Thompson 2002.
[89] Correlates of War Militarized Dispute #274.

For Thatcher, the stakes were high in 1982. When the Falklands crisis occurred, her status as prime minister, in the eyes of both the public and her party, was at a nadir. This reinforced her commitment to fight and win the war.[90] Thatcher also felt strongly that the standing of Britain was at stake. As most of her Conservative Party policies and deeply held conservative beliefs were related to rescuing the prestige of a declining England, the provocation of Argentina triggered genuine outrage on her part.[91] Thatcher personally gave the order to sink the Argentine ship *Belgrano*, killing more than 300 sailors. In contrast to the image of women leaders as more prone toward pacifism, Thatcher was comfortable with further provocation:

In the latter stages she was very hyped up and sometimes, in the words of one member of the War Cabinet, "dangerously gung-ho": she had to be restrained from ordering an attack on the Argentine aircraft *Veinticinco de Mayo* which at that stage would have been seen as a gratuitous provocation of world opinion, far worse than the *Belgrano*.[92]

In some ways, Thatcher's military behavior supports the theory that women leaders are selected into office in part because their behavior is consistent with what society would expect of men, which means we should not observe significant differences between male and female leaders.

Stepping back to look at the broader picture, Table 5.1 shows the list of women leaders who initiated militarized disputes, authorizing the use or threatening the use of military force against another state.

Of the women leaders in the LEAD dataset, 36 percent initiated at least one militarized interstate dispute. For males, this figure is 30 percent. This does not mean that women are generally more aggressive, however. Men were responsible for 694 acts of aggression, including eighty-six wars, while women were responsible for just thirteen acts of aggression and only one war (Indira Gandhi). The small number of cases is a problem; nevertheless, two explanations account for the small difference between men and women leaders. The first is that women leaders expect their opponents to view them as risk-averse, and their opponents do in fact expect women to be risk-averse. To counter that perception, or due to selection effects, the women who make it to the top office of the land behave somewhat aggressively. Alternatively, based on gender stereotypes, women's opponents expect them to back down or to behave in what political scientists refer to as a "dovish" fashion. Because their opponents expect them to back down, not wanting to be taken advantage of, in this story, women (regardless of their dovishness level) must actually fight more often than potentially more hawkish men must.

If we focus on our Risk Index, taking into account the length of time a leader may be in office,[93] there is no difference at all between the average Risk Index score for men and women. The women who rise to the top have the same risk propensity as men. This suggests that it may be the stereotypical expectations

---

[90] Berlinski 2011.   [91] Campbell 2004.   [92] Campbell 2001, 201.
[93] There is a small correlation between how risk-acceptant leaders are and how long they survive in office.

TABLE 5.1. *Women Military Dispute Initiators*

Name	Country	Number	Risk Score
Indira Gandhi	India	10	0.40
Tansu Çiller	Turkey	5	0.39
Golda Meir	Israel	3	0.47
Violeta Chamorro	Nicaragua	3	0.32
Tz'u Hsi	China	3	0.18
Margaret Thatcher	Britain	2	0.24
Kim Campbell	Canada	1	0.39
Benazir Bhutto	India	1	0.25
Gro Harlem Brundtland	Norway	1	0.29
Isabel Perón	Argentina	1	0.14
Khaleda Zia	Bangladesh	1	0.04
Helen Clark	New Zealand	1	0.00

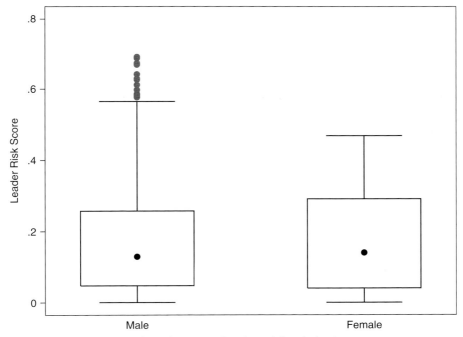

FIGURE 5.3. Comparing the risk scores of male and female leaders.

that women in general should be more dovish, or selection effects, that lead women to be slightly more aggressive than men once in office. Figure 5.3 shows the average Risk Index scores of men and women leaders. For each gender, this shows the average risk score and then the confidence interval, or the range that

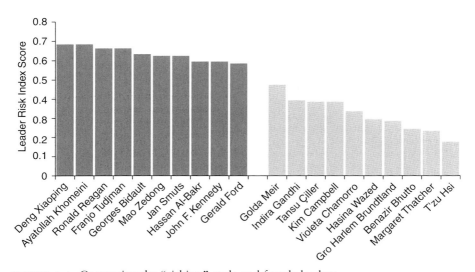

FIGURE 5.4. Comparing the "riskiest" male and female leaders.

the risk score generally falls between. Note the overwhelming extent of overlap between the figures, suggesting, on a broad scale, insignificant differences.

The small number of women leaders makes it extremely difficult to generalize from this data in any direction. However, if you look more closely at Figure 5.3, for male leaders the series of dots that are outside the bounds of the upper end of the confidence interval represent extremely risky male leaders – the riskiest leaders in the LEAD dataset, such as Tudjman, Deng Xiaoping, and Ayatollah Khomeini. In contrast, there are no outlying women leaders with extremely high risk scores. The highest woman in the Risk Index, Golda Meir, is in the top overall, but trails the most conflict-prone men by a good deal. This is extremely interesting, so we turn to Figure 5.4, which shows the Risk Index scores of the ten riskiest men and key women in the LEAD dataset.

One explanation for this is that while, on average, women leaders behave similarly to men, there has not yet been an excessively risk-tolerant female leader. Even more bluntly, there are so far no hyper-aggressive women leaders when it comes to the probability of entering a military conflict. It is important to keep in mind, however, because of the small overall number of women leaders, that this is a very preliminary take on the issue of gender and conflict propensity. It is possible over the next few decades, as more women leaders take office, even this difference may disappear. Alternatively, clearer differences may emerge. The existing data suggest that the former is more likely than the latter, but many in psychology and political science[94] who study gender differences and behavior might disagree.

[94] Hudson et al. 2012.

CONCLUSION

Women face challenges and have opportunities that are unique for leaders in our dataset. Although there are too few to make defensible statistical observations about their systematic characteristics, we nonetheless can draw on rich biographical data to learn about their experiences. Contrary to conventional wisdom (e.g., Fukuyama 1998), women leaders do not necessarily come to power by emulating or trying to outdo their male counterparts, though that potentially happens as well. Nor are they, by definition, weak, conciliatory, and cooperative when facing international crises. As demonstrated by Thatcher and Meir, women can be aggressive leaders, willing to take risks that men with more exposure to war would avoid. As more women leaders join the world stage, the potential for a more sophisticated understanding of the relationship between their background experiences, institutional selection effects, and conflict behavior is fertile ground for future quantitative analysis.

6

"L'état, c'est moi" – or Is It?

"I am the state."
– Louis XIV (1638–1715)

We have two things left to accomplish before closing this book. First, there is a serious question that we have assiduously avoided to sustain our focus on leaders and their personal attitudes and beliefs about risk and disinhibited behavior. For consistency's sake, we have focused solely on the decision to threaten or use military force against other nations, but what happens when a war occurs? Do the leaders who engage in what most would judge to be high-risk behavior take these risks prudentially, or are they foolhardy? To answer these questions, we turn to the relationship between leaders' risk scores and the outcomes, costs, and durations of the wars in which they participate. Following that, we lay out the utility of this research agenda for the public policy world, as well as for future academic investigation.

Risk is a funny thing. The people who engage in what others view as high-risk behavior usually do not see their behavior as particularly dangerous for themselves. Rather, they tend to see their choices as something that might be foolhardy for others, but they also believe that either through training or superior talent, they have a better way of managing or ameliorating danger than everyone else. So, for example, most skydivers do not see the sport nearly as risky as does the rest of the earth-bound population. To be sure, there are risks involved in jumping out of a plane, but trained skydivers are willing to place their trust in their equipment and training. The skydivers' critics see the choice as reckless or foolhardy. Driving at high speed is another example. While it is a fact that at higher speeds, accidents are associated with greater vehicular damage and occupant harm, it does not follow that driving quickly places everyone at equal risk. Skilled drivers can drive safely at seventy miles per hour or more. Unskilled and inattentive drivers put themselves and others at great risk at far slower speeds. Tragically, the substantial majority of drivers in America all believe they are better than average drivers, something that cannot possibly be true – and therein may lie the rub for politics. Are some risk acceptant leaders substantially better at judging the risks of military action, or are they simply more cost tolerant than their counterparts?

Some people view the decision to go to war as so inherently dangerous that it would be almost impossible to conceive of initiating the use of force under any circumstances. Costa Rica, taking this position, dismantled its armed forces decades ago and remains an independent state in an otherwise potentially dangerous system and region. Obviously, however, there are others who feel differently. The LEAD Risk Index, in contrast, is not built on leader self-perception of risk behavior, but rather is built objectively, assuming that most of us would judge the decision to go to war as profoundly risky.

THE RETURN OF THE LEADER

In this book, we focus on how the variation in the risk profiles of individual leaders can uniquely explain many observed conflict outcomes. Where systemic and institutional theories fail, we find rich explanations in the detail of biographies and primary source documents. Individual leaders do matter; heads of state are not simply interchangeable or continuously overwhelmed by exogenous factors. These executives can change the course of history in powerful ways, overcoming constraints of regime type, bureaucratic obstacles, and the will of the individuals who select them to office.

Interpersonal psychology covers a number of different constructs that are important to the study of international relations. International relations theory that does not focus on leaders has tended to adopt the logic of these constructs, implicitly applying them to state behavior.[1] Including leaders as valid subjects for analysis allows us to apply the empirical findings of psychology directly, without the hand-waving assumptions needed to believe that corporations act with the same drives as individuals. Trust, for example, is one well-studied psychological construct that is dependent on two individuals making assessments of each other, as Margaret Thatcher famously described of Mikhail Gorbachev when she called him "a man we can do business with."[2]

The evidence presented in this book demonstrates that risky leaders do not act in a vacuum; they are aware of and respond to their contemporaries. During the 1961 Vienna Summit, which was so disastrous for Kennedy and so encouraging to Khrushchev, their interpersonal interactions served as a learning experience, a way for each leader to assess the other, in person. This interaction provided a wealth of information that Khrushchev used, among other things, to begin the process of erecting the Berlin Wall.

---

[1] Tetlock and Goldgeier 2007.   [2] Campbell 2001.

Similarly, as explained by Diggins, Ronald Reagan's personal assessment of Mikhail Gorbachev provided an important, unobservable background to U.S.-Soviet relations during the Cold War:

The *Challenger* disaster shook Reagan in much the same way that the nuclear explosion at Chernobyl shattered Gorbachev's confidence in continuing the arms race. When Reagan heard Gorbachev say, "God help us," he knew there were grounds to begin negotiation, to follow the biblical injunction and turn swords into ploughshares.[3]

These personal interactions are largely absent from much of what constitutes modern international relations research, yet they are important for filling in our understanding of why conflicts do or do not occur. These anecdotes are in line with empirical psychological research. For example, assuming that personal beliefs, rather than rational decisions, are the main factors driving trust (or the lack thereof) between individuals, some research posits that trust develops when individuals come to believe, either with the help of a mediator or some other process, that the "core beliefs" of others line up with their own.[4] To be fair, the LEAD dataset does not capture all relevant aspects of a leader's background, such as religious beliefs or the psychological effects of specific experiences. However, for the first time, it opens the door to incorporating these characteristics in a systematic way.

AFTER LEADERS GO TO WAR

Looking at the population of all leaders and, in particular, those in power at the end of wars, there appears to be a strong correlation between a leader's risk score and how his or her country performs in war. Figure 6.1 shows the relationship between war outcomes (0 = lose, 1 = draw, 2 = win) on the vertical axis and leader risk in quartiles, with low-risk leaders to the left and high-risk leaders to the right. The figure suggests that very low-risk leaders are far more likely to lose the fights they become ensnared in. However, this might be solely a result of focusing on the wrong population.

If we focus only on the leaders who fight in wars, there is no such relationship. Moreover, for these leaders, there is little relationship between their risk scores and how well the war turns out for their countries. For the population of leaders who are sufficiently risk acceptant to fight, rather than giving up without a struggle, willingness to countenance greater risk seems to convey little if any advantage in winning a war.

Why might this be? Bargaining theory suggests that leaders factor information about each other and each side's chances of victory into their calculations about the relative value of fighting. Among the leaders who choose to fight, whether as the initiator or the target of an eventual attack, both sides are

---

[3] Diggins 2007, 35.   [4] Zafonte and Sabatier 1998.

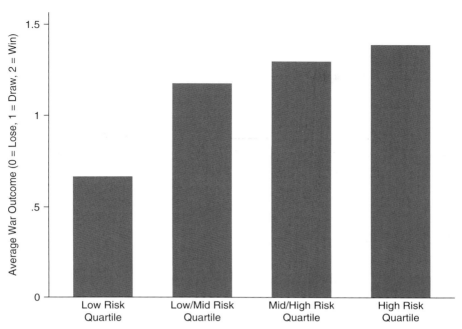

FIGURE 6.1. War outcomes (0 = lose, 1 = draw, 2 = win) by leader risk in quartiles.

likely to be relatively high risk, as low-risk leaders often simply back down when faced with the prospect of war. If we look at the risk scores for initiators versus targets (when both sides fight rather than one side preventively backing down to avoid the military crisis in the first place), we see a pattern that supports bargaining theory. Unlike the pattern in Figure 6.1, among those who go to war anyway, greater risk acceptance seems to bring little reward for noninitiators.

There is a substantial difference in the types of leaders who are willing to fight and those who are not. There is also a systematic difference within the population of fighters but a difference that is much smaller, as is the case with war outcomes. If we focus only on those leaders who brought their states into wars either as initiators or targets, consistent with bargaining theory, the difference between the targets and initiators narrows greatly, although it still remains.

Looking at the relationship between leader risk scores and how wars turn out reveals several things. First, leaders appear to consider the risks of war when making their decision to use force or not. Wars do not simply "happen." They appear to result from careful consideration. These considerations filter through each leader's personal biases about the nature of what constitutes prudential risk. Those in the population of fighters, those who either start wars or are targeted by those who are willing to fight, are more risk-acceptant than

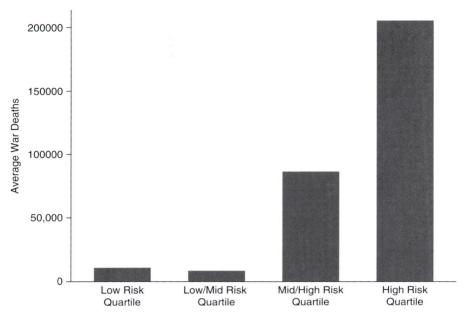

FIGURE 6.2. The human costs of war (fatalities) by leader risk in quartiles.

the typical leader in the system. In the group of fighters, those who start fights are somewhat more risk prone than those who respond. As anticipated by rational choice bargaining theory, in the population of fighters, the differences are smaller than those in the general population, more of kind than of type.

The cost of war is also an area in which differences in leader risk can help us understand why some wars are so devastating, while others end quickly and with relatively less bloodshed. While leader risk has little effect on how long wars seem to last, on average, some leaders are willing to accept far greater costs associated with fighting than are others.

If we focus only on those leaders who are willing to fight, the place where we might reasonably expect there to be the smallest differences across our leaders, we still see a powerful relationship between leader risk score and casualties in war. Figure 6.2 shows how, as leaders' risk scores rise, so too does the associated deadliness of the wars they fight. Bear in mind, this is the population of fighters. In the population of all leaders, the finding is even starker. What distinguishes the high-risk leaders is not their better judgment, although those who do stay in power to the end of wars do somewhat better than we would expect by chance. Nor do they fight wars that are qualitatively longer than those fought by lower-risk leaders. What separates the high-risk leaders is their willingness to bear huge human costs in pursuit of their aims. Among our highest-risk leaders who go to war, we see numerous leaders whose behavior borders on sociopathic. Stalin, Hitler, Hussein, López, and Khomeini all were high-risk leaders who were willing to accept huge casualties in pursuit of their aims. In the cases of Hitler, Hussein, and López, they lost the wars they initiated. In Hussein's case, one of his wars, that against the United States, was over quickly, but his war with Iran took years. Both wars were costly in terms of Iraqi lives lost.

PUBLIC POLICY IMPLICATIONS

The questions asked in this book are not simply academic items of curiosity but topics with great importance in the real world. U.S. intelligence agencies, such as the Central Intelligence Agency, allegedly keep significant profile information on every leader or potential leader around the world. The logic is twofold. First, gathering profile data on world leaders helps the intelligence community be better prepared when the president is going to meet with someone and needs information on his or her background and likely behaviors. Second, profile data on world leaders comprise a valuable source of information for understanding the baseline behaviors to expect from each leader and the potential replacements for that leader.

The LEAD dataset takes one of the first major steps to building that sort of analytical capacity from an academic perspective. It has the potential, especially in combination with more traditional political analysis, to provide useful information to those in the policy community interested in establishing baselines for behavior of leaders, based on the behavior of prior leaders with similar attributes. The LEAD dataset could also be used to plug in particular attributes and model how, for example, the replacement of Maliki in Iraq with a leader who has a different set of background experiences could influence Iraqi policy making.

This is the real-world analogue to the fact that, when models combine structural factors, domestic political factors, and individual-level factors such as leader attributes, they become most likely to actually capture behaviors in the world around us.

FUTURE AVENUES FOR RESEARCH

What does this mean for future research on leader characteristics and how they may shape international politics? One potentially promising avenue involves the nature of personal interaction and its effect on national-level behavior. First, when leaders have had the opportunity to interact in person, some of the evidence presented in prior chapters suggests that they are more likely to make accurate assessments about each other, with more interaction leading to better assessments. Specifically, they are more likely to accurately assess leader-level beliefs about the resolve of their opponents. Unfortunately, the LEAD dataset does not capture prior interpersonal interactions. We do not know, systematically, whether leaders had the opportunity to meet at summits, regional events, or other nonconflict situations. We can know, however, whether individual leaders met as opponents when their nations were involved in war.

Adding leader information to existing datasets enriches our understanding of variables relating to prior military conflict. For example, while it may be true that countries that experienced conflict in the past are more likely to experience conflict in the future, the LEAD dataset allows us to assess the effects of leader reputation and past leader behavior, not just past national behavior.[5] This could improve our understanding of how all states behave. In democracies, due to the demands of campaigns and competing parties, leaders may support policies significantly different from those of their predecessors. George W. Bush and Barack Obama were both U.S. presidents, but their approach to foreign policy was quite different, and this is observed in the military conflicts (MIDs, using the shorthand again as defined in Chapter 2) ascribed to each leader. In autocracies, because transitions from leader to leader often involve coups and other irregular forms of entry, differences in behavior from leader to leader can be quite large as well. This illustrates the practical power of the leader-level analyses presented here.

Another way in which the leader level of analysis provides new insights into observed conflict outcomes comes from considering what happens when different types of leaders collide. Do risky leaders act as predators, taking advantage of their timid opponents? Anecdotally, cases of leaders such as Adolf Hitler show that leaders do act differently when confronted by leaders they perceive as of different types. Hitler took advantage of multiple domestic and international opportunities to consolidate power and trigger World War II. He also used Germany's growing conflicts with the rest of Europe in the 1930s as an opportunity to "test" his opponents and learn about them. In this way, Adolf Hitler was able to aggressively learn about the personal characteristics of his adversaries.

Theories that privilege structural, systemic, and institutional factors cannot account for this personal level of state interaction. These theories imply that Hitler acted no differently from any of the other leaders who could have taken his place. If any leader would have done as Hitler did, as most traditional international relations theories would conclude, there is nothing special about Adolf Hitler as an individual and nothing that we need to know about him as a person in order to understand the onset and escalation of World War II. To experts and laymen alike, this simply makes no sense.

Another way in which risky leaders may act as predators is the way in which they form alliances. Hitler and Mussolini, both of whom score high on the Risk Index, are illustrative examples. So is Franjo Tudjman, whom we profiled earlier. Tudjman, one of the riskiest leaders identified by the LEAD data, collaborated with Slobodan Milosevic to start the Balkan War and carve up Bosnia for mutually beneficial territorial gains.

---

[5] This could build on the recent work of Weisiger and Yarhi-Milo 2015.

So, which theory better explains the observed outbreak of interstate wars: the characteristics of leadership at the individual level or the structural constraints identified by authors such as Nordhaus et al.?[6] In fact, they are complementary and intertwined. More than most individuals, world leaders are both the products of their environment and the shapers of future environments. Sometimes, but not always, the inclusion of analysis at the leader level will reveal important information overlooked by other theories.

What this book demonstrates, however, is that we should include leader characteristics on the same terms as the other variables we use to better understand the phenomena of interstate war. With this data, we can now compare theories in a way that was not possible before. As we argue throughout this book, the systematic inclusion of individual leader-level variables tells an important story that traditional international relations theory overlooks. There are many ways to test the implications of this argument; this book is only a first step.

The systematic inclusion of leaders in empirical analyses opens many more avenues for further research beyond simply war. In this book, we have not studied the role of leaders with respect to civil wars. We do not know, for example, the effect of leader background characteristics on the propensity for domestically oppressive behavior. Such actions are important but are not captured in our analysis of interstate martial aggression. Because civil wars also have significant effects on the population of future leaders – for example, leaders who survive a civil war and go on to become state leaders – this is a rich area for future study.

We also do not know about the effect of leader background characteristics on interactions with legislatures. We know that leaders in democratic systems must negotiate with powerful political opponents who may have different ideas about interstate war. This is also related to the discussion on selection effects, because many leaders in democratic regimes come from prior political backgrounds.

There is a potentially very useful line of research on gender and family issues that can be opened up by expanding beyond simply the head of state. Rather than just evaluating leaders, this book suggests that the background experiences of other political actors may also play an important role in shaping leaders' behavior. Some research suggests, for example, that having daughters makes legislators more likely to support "women-friendly" policies, while judges with daughters are more likely to issue favorable rulings on women's issues.[7] Expanding on this book to further the investigation of how the background experiences of other political actors may shape the later behaviors of leaders is also very promising.

---

[6] Nordhaus et al. 2012.　　[7] Washington 2008.

CONCLUSION

Focusing on leaders as actors with agency, rather than just black boxes that international structure and domestic politics incentivize, provides a lens into international politics that existing, competing approaches cannot accommodate. Institutionalists, focusing on either domestic or international institutions, have little to say about the course of war, the democratic peace literature notwithstanding. Classical realism, while recognizing the importance of leadership, discounts any systematic relationship between institutions, domestic or otherwise, and the onset or course of war. Realists also tend to view quality leadership as an idiosyncratic aspect of humans rather than something we can measure and test systematically. Structural, or neo-realist, models tell us little if anything about the course of any single war or conflict. By focusing on leaders and accounting for system structure and institutional constraints, we begin to see for the first time a more complete picture of international relations.

Our focus on leaders allows us to draw inferences about the danger levels of entire regions and the system. As we saw in the interaction of Kennedy and Khrushchev in the Cuban Missile Crisis, understanding the leaders involved allows us to gain insights into pairs of states, or dyads. It also allows us to understand better, and to anticipate, which states are at high risk for conflict and, as we have just learned, which conflicts are likely to be especially costly.

In fact, this is what the data show us, consistently. We find that leaders in most types of political regimes who have seen combat seem to be more cautious about military engagements than those who have served in the military but have not seen combat. There is some learning mechanism in place that needs to be acknowledged as part of larger theoretical debates. We are not suggesting that individuals trump their circumstances. We give due weight to the importance of systemic and institutional factors that constrain leaders or enable certain kinds of behavior. Nonetheless, the results presented in the previous chapters show that completely ignoring individual agency is similarly counterproductive.

Of course, international relations is about the relations between states. But it is also about the relations between individuals. We are not arguing that understanding leaders will provide a comprehensive theory that explains conflict. In Chapter 3, we included leaders such as Woodrow Wilson, for whom systemic and institutional-level explanations tell us much more about war than his personal characteristics. However, it is short-sighted to claim that the theory of international conflict is fully developed when it treats state leaders as automatons. We know that this is simply not true and that overlooking these leaders, their unique characteristics, and individual agency ignores important sources of explanatory power.

While we may never know how the experience of being a combat veteran, for example, precisely affects the psychology of one individual versus another, this experience cannot be undone. It is a fixed part of the history of every individual leader to whom it applies. These are experiences that leaders themselves draw on to make decisions and that we, as scholars, can also draw on to make observations. Incorporating the background experiences of leaders into our thinking about the behavior of countries thus not only is a means to generate good stories, but also results in a systematic improvement in our ability to understand how countries go to war.

08032017

Bibliography

Abdullah, Halimah, and Joe Van Kanel. 2012. "Economy tops voter concerns in exit polls." *CNNPolitics*, November 6. Retrieved from www.cnn.com/2012/11/06/politics/exit-polls/index.html.

Abdelal, Rawi, Yoshiko M. Herrera, Alastair Iain Johnston, and Rose McDermott. 2006. "Identity as a variable." *Perspectives on Politics* 4 (4):695–711.

Achen, Christopher H. 1986. *The statistical analysis of quasi-experiments*. Berkeley: University of California Press.

Altman, Lawrence K. 2004. "The doctor's world: A recollection of early questions about Reagan's health." *The New York Times*. June 15.

Ameringer, Charles D. 1978. *Don Pepe: A political biography of José Figueres of Costa Rica*. Albuquerque, NM: University of New Mexico Press.

Anda, Robert F., Vincent J. Felitti, J. Douglas Bremner, John D. Walker, Charles Whitfield, Bruce D. Perry, Shanta R. Dube, and Wayne H. Giles. 2006. "The enduring effects of abuse and related adverse experiences in childhood: A convergence of evidence from neurobiology and epidemiology." *European Archives of Psychiatry and Clinical Neuroscience* 256: 174–86.

Angell, Norman. 1914. *The great illusion: A study of the relation of military power to national advantage*. London: W. Heinemann.

Aquino, Corazon C. 1995. *In the name of democracy and prayer: Selected speeches of Corazon C. Aquino*. Pasig City, Philippines: Anvil Publishing.

Associated Press. 2008. "McCain raps Obama for lack of military service." *NBCNews.com*. May 23. Retrieved from www.nbcnews.com/id/24786523/ns/politics-decision_08/t/mccain-raps-obama-lack-military-service.

Bacani, Cesar R. Jr. 2010. "Essential Cory Aqunio." Retrieved from www.coryaquino.ph/index.php/essential/.

Balcells, Laia. 2010. "Rivalry and revenge: Violence against civilians in conventional civil wars." *International Studies Quarterly* 54 (2):291–313.

Bandura, Albert. 1982. "The psychology of chance encounters and life paths." *American Psychologist* 37 (7):747–55.

Bar-Joseph, Uri, and Rose McDermott. 2008. "Personal functioning under stress." *Journal of Conflict Resolution* 52 (1):144–70.

Barber, James D. 1972. *The presidential character: Predicting performance in the White House*. Englewood Cliffs, NJ: Prentice-Hall.

1992. *The presidential character*. Englewood Cliffs, NJ: Prentice-Hall.

Baron-Cohen, Simon. 2004. *Prenatal testosterone in mind: Amniotic fluid studies*: Cambridge, MA: MIT Press.

BBC News. 1999. "Franjo Tudjman: Father of Croatia." Retrieved from http://news.bbc.co.uk/2/hi/europe/294990.stm.

Bennett, Christopher. 1997. *Yugoslavia's bloody collapse: Causes, course and consequences*. New York: NYU Press.

Bennett, Clinton. 2010. *Muslim women of power: Gender, politics and culture in Islam*. London: Bloomsbury Publishing.

Bennett, D. Scott, and Allan C. Stam. 2000. "EUGene: A conceptual manual." *International Interactions* 26 (2):179–204.

2005. *The behavioral origins of war*. Princeton, NJ: Princeton University Press.

Berlinski, Claire. 2011. *There is no alternative: Why Margaret Thatcher matters*. 2nd ed. New York: Basic Books.

Besley, Timothy, and Marta Reynal-Querol. 2011. "Do democracies select more educated leaders?" *American Political Science Review* 105 (3):552–66.

Besley, Timothy, Jose G. Montalvo, and Marta Reynal-Querol. 2011. "Do educated leaders matter for growth?" *Economic Journal* 121 (554):205–27.

Bettencourt, B., and N. Miller. 1996. "Gender differences in aggression as a function of provocation: A meta-analysis." *Psychological Bulletin* 119 (3):422–47.

Betts, Richard K. 1977. *Soldiers, statesmen, and Cold War crises*. Cambridge, MA: Harvard University Press.

Bhutto, Benazir. 2008. *Daughter of destiny: An autobiography*: London: Harper Perennial.

Binder, David. 1999. "Tudjman is dead; Croat led country out of Yugoslavia." *The New York Times*. December 11:A1.

Boettcher, William A. 2005. *Presidential risk behavior in foreign policy: Prudence or peril?* New York: Palgrave Macmillan.

Boomsma, Dorret, Andreas Busjahn, and Leena Peltonen. 2002. "Classical twin studies and beyond." *Nature Reviews Genetics* 3 (11):872–82.

Bradley, Robert H., and Rorbert F. Corwyn. 2002. "Socioeconomic status and child development." *Annual Review of Psychology* 53:371–400.

Brands, Henry William. 2003. *Woodrow Wilson*. New York: Henry Holt and Company.

Bray, Arturo. 1957. *Hombres y épocas del Paraguay*. Buenos Aires, Argentina: Ediciones Nizza.

Brecher, Michael. 1996. "Crisis escalation: Model and findings." *International Political Science Review* 17 (2):215–30.

Brinkley, Douglas. 2005. *The boys of Point du Hoc: Ronald Reagan, D-Day, and the U.S. Army 2nd Ranger Battalion*. New York: William Morrow.

Bruni, Frank. 2000. "Bush claims victory, urging Gore to bow out." *New York Times*. November 27:A1.

Brunk, Gregory G., Donald Secrest, and Howard Tamashiro. 1990. "Military views of morality and war: An empirical study of the attitudes of retired American officers." *International Studies Quarterly* 34 (1):83–109.

Bueno de Mesquita, Bruce. 1981. *The war trap*. New Haven, CT: Yale University Press.

Bueno de Mesquita, Bruce, Alistair Smith, Randolph M. Siverson, and James D. Morrow. 2003. *The logic of political survival*. Cambridge, MA: MIT Press.

Burlingame, Michael. 1987. *The inner world of Abraham Lincoln*. Urbana-Champaign: University of Illinois Press.

Byman, Daniel, and Kenneth M. Pollack. 2001. "Let Us Now Praise Great Men: Bringing the Statesman Back In." *International Security* 25 (4): 107–146.

Calhoun, Todd R. 1998. "Evaluating security assistance programs: Performance evaluation and the Expanded International Military Education and Training (E-IMET) Program." Thesis, Naval Postgraduate School. Retrieved from http://calhoun.nps.edu/bitstream/handle/10945/8326/evaluatingsecurioocalh.pdf?sequence=1.

Campbell, John. 2001. *Margaret Thatcher*, vol. 1: *The grocer's daughter*. London: Pimlico. 2004. *Margaret Thatcher*, vol. 2: *Iron lady*. New ed. London: Pimlico.

Campbell, Kim. 1996. *Time and change: The political memoirs of Canada's first prime minister*. Toronto: Doubleday Canada.

Cannon, Lou. 1982. *Reagan*. New York: G. P. Putnam's Sons.

Caprioli, Mary, and Mark A. Boyer. 2001. "Gender, violence, and international crisis." *Journal of Conflict Resolution* 45 (4):503–18.

Carlyle, Thomas. 1935. *On heroes, hero-worship, and the heroic in history*. London: Oxford University Press.

Carr, Edward H. 1946. *The twenty years' crisis, 1919–1939*. 2nd ed. London: Macmillan.

Caspi, Avshalmon, and Brent W. Roberts. 2005. "Personality development: Stability and change." *Annual Review of Psychology* 56:454–84.

Chand, Attar. 1991. *Prime Minister P.V. Narasimha Rao: The scholar and the statesman*. New Delhi: Gian Publishing House.

Chang, Lei, Hui Jing Lu, Hongli Li and Tong Li. 2011. "The face that launched a thousand ships: The mating-warring association in men." *Personality and Social Psychology Bulletin* 37 (7):976–84.

Cheibub, Jose A., Jennifer Gandhi, and James R. Vreeland. 2010. "Democracy and dictatorship revisted." *Public Choice* 143 (1–2):67–101.

Chiozza, Giacomo, and Ajin Choi. 2003. "Guess who did what: Political leaders and the management of territorial disputes, 1950–1990." *Journal of Conflict Resolution* 47 (3):251–78.

Chiozza, Giacomo, and Hein E. Goemans. 2003. "Peace through insecurity – Tenure and international conflict." *Journal of Conflict Resolution* 47 (4):443–67.
2004. "International conflict and the tenure of leaders: Is war still ex post inefficient?" *American Journal of Political Science* 48 (3):604–19.
2011. *Leaders and international conflict*. New York: Cambridge University Press.

Churchill, Winston. 1948. *The Second World War*, vol. 1: *The gathering storm*. Boston: Houghton Mifflin.

Cicero, Scott D., Kate Nooner, and Raul Silva. 2011. "Vulnerability and resilience in childhood trauma and PTSD." In *Post-traumatic syndromes in childhood and adolescence: A handbook of research and practice*, ed. V. Ardino. New York: Wiley-Blackwell.

Clark, Christopher M. 2000. *Kaiser Wilhelm II: Profiles in power*. London: Pearson Education.

Clements, Kendrick A. 1987. *Woodrow Wilson: World statesman*. Boston: Twayne Publishers.

Coccaro, Emil F., C.S. Bergeman, Richard J. Kavoussi, and A.D. Seroczynski. 1997. "Heritability of aggression and irritability: A twin study of the Buss-Durkee Aggression Scales in adult male subjects." *Society of Biological Psychiatry* 41:273–84.

Colgan, Jeff. 2010. "Oil and revolutionary governments: Fuel for international conflict." *International Organization* 64 (4):661–94.

2013. "Domestic revolutionary leaders and international conflict." *World Politics* 65 (4): 656–90.

Colgan, Jeff, and Jessica Weeks. 2015. "Revolution, personalist dictatorships, and international conflict." *International Organization* 69 (1): 163–94.

Coll, Steve. 1993. "Franjo Tudjman, at war with history: Croatia's president and a past that's shaping the present." *The Washington Post*. March 1:B1.

2013. "Remote control: Our drone delusion." *The New Yorker*. May 6:76.

Collier, Paul, Anke Hoeffler, and Måns Söderbom. 2004. "On the duration of civil war." *Journal of Peace Research* 41 (3):253.

Collins, Joseph J., and Ole R. Holsti. 1999. "Civil-military relations: How wide is the gap?" *International Security* 24 (2):199–207.

Conger, Rand D., and M. Brent Donnellan. 2007. "An interactionist perspective on the socioeconomic context of human development." *Psychology* 58 (1):175–99.

Conover, Pamela Johnston, and Virginia Sapiro. 1993. "Gender, feminist consciousness, and war." *American Journal of Political Science*:1079–99.

Cooper, John Milton Jr. 2009. *Woodrow Wilson: A biography*. New York: Alfred A. Knopf.

Corr, Philip J. 2004. "Reinforcement sensitivity theory and personality." *Neuroscience & Biobehavioral Reviews* 28 (3):317–32.

Corwin, Edward Samuel. 1948. *The President, office and powers, 1787–1948: History and analysis of practice and opinion*. New York: New York University Press.

Covizzi, Ilaria. 2008. "Does union dissolution lead to unemployment? A longitudinal study of health and risk of unemployment for women and men undergoing separation." *European Sociological Review* 24 (3):347–61.

Cox, Gary W. 1999. "The empirical content of Rational Choice Theory: A reply to Green and Shapiro." *Journal of Theoretical Politics* 11 (2):147–69.

Crisostomo, Isabelo T. 1987. *Cory: Profile of a president*. Selangor, Malaysia: Pelanduk Publications.

Croco, Sarah E. 2011. "The decider's dilemma: Leader culpability, war outcomes, and domestic punishment." *American Political Science Review* 105 (3):457–77.

Crowley, Candy. 2011. "CNN Live Event/Special: 9/11 memorial; Truck bombing at NATO base in Afghanistan; Vice President Biden visits hallowed ground." *CNN Transcripts*, September 11. Retrieved from http://transcripts.cnn.com/TRAN SCRIPTS/1109/11/se.06.html.

Cutchin, Malcolm P., Kathryn Remmes Martin, Steven V. Owen, and James S. Goodwin. 2008. "Concern about petrochemical health risk before and after a refinery explosion." *Risk Analysis* 28 (3):589–601.

Dabbs, James M. Jr., Robert L. Frady, Timothy S. Carr, and Norma F. Besch. 1987. "Saliva testosterone and criminal violence in young adult prison inmates." *Psychosomatic medicine* 49 (2):174–82.

Dabbs, James M. Jr., Timothy S. Carr, Robert L. Frady, and Jasmin K. Riad. 1995. "Testosterone, crime, and misbehavior among 692 male prison inmates." *Personality and Individual Differences* 18 (5):627–33.

Dafoe, Allan. 2011. "Statistical critiques of the democratic peace: Caveat emptor." *American Journal of Political Science* 55 (2):247–62.

Dawisha, Karen, and Bruce Parrott, eds. 1997. *Politics, power, and the struggle for democracy in South-East Europe*. Cambridge, UK: Cambridge University Press.

de Gaulle, Charles. 1960. *The edge of the sword*. Translated by G. Hopkins. London: Faber & Faber.

de Tocqueville, Alexis 2000. *Democracy in America*. Translated by H. C. M. a. D. Winthrop. Chicago, IL: University of Chicago Press.

de Vries, Aiko P. J., Nancy Kassam-Adams, Avital Cnaan, Elisabeth Sherman-Slate, Paul R. Gallagher, and Flaura K. Winston. 1999. "Looking beyond the physical injury: Posttraumatic stress disorder in children and parents after pediatric traffic injury." *Pediatrics* 104 (6):1293–9.

Dean, Robert D. 1998. "Masculinity as ideology: John F. Kennedy and the domestic politics of foreign policy." *Diplomatic History* 22 (2):29–61.

Debs, Alexandre, and Hein E. Goemans. 2010. "Regime type, the fate of leaders, and war." *American Political Science Review* 104 (3):430–45.

Dempsey, Jason K. 2009. *Our army: Soldiers, politics, and American civil-military relations*. Princeton, NJ: Princeton University Press.

Desai, Sonalde, and Linda J. Waite. 1991. "Women's employment during pregnancy and after the first birth: Occupational characteristics and work commitment." *American Sociological Review*:551–66.

Diehl, Paul F. 1985. "Contiguity and military escalation in major power rivalries, 1816–1980." *The Journal of Politics* 47 (4):1203–11.

Diggins, John Patrick. 2007. *Ronald Reagan: Fate, freedom, and the making of history*. New York: W. W. Norton.

DiLalla, Lisabeth F. 2002. "Behavior genetics of aggression in children: Review and future directions." *Developmental Review* 22 (4):593–622.

Dorman, Andrew M. 2002. *Defence under Thatcher*. Hampshire, UK: Palgrave.

Dupuy, Kendra E., and Krijn Peters. 2010. *War and children: A reference handbook*. Santa Barbara, CA: Praeger Security International.

Dyson, Stephen B., and Thomas Preston. 2006. "Individual characteristics of political leaders and the use of analogy in foreign policy decision making." *Political Psychology* 27 (2):265–88.

Easterbrooks, M. Ann, and Wendy A. Goldberg. 1984. "Toddler development in the family: Impact of father involvement and parenting characteristics." *Child Development* 55 (3):740–52.

Eaves, Lindon J., H.J. Eysenck, and Nicholas G. Martin. 1989. *Genes, culture and personality: An empirical approach*. London: Academic Press.

Economist. 2010. "Xi who must be obeyed." *The Economist*, October 21. Retrieved from www.economist.com/node/17309197.

Efron, Bradley. 1983. "Estimating the error rate of a prediction rule: Improvement on cross-validation." *Journal of the American Statistical Association* 78 (382):316–31.

Eliot, Marc. 2008. *Reagan: The Hollywood years*. New York: Harmony Books.

Ernst, Cecile, and Jules Angst. 1983. *Birth order: Its influence on personality*. New York: Springer-Verlag.

Etheredge, Lloyd S. 1978. "Personality effects on American foreign policy, 1898–1968: A test of interpersonal generalization theory." *American Political Science Review* 72 (2):434–51.

Evans, Thomas W. 2006. *The education of Ronald Reagan: The General Electric years and the untold story of his conversion to conservatism*. New York: Columbia University Press.

F.R. [*New York Times* correspondent]. 1901. "Duelling in Germany." *The New York Times Magazine Supplement*. December 1:SM6.

Farrington, David P. 1991. "Childhood aggression and adult violence: Early precursors and later life outcomes." In K.H. Rubin and D.J. Pepler (eds.), *The development and treatment of childhood aggression* (pp. 5–29). Hillsdale, NJ: Lawrence Erlbaum Associates.

Feaver, Peter, and Christopher Gelpi. 2004. *Choosing your battles: American civil-military relations and the use of force.* Princeton, N.J.: Princeton University Press.

Fiebig-von Hase, Ragnhild. 2003. "The uses of 'friendship': The 'personal regime' of Wilhelm II and Theodore Roosevelt, 1901–1909." In A. Mombauer and W. Deist (eds.), *The Kaiser: New research on Wilhelm II's role in imperial Germany* (pp. 143–75). Cambridge, UK: Cambridge University Press.

Fife, Robert. 1993. *Kim Campbell: The making of a politician.* Toronto, Canada: HarperCollins.

Forer, Lucille K. 1976. *The birth order factor: How your personality is influenced by your place in the family.* New York: D. McKay.

Foyle, Douglas C. 1999. *Counting the public in: Presidents, public opinion, and foreign policy.* New York: Columbia University Press.

Frankland, Mark. 1966. *Khrushchev.* Harmondsworth, Middlesex, UK: Penguin Books.

Frevert, Ute. 1998. "The taming of the noble ruffian: Male violence and dueling in early modern and modern Germany." In P. Spierenburg (ed.), *Men and violence: Gender, honor, and ritual in modern Europe and America* (pp. 37–62). Columbus: Ohio State University Press.

Friedman, Naomi P., Akira Miyake, Susan E. Young, John C. DeFries, Robin P. Corley, and John K. Hewitt. 2008. "Individual differences in executive functions are almost entirely genetic in origin." *Journal of Experimental Psychology* 137 (2):201–25.

Frutos, Julio Cesar (ed.) 2007. *Testimonios de la Guerra Grande y muerte del Mariscal López.* Asunción, Paraguay: Color ABC.

Fuhrmann, Matthew, and Michael C. Horowitz. 2015. "When leaders matter: Rebel experience and nuclear proliferation." *The Journal of Politics* 77 (1): 72-87.

Fukuyama, Francis. 1998. "Women and the evolution of world politics." *Foreign Affairs* 77 (5):24–40.

Fussell, Paul. 1991. *The Norton book of modern war.* New York: W. W. Norton.

Gäbler, Ira, and Andreas Maercker. 2011. "Revenge after trauma: Theoretical outline." In M. Linden and A. Maercker (eds.), *Embitterment* (pp. 42–69). Vienna, Austria: Springer-Verlag Wien.

Gallagher, Maryann E. 2010. *Who ups the ante? Personality traints and risky foreign policy [Dissertation].* Atlanta, GA: Emory University.

Gallagher, Maryann E., and Susan H. Allen. 2013. "Presidential personality: Not just a nuisance." *Foreign Policy Analysis* 10 (1):1–21.

Gamble, Richard M. 2001. "Savior nation: Woodrow Wilson and the gospel of service." *Humanitas* 14 (1):4–22.

Gardner, Margo, and Laurence Steinberg. 2005. "Peer influence on risk taking, risk preference, and risky decision making in adolescence and adulthood: An experimental study." *Developmental Psychology* 41 (4):4.

Garnett, Mark. 2007. "Banality in politics: Margaret Thatcher and the biographers." *Political Studies Review* 5:172–82.

Gartzke, Erik, and Dong-Joon Jo. 2005. "Determinents of nuclear weapons proliferation: A quantitative model." *Journal of Conflict Resolution* 51 (1): 167–94.

Gelpi, Christopher, and Peter D. Feaver. 2002. "Speak softly and carry a big stick? Veterans in the political elite and the American use of force." *American Political Science Review* 96 (4):779–93.

Gelpi, Christopher, Peter D. Feaver, and Jason Reifler. 2009. *Paying the human costs of war: American public opinion and casualties in military conflicts.* Princeton, NJ: Princeton University Press.

George, Alexander L. 1980. *Presidential decisionmaking in foreign policy: The effective use of information and advice.* Boulder, CO: Westview Press.

George, Alexander L., and Andrew Bennett. 2005. *Case studies and theory development in the social sciences*: Cambridge, MA: MIT Press.

George, Alexander L., and Juliette L. George. 1964. *Woodrow Wilson and Colonel House: A personality study.* Mineola, NY: Dover Publications.

Ghosn, Faten, and Scott Bennett. 2003. Codebook for the Dyadic Militarized Interstate Incident Data, Version 3.10. Online: http://correlatesofwar.org.

Gilbert, Robert E. 2003. *Tormented president: Calvin Coolidge, death, and clinical depression.* Westport, CT: Praeger Publishers.

Gilens, Martin. 2001. "Political ignorance and collective policy preferences." *American Political Science Review* 95 (2):379–96.

Goddard, S.E. 2006. "Uncommon ground: Indivisible territory and the politics of legitimacy." *International Organization* 60 (1):35–68.

Goemans, Hein E., Kristian S. Gleditsch, and Giacomo Chiozza. 2009. "Introducing Archigos: A dataset of political leaders." *Journal of Peace Research* 46 (2):269–83.

Goldgeier, James M. 1994. *Leadership style and Soviet foreign policy: Stalin, Khrush-chev, Brezhnev, Gorbachev.* Baltimore, MD: Johns Hopkins University Press.

Goldstein, Avery. 2005. *China's grand strategy and international security.* Palo Alto, CA: Stanford University Press.

Goodhand, Jonathan, David Hulme, and Nick Lewer. 2000. "Social capital and the political economy of violence: A case study of Sri Lanka." *Disasters* 24 (4):390–406.

Gourevitch, Philip. 1999. *We wish to inform you that tomorrow we will be killed with our families: Stories from Rwanda.* 1st ed. New York: Picador.

Gourevitch, Philip, and Paul Kagame. 1996. "After genocide: A conversation with Paul Kagame." *Transition* 72:162–94.

Greenstein, Fred I. 1969. *Personality and politics: Problems of evidence, inference, and conceptualization.* Chicago, IL: Markham Publishing.

   1992. "Can personality and politics be studied systematically?" *Political Psychology* 13 (1):105–28.

Grieco, Joseph M., Christopher Gelpi, Jason Reifler, and Peter D. Feaver. 2011. "Let's get a second opinion: International institutions and American public support for war." *International Studies Quarterly* 55 (2):563–83.

Gronke, Paul, and Peter D. Feaver. 2001. "Uncertain confidence: Civilian and military attitudes about civil-military relations." *Soldiers and Civilians*:129–61.

Guerra, Tomás. 1997. *José Figueres Ferrer y la justicia social.* San José, Costa Rica: Educa.

Halpert, Jane A., Midge L. Wilson, and Julia L. Hickman. 1993. "Pregnancy as a source of bias in performance appraisals." *Journal of Organizational Behavior* 14 (7):649–63.

Haridas, Nalini. 1998. *Rao and Nixon: Sinners and patriots*: Nalini Haridas.

Harris, Judith R. 1998. *The nurture assumption: Why children turn out the way they do* New York: New York Free Press.

Hartup, Willard W. 2005. "Introduction." In R.E. Tremblay, W.W. Hartup, and J. Archer (eds.), *Developmental origins of aggression* (pp. 3–24). New York: Guilford Press.

Harvey, Frank P. 2011. *Explaining the Iraq War: Counterfactual theory, logic, and evidence.* New York: Cambridge University Press.

Harvey, Michael, and Jo Ann Danelo Barbour (eds.) 2009. *Global leadership: Portraits of the past, visions for the future.* Silver Spring, MD: International Leadership Association.

Hatemi, Peter K. 2013. "The influence of major life events on economic attitudes in a world of gene-environment interplay." *American Journal of Political Science* 57 (4):987–1007.

Hatemi, Peter K., and Rose McDermott. 2012. "A neurobiological approach to foreign policy analysis: Identifying individual differences in political violence." *Foreign Policy Analysis* 8 (2):111–29.

Hayden, Robert M. 1992. "Balancing discussion of Jasenovac and the manipulation of history." *East European Politics and Societies* 6 (2):207–12.

Heckscher, August. 1991. *Woodrow Wilson.* New York: Macmillan.

Hedl, Drago. 2000. "Living in the past Franjo Tudjman's Croatia." *Current History* 99 (635):104–9.

Henderson, Peter V. N. 1984. "Woodrow Wilson, Victoriano Huerta, and the recognition issue in Mexico." *The Americas* 41 (2):151–76.

Hermann, Margaret G. 1974. "Leader personality and foreign policy behavior." In J. N. Rosenau (ed.), *Comparing foreign policies: Theories, findings and methods* (pp. 101–34). New York: Sage-Halsted.

    1980. "Explaining foreign policy behavior using the personal characteristics of political leaders." *International Studies Quarterly* 24 (1):7–46.

    2001. "How decision units shape foreign policy: A theoretical framework." *International Studies Review* 3 (2):47–81.

    2003. "Assessing leadership style: Trait analysis." In J. M. Post (ed.), *Psychological Assessment of Political Leaders* (pp. 178–212). Ann Arbor: University of Michigan Press.

Herrmann, Richard K., and Jonathan W. Keller. 2004. "Beliefs, values, and strategic choice: U.S. leaders' decisions to engage, contain, and use force in an era of globalization." *Journal of Politics* 66 (2):557–80.

Herz, John H. 1951. *Political realism and political idealism.* Chicago, IL: University of Chicago Press.

Hockenos, Paul. 2003. *Homeland calling: Exile patriotism and the Balkan Wars.* Ithaca, NY: Cornell University Press.

Hoover, Herbert. 1951. *The memoirs of Herbert Hoover: Years of adventure 1874–1920.* New York: Macmillan.

Horowitz, Michael C., and Allan C. Stam. 2014. "How prior military experience influences the future militarized behavior of leaders." *International Organization* 68 (3): 527–59.

Horowitz, Michael C., Erin M. Simpson, and Allan C. Stam. 2011. "Domestic institutions and wartime casualties." *International Studies Quarterly* 55 (4):909–36.

Horowitz, Michael C., Rose McDermott, and Allan C. Stam. 2005. "Leader age, regime type, and violent international relations." *Journal of Conflict Resolution* 49 (5):661–85.

Hudson, Valerie M. 1990. "Birth order of world leaders: An exploratory analysis of effects on personality and behavior." *Political Psychology* 11 (3):583–602.

Hudson, Valerie, Bonnie Ballif-Spanvill, Mary Capriolo, and Chad Emmett. 2012. *Sex and world peace.* New York: Columbia University Press.

Huesmann, L.R., and N.G. Guerra. 1997. "Children's normative beliefs about aggression and aggressive behavior." *Journal of Personality and Social Psychology* 72:408–19.

Huntington, Samuel P. 1957. *The soldier and the state: The theory and politics of civil-military relations*. Cambridge, MA: Belknap Press of Harvard University Press.

Husain, Syed Arshad, Jyotsna Nair, William Holcomb, John C. Reid, Victor Vargas, and Satish S. Nair. 1998. "Stress reactions of children and adolescents in war and siege conditions." *American Journal of Psychiatry* 155 (12):1718–19.

Husic, Sead. 2007. "Franjo Tudjman – Der nationalist. 1922–1990." In *Psychopathologie der Macht: die Zerstorung Jugoslawiens im Spiegel der Biografien von Milosevic, Tudjman und Izetbegovic*: Berlin, Germany: Schiler Verlag.

Hutchison, M.L., and D.M. Gibler. 2007. "Political tolerance and territorial threat: A cross-national study." *Journal of Politics* 69 (1):128–42.

Huth, Paul. 2009. *Standing your ground: Territorial disputes and international conflict*. Ann Arbor: University of Michigan Press.

Jai, Janak Raj. 1996. *Narasimha Rao: The best prime minister*. New Delhi: Regency Publications.

Jalalzai, Farida. 2010. "Madam president: Gender, power, and the comparative presidency." *Journal of Women, Politics and Policy* 31 (2):132–65.

Jalalzai, Farida, and Mona Lena Krook. 2010. "Beyond Hillary and Benazir: Women's political leadership worldwide." *International Political Science Review* 31 (1):5–21.

Janowitz, Morris. 1960. *The professional soldier: A social and political portrait*. New York: Free Press.

Jennings, M. Kent, and Gregory B. Markus. 1977. "The effects of military service on political attitudes: A panel study." *American Political Science Review* 71 (1):131–47.

Jennings, M. Kent, Gregory B. Markus, and Richard G. Niemi. 1991. *Youth-parent socialization panel study, 1965–1982: Three waves combined*. Ann Arbor, MI: Inter-university Consortium for Political and Social Research.

Jerusalem Post. 1970. "2nd Algerian also security officer." *Jerusalem Post*: August 25.
1973. "Cabinet meets, Meir voices Israel's sorrow." *Jerusalem Post*: February 23.

Jervis, Robert. 1988. "War and misperception." *The Journal of Inderdisciplinary History* 18 (4):675–700.
2013. "Do leaders matter and how would we know?" *Security Studies* 22 (2):153–79.

Jo, Dong-Joon, and Erik Gartzke. 2007. "Determinants of nuclear weapons proliferation." *Journal of Conflict Resolution* 51 (1):167–94.

John F. Kennedy Presidential Library and Museum. 1962. "Department of State telegram transmitting letter from Chairman Khrushchev to President Kennedy, October 26, 1962." Retrieved from http://microsites.jfklibrary.org/cmc/oct26/doc4.html.

Joes, Anthony James. 2007. *Urban guerrilla warfare*. Lexington: University Press of Kentucky.

Johnson, Dominic D. P., Rose McDermott, Jon Cowden, and Dustin Tingley. 2012. "Dead certain." *Human Nature* 23 (1):98–126.

Johnson, Kirk. 2012. "For the vice president of China, tea time in Iowa." *New York Times*. February 15:A4.

Jones, Benjamin F., and Benjamin A. Olken. 2005. "Do leaders matter? National leadership and growth since World War II." *Quarterly Journal of Economics* 120 (3):835–64.

Kadera, Kelly M., and Dina Zinnes. 2010. "Evolution/history of the scientific study of international processes." In R. A. Denemark (ed.), *The International studies encyclopedia*. Malden, MA: Wiley-Blackwell.

Kaga, Yoshie, John Bennett, and Peter Moss. 2010. *Caring and learning together: A cross-national study on the integration of early childhood care and education within education.* Paris: UNESCO.

Kagan, Robert, and William Kristol. 2004. "The right war for the right reasons." *The Weekly Standard* 9 (23): Retrieved from www.weeklystandard.com/Content/Public/Articles/000/3/735tahyk.asp.

Kant, Immanuel. 2006. *Anthropology from a practical point of view.* Translated and edited by Robert B. Louden. New York: Cambridge University Press.

Katz, Friedrich. 1978. "Pancho Villa and the attack on Columbus, New Mexico." *The American Historical Review* 83 (1):101–30.

Kavanagh, Dennis. 1998. *A dictionary of political biography: Who's who in twentieth-century world politics.* New York: Oxford University Press.

Keenan, Kate, and Daniel S. Shaw. 1994. "The development of aggression in toddlers: A study of low-income families." *Journal of Abnormal Child Psychology* 22 (1):53–77.

Keiger, John. 2008. "Raymond Poincaré." In J. Wright and S. Casey (eds.), *Mental maps in the era of two world wars* (pp. 1–20). New York: Palgrave Macmillan.

Keizer, Renske. 2010. "*Remaining childless: Causes and consequences from a life course perspective.*" Dissertation, Utrecht University.

Keller, J.W. 2005. "Leadership style, regime type, and foreign policy crisis behavior: A contingent monadic peace?" *International Studies Quarterly* 49 (2):205–32.

Kengor, Paul. 2004. *God and Ronald Reagan: A spiritual life.* New York: HarperCollins.

Kennedy, Andrew B. 2011. *The international ambitions of Mao and Nehru: National efficacy beliefs and the making of foreign policy.* New York: Cambridge University Press.

Kerry, John F. 2004. "Text of John Kerry's acceptance speech at the Democratic National Convention." *Washington Post.* July 29. Retrieved from www.washingtonpost.com/wp-dyn/articles/A25678-2004Jul29.html.

Khong, Yuen Foong. 1992. *Analogies at war: Korea, Munich, Dien Bien Phu, and the Vietnam decisions of 1965.* Princeton, NJ: Princeton University Press.

Khrushchev, Nikita. 2004. *Memoirs of Nikita Khrushchev,* vol. 1: *Commisar, 1918–1945.* University Park: Pennsylvania State University Press.

Kim-Cohen, Julia, Terrie E. Moffitt, Avshalom Caspi, and Alan Taylor. 2004. "Genetic and environmental processes in young children's resilience and vulnerability to socioeconomic deprivation." *Child Development* 75 (3):651–68.

King, Gary, Michael Tomz, and Jason Wittenberg. 2000. "Making the most of statistical analyses: Improving interpretation and presentation." *American Journal of Political Science* 44 (2):347–61.

Kinzer, Stephen. 2008. *A thousand hills: Rwanda's rebirth and the man who dreamed it.* Hoboken, NJ: Wiley & Sons.

Kirkpatrick, David D. 2011. "Egypt erupts in jubilation as Mubarak steps down." *The New York Times.* February 11. Retrieved from www.nytimes.com/2011/02/12/world/middleeast/12egypt.html.

Kissinger, Henry A. 1957. *A world restored: Metternich, Castlereagh and the problems of peace.* Boston: Houghton Mifflin.

  1958. *Nuclear weapons and foreign policy.* Boston: Houghton Mifflin.

Klonsky, Bruce. 1983. "The socialization and development of leadership ability." *Genetic Psychology Monographs* 108 (1):97–135.

Koenen, Karestan C., Michael J. Lyons, Jack Goldberg, John Simpson, Wesley M. Williams, Rosemary Toomey, Seth A. Eisen, William True, and Ming T. Tsuang. 2003. "Co-twin control study of relationships among combat exposure, combat-related PTSD, and other mental disorders." *Journal of Traumatic Stress* 16 (5):433–8.

Kohn, Melvin L., and Carmi Schooler. 1982. "Job conditions and personality: A longitudinal assessment of their reciprocal effects." *American Journal of Sociology* 87 (6):1257–86.

Kolb, D.A. 1984. *Experiential learning: Experience as the source of learning and development*. Englewood Cliffs, NJ: Prentice Hall.

Komisar, Lucy. 1987. *Corazon Aquino: The story of a revolution*. New York: George Braziller.

Kowert, Paul A., and Margaret G. Hermann. 1997. "Who takes risks?" *Journal of Conflict Resolution* 41 (5):611–37.

Krepon, Michael. 2009. *Better safe than sorry: The ironies of living with the bomb*. Palo Alto, CA: Stanford University Press.

Kristof, Nicholas D. 2000. "How Bush came to tame his inner scamp." *The New York Times*. July 29. Retrieved from www.nytimes.com/2000/07/29/us/how-bush-came-to-tame-his-inner-scamp.html.

Lambert, Nicholas A. 2004. "Transformation and technology in the Fisher era: The Impact of the communications revolution." *Journal of Strategic Studies* 27 (2):272–97.

Le Billon, Philippe. 2001. "The political ecology of war: Natural resources and armed conflicts." *Political Geography* 20 (5):561–84.

Lebow, Richard Ned. 1981. *Between peace and war: The nature of international crisis*. Baltimore, MD: Johns Hopkins University Press.
    1983. "Miscalculation in the South Atlantic: The origins of the Falkland War." *Journal of Strategic Studies* 6 (1):5–35.

Lee, Stephen J. 1988. *Aspects of European history 1789–1980*. Reprint, illustrated ed. London: Routledge.

Lemer, Jennifer S., and Dacher Keltner. 2001. "Fear, anger, and risk." *Journal of Personality and Social Psychology* 81 (1):146–59.

Lentz, Harris M. 1994. *Heads of states and governments: A worldwide encyclopedia of over 2,300 leaders, 1945 through 1992*. Jefferson, NC: McFarland.
    1999. *Encyclopedia of heads of states and governments: 1900–1945*. Jefferson, NC: McFarland.

Leuchars, Christopher. 2002. *To the bitter end: Paraguay and the War of the Triple Alliance*. Westport, CT: Greenwood Press.

Levy, Jack S. 1997. "Prospect theory, rational choice, and international relations." *International Studies Quarterly* 41 (2):87–112.

Lewis, John, and Litai Xue. 1988. *China builds the bomb*. Palo Alto, CA: Stanford University Press.

Liswood, Laura A. 1996. *Women world leaders: Fifteen great politicians tell their stories*. San Francisco, CA: Pandora.

Loeber, Rolf, and Dale Hay. 1997. "Key issues in the development of aggression and violence from childhood to early adulthood." *Annual Review of Psychology* 48 (1):371–410.

Loehlin, John C. 1992. *Genes and environment in personality development*. New York: Sage Publications.

Loewenstein, G., and D. Prelec. 1992. "Anomalies in intertemporal choice: Evidence and an interpretation." *The Quarterly Journal of Economics* 107 (2):573–97.

Lopes-Cardozo, Barbara, Reinhard Kaiser. Carol A. Gotway, and Ferid Agani. 2003. "Mental health, social functioning, and feelings of hatred and revenge of Kosovar Albanians one year after the war in Kosovo." *Journal of Traumatic Stress* 16 (4):351–60.

Lopes-Cardozo, Barbara, Leisel Talley, Ann Burton, and Carol Crawford. 2004a. "Karenni refugees living in Thai-Burmese border camps: Traumatic experiences, mental health outcomes, and social functioning." *Social Science & Medicine* 58 (12):2637–44.

Lopes-Cardozo, Barbara, Oleg O. Bilukha, Carol A. Gotway Crawford, Irshad Shaikh, Mitchell I. Wolfe, Michael L. Gerber, and Mark Anderson. 2004b. "Mental health, social functioning, and disability in postwar Afghanistan." *Journal of the American Medical Association* 292:575–84.

López, Carlos A. 1845. "Prevención del Presidente al Coronel Francisco Solano López del Ejercito destinado a Corrientes." Vol. 272, No. 22, Folder 5. Catalogo SH de Ana, Sección Historia. Archivo Nacional de Asunción, Paraguay. Accessed November 20, 2010.

López, Francisco Solano. 1849a. "Comunicaciones del General Francisco Solano López al Presidente." Vol. 287, No. 3, Folder 29. Catalogo SH de Ana, Sección Historia. Archivo Nacional de Asunción, Paraguay. Accessed November 20, 2010.

1849b. "Diario de una excursión real zados por el ejercito al mando del General Francisco Solano López." Vol. 287, No. 5, Folder 5. Catalogo SH de Ana, Sección Historia. Archivo Nacional de Asunción, Paraguay. Accessed November 20, 2010.

1850. "Correspondencias del general Francisco Solano López al Presidente." Vol. 292, No. 20, Folder 19. Catalogo SH de Ana, Sección Historia. Archivo Nacional de Asunción, Paraguay. Accessed November 20, 2010.

Louis, William R. 1992. *In the name of God, go!: Leo Amery and the British Empire in the age of Churchill*. New York: W.W. Norton.

Lucas, John. 1996. *5 days in London*. New Haven, CT: Yale University Press.

Ludeke, Steven G., and Robert F Krueger. 2013. "Authoritarianism as a personality trait: Evidence from a longitudinal behavior genetic study." *Personality and Individual Differences* 55 (5):480–4.

Ludwig, Arnold M. 2002. *King of the mountain: The nature of political leadership*. Lexington: University Press of Kentucky.

Luecken, Linda J., and Jenna L. Gress. 2010. "Early adversity and resilience in emerging adulthood." In J. W. Reich, A. J. Zautra, and J. S. Hall (eds.), *Handbook of adult resilience* (pp. 238–57). New York: Guilford Press.

Lukas, John. 1991. *Five days in London*. New Haven, CT: Yale University Press.

Lynch, Allen. 2002. "Woodrow Wilson and the principle of 'National Self-Determination': A reconsideration." *Review of International Studies* 28 (2):419–36.

Macdonald, David Bruce. 2003. *"Balkan holocausts?: Serbian and Croatian victim centered propaganda and the war in Yugoslavia."* Manchester, UK: Manchester University Press.

Machel, Graça. 1996. *The impact of armed conflict in children*. New York: UNICEF.

Mahoney, Richard D. 2011. *The Kennedy brothers: The rise and fall of Jack and Bobby*. Reprint edition. New York: Arcade Publishing.

Maiolo, Joseph. 2009. *Cry havoc: How the arms race drove the world to war, 1931–1941*. New York: Basic Books.

Mamdani, Mahmood. 2001. *When victims become killers: Colonialism, nativism, and the genocide in Rwanda*. Princeton, NJ: Princeton University Press.

Marshall, Monty G., Ted R. Gurr, and Keith Jaggers. 2014. *Polity IV project: Dataset users manual.* Vienna, VA: Center for Systemic Peace. Retrieved from www.system icpeace.org/inscr/p4manualv2013.pdf.

Martin, Nicholas, Dorret Boomsma, and Geoffrey Machin. 1997. "A twin-pronged attack on complex traits." *Nature Genetics* 17:387–92.

Martin, Ralph G. 1998. *Golda Meir: The romantic years.* New York: Charles Scribners.

Masten, Ann S., and Margaret O'Dougherty Wright. 2010. "Resilience over the life-span: Developmental perspectives on resistance, recovery, and transformation." In J. W. Reich, A. J. Zautra, and J. S. Hall (eds.), *Handbook of adult resilience* (pp. 213–37) New York: Guilford Press.

Masterman, George F. 1870. *Seven eventful years in Paraguay: A narrative of personal experience amongst the Paraguayans.* London: S. Low, Son and Marston.

Matthews, David R. 1954. *The social background of political decision-makers.* New York: Random House.

Mazur, Allan, and Alan Booth. 1998. "Testosterone and dominance in men." *Behavioral and Brain Sciences* 21 (3):353–97.

McCord, Joan. 1979. "Some child-rearing antecedents of criminal behavior in adult men." *Journal of Personality and Social Psychology* 37 (9):1477–86.

McCullough, David. 2005. *1776.* New York: Simon & Schuster.

McDermott, Rose. 2008. *Presidential leadership, illness, and decision making.* Cambridge, UK: Cambridge University Press.

  2014. "The biological bases for aggressiveness and nonaggressiveness in presidents." *Foreign Policy Analysis* 10 (4):313–27.

McDougall, Walter. 1997. *Promised land, crusader state: The American encounter with the world since 1776.* New York: Houghton Mifflin.

McLoyd, Vonnie C. 1998. "Socioeconomic disadvantage and child development." *American Psychologist* 53 (2):185–204.

McPherson, James M. 2003. *Battle cry of freedom: The Civil War era.* New York: Oxford University Press.

Meagher, Michael, and Larry D. Gregg. 2011. *John F. Kennedy: A biography.* Westport, CT: Greenwood Press.

Mearsheimer, John J. 2001. *The tragedy of Great Power politics.* 1st ed. New York: Norton.

Medland, Sarah E., and Peter K. Hatemi. 2009. "Political science, biometric theory, and twin studies: A methodological introduction." *Political Analysis* 17 (2):191–214.

Medvedev, Roy. 1982. *Khrushchev.* T. Brian Pearce (ed.). Oxford, UK: Basil Blackwell.

Meier, Viktor. 1999. *Yugoslavia: A history of its demise.* London: Routledge.

Meir, Golda. 1973. *A land of our own: An oral autobiography.* M. Syrkin (ed.). New York: G. P. Putnam's Sons.

Mersky, Joshua P., James Topitzes, and Arthur J. Reynolds. 2012. "Unsafe at any age: Linking childhood and adolescent maltreatment to delinquency and crime." *Journal of Research in Crime and Delinquency* 49 (2):295–318.

Miller, Edward. 2013a. *Misalliance: Ngo Dinh Diem, the United States, and the fate of South Vietnam.* Boston: Harvard University Press.

Miller, Manjari C. 2013b. *Wronged by empire.* Palo Alto, CA: Stanford University Press.

Mommsen, Wolfgang J. 1990. "Kaiser Wilhelm II and German politics." *Journal of Contemporary History* 25 (2/3):289–316.

Morgenthau, Hans J. 1948. *Politics among nations: The struggle for power and peace.* New York: Knopf.

Morgos, Dorothy, J. William Worden, and Leila Gupta. 2007. "Psychosocial effects of war experiences among displaced children in Southern Darfur." *OMEGA: The Journal of Death and Dying* 56 (3):229–53.

Mousa, F., and H. Madi. 2003. *Impact of the humanitarian crisis in the occupied Palestinian territory on people and services.* Gaza: United Nations Relief and Works Agency for Palestinian Refugees in the Near East (UNRWA).

Mukunda, Gautam. 2012. *Indispensible: When leaders really matter.* Boston: Harvard Business Review Press.

Mumpower, Jeryl L., Liu Shi, James W. Stoutenborough, and Arnold Vedlitz. 2013. "Psychometric and demographic predictors of the perceived risk of terrorist threats and the willingness to pay for terrorism risk management programs." *Risk Analysis* 33 (10):1802–11.

Nagin, Daniel S., and Richard E. Tremblay. 2001. "Parental and early childhood predictors of persistent physical aggression in boys from kindergarten to high school." *Archives of General Psycviatry* 58 (4):389–94.

Narang, Vipin, and Paul Staniland. 2013. "Democratic accountability and foreign security policy." Working paper.

Nash, George H. 1983. *The life of Herbert Hoover.* 1st ed. New York: W.W. Norton.

Nau, Henry. 2013. *Conservative internationalism: Armed diplomacy under Jefferson, Polk, Truman, and Reagan.* Princeton, NJ: Princeton UniversityPress.

Navarro Bolandi, Hugo. 1953. *José Figueres en la evolución de Costa Rica.* Mexico City, Mexico: Imprenta Quiros.

Newbury, Catharine. 1998. "Ethnicity and the politics of history in Rwanda." *Africa Today* 45 (1):7–24.

NHTSA's National Center for Statistics and Analysis. 2007. *NHTSA: Motorcycles traffic safety fact sheet (DOT-HS-810–990).* Washington, DC: National Highway Traffic Safety Administration. Retrieved from www-nrd.nhtsa.dot.gov/Pubs/810990.PDF.

Nicholson, Nigel, Emma Soane, Mark Fenton-O'Creevy, and Paul Willman. 2005. "Personality and domain-specific risk taking." *Journal of Risk Research* 8 (2):157–76.

Niemi, Richard G., and Mary A. Hepburn. 1995. "The rebirth of political socialization." *Perspectives on Political Science* 24 (1):7–16.

Nigg, Joel T. 2000. "On inhibition/disinhibition in developmental psychopathology: Views from cognitive and personality psychology and a working inhibition taxonomy." *Psychological Bulletin* 126 (2):220.

Noonan, Peggy. 2001. *When character was king: A story of Ronald Reagan.* Large print, reprint ed. New York: Random House Large Print.

Nordhaus, William, John R. Oneal, and Bruce M. Russett. 2012. "The effects of the international security environment on national military expenditures: A multicountry study." *International Organization* 66 (3):491–513.

Nye, Joseph S. Jr. 2013. *Presidential leadership and the creation of the American era.* Princeton, NJ: Princeton University Press.

O'Brien, Michael. 2005. *John F. Kennedy: A biography.* New York: Thomas Dunne Books.

Oneal, John R., and Bruce M. Russett. 2000. *Triangulating peace: Democracy, interdependence, and international organizations.* New York: W.W. Norton.

Opfell, Olga S. 1993. *Women prime ministers and presidents.* Jefferson, NC: McFarland.

Overy, Richard. 1995. *Why the Allies won.* New York: W. W. Norton.

Oxley, Douglas R., Kevin B. Smith, John R. Alford, Matthew V. Hibbing, Jennifer L. Miller, Mario Scalora, Peter K. Hatemi, and John R. Hibbing. 2008. "Political attitudes vary with physiological traits." *Science* 321 (5896):1667–70.

Page, Benjamin I., and Jason Barabas. 2000. "Foreign policy gaps between citizens and leaders." *International Studies Quarterly* 44 (3):339–64.

Parcel, Toby L., and Elizabeth G. Menaghan. 1990. "Maternal working conditions and children's verbal facility: Studying the intergenerational transmission of inequality from mothers to young children." *Social Psychology Quarterly* 53 (2):132–47.

Parsons, Craig. 2007. *How to map arguments in political science*. Oxford, UK: Oxford University Press.

Paxson, Christina. 2002. "Comment on Alan Krueger and Jitka Maleckova, 'Education, poverty, and terrorism: Is there a causal connection?'" Unpublished manuscript, Princeton University.

Perkins, Anne. 2013. "Margaret Thatcher obituary: Britain's first female prime minister whose three terms broke the pattern of postwar politics." *The Guardian*. April 8.

Pham, Phuong, Harvey Weinstein, and Timothy Longman. 2004. "Trauma and PTSD symptoms in Rwanda: Implications for attitudes toward justice and reconciliation." *JAMA: The Journal of the American Medical Association* 292 (5):602–12.

Phelps, John T. 1985. "Aerial intrusions by civil and military aircraft in a time of peace." *Military Law Review* 107:255–303.

Pickering, A.D., Philip J. Corr, Jane H. Powell, Veena Kumari, Jasper C. Thornton, and Jeffrey A. Gray 1997. "Individual differences in reactions to reinforcing stimuli are neither black nor white: To what extent are they gray?" In H. Nyborg (ed.), *The scientific study of human nature: Tribute to Hans J. Evsenck at eighty* (pp. 36–67). Amsterdam, The Netherlands: Pergamon/Elsevier.

Pinker, Steven. 2011. *The better angels of our nature: Why violence has declined*. New York: Viking Adult.

Pitts, David. 2007. *Jack and Lem: John F. Kennedy and Lem Billings: The untold story of an extraordinary friendship*. New York: Carroll & Graf.

Plomin, Robert. 2008. *Behavioral genetics*. New York: Macmillan.

Plotz, David. 1999. "Croatian President Franjo Tudjman: The Balkans' (not much) lesser evil." Slate.com. December 10. Retrieved from www.slate.com/articles/news_and_politics/assessment/1999/12/croatian_president_franjo_tudjman.html.

Posen, Barry R. 1984. *The sources of military doctrine: France, Britain, and Germany between the world wars*. Ithaca, NY: Cornell University Press.

Post, Jerrold M. 2003. *The psychological assessment of political leaders: With profiles of Saddam Hussein and Bill Clinton*. Ann Arbor: University of Michigan Press.

Post, Jerrold M., and Robert S. Robins. 1993. *When illness strikes the leader: The dilemma of the captive king*. New Haven, CT: Yale University Press.

Powell, Colin L., and Joseph E. Persico. 1995. *My American journey*. New York: Random House.

Prelec, D., and G. Loewenstein. 1991. "Decision making over time and under uncertainty: A common approach." *Management Science* 37 (7):770–86.

Prunier, Gérard. 1995. *The Rwanda crisis: History of a genocide*. New York: Columbia University Press.

Pynoos, Robert S., Alan M. Steinberg, and Ruth Wraith. 1995. "A developmental model of childhood traumatic stress." In D. Cicchetti and D. J. Cohen (eds.),

Developmental psychopathology, vol. 2: *Risk, disorder and adaptation* (pp. 72–94). New York: John Wiley and Sons.

Quirk, Joel. 2010. "Historical methods." In C. Reus-Smit and D. Snidal (eds.), *The Oxford handbook of international relations* (pp. 518–37). Oxford, UK: Oxford University Press.

Ramadan, Samir, and Ibrahiem Qouta. 2000. *Trauma, violence and mental health: The Palestinian experience.* S.R.I Quta.

Ramet, Sabrina P. 2010. *Central and Southeast European politics since 1989.* Cambridge, UK: Cambridge University Press.

Ranis, G. 1987. "Towards a model of development for the natural resources poor economy." *Discussion Paper 529.* Yale Economic Growth Center, Yale University.

Rasler, Karen, and William R. Thompson. 2006. "Contested territory, strategic rivalries, and conflict escalation." *International Studies Quarterly* 50 (1):145–68.

2010. "Systemic theories of conflict." In R. A. Denemark (ed.), *The international studies encyclopedia.* Hoboken, NJ: Wiley-Blackwell.

2011. "Borders, rivalry, democracy, and conflict in the European region, 1816–1994." *Conflict Management and Peace Science* 28 (3):280–305.

Ray, James Lee. 2001. "Integrating levels of analysis in world politics." *Journal of Theoretical Politics* 13 (4):355–88.

Reeves, Richard. 1994. *President Kennedy: Profile of power.* New York: Simon & Schuster.

Reiter, Dan, and Allan C. Stam. 2002. *Democracies at war.* Princeton, N.J.: Princeton University Press.

Renehan, Edward J. Jr. 2002. *The Kennedys at war: 1937–1945.* New York: Doubleday.

Resquin, Isiodoro. 1875. "Memorias del General Isiodoro Resquin sobre la guerra de la Triple Alianza." Vol. 356, No. 32, Folder 87. Catalogo SH de Ana, Sección Historia. Archivo Nacional de Asunción, Paraguay. Accessed November 20, 2010.

Rhodes, Richard. 1996. *Dark sun: The making of the hydrogen bomb.* New York: Simon & Schuster.

Rice, Edward. 1972. *Mao's way.* Berkeley: University of California Press.

Riker, William. 1990. "Political science and rational choice." In J. E. Alt and K. A. Shepsle (eds.), *Perspectives on positive political economy* (pp. 163–81). New York: Cambridge University Press.

Rimer, Sara. 2004. "Portrait of George Bush in '72: Unanchored in turbulent time." *New York Times.* September 20:A1.

Roberts, Bayard, Kaducu Felix Ocaka, John Browne, Thomas Oyok, and Egbert Sondorp. 2008. "Factors associated with post-traumatic stress disorder and depression amongst internally displaced persons in northern Uganda." *BMC Psychiatry* 8 (1):38.

Roberts, Brent, Nathan R. Kuncel, Rebecca Shiner, Avshalom Caspi, and Lewis R. Goldberg. 2007. "The power of personality: The comparative validity of personality traits, socioeconomic status, and cognitive ability for predicting important life outcomes." *Perspectives on Psychological Science* 2 (4):313–45.

Roberts, Brent W., Avshalmon Caspi, and Terrie E. Moffitt. 2003. "Work experiences and personality development in young adulthood." *Journal of Personality and Social Psychology* 84 (3):582–93.

Rodgers, Joseph L. 2001. "What causes birth order–intelligence patterns." *American Psychologist* 56 (6/7):505–10.

Rodgers, Joseph L., H. Harrington Cleveland, Edwin van den Oord, and David C. Rowe. 2000. "Resolving the debate over birth order, family size, and intelligence." *American Psychologist* 55 (6):599–612.

Rogel, Carole. 2004. *The breakup of Yugoslavia and its aftermath*. Westport, CT: Greenwood Press.

Romano, Elisa, Richard E. Tremblay, Bernard Boulerice, and Raymond Swisher. 2005. "Multilevel correlates of childhood physical aggression and prosocial behavior." *Journal of Abnormal Child Psychology* 33 (5):565–78.

Romero, Simon. 2013. "After years in solitary, an austere life as Uruguay's President." *The New York Times*. January 4:A1.

Rosenau, James N. 1971. *The scientific study of foreign policy*. New York: Free Press.

Rosenthal, A.M. 1992. "On my mind; It's the economy, Stupid." *New York Times*. October 30:A31.

Rumsfeld, Donald. 2002. "DoD news briefing – Secretary Rumsfeld and Gen. Myers." US Department of Defense, Press Operations, news transcript. February 12. Retrieved from www.defense.gov/transcripts/transcript.aspx?transcriptid=2636.

Russell, Douglas S. 2005. *Winston Churchill, soldier: The military life of a gentleman at war*. London: Brassey's.

Russett, Bruce M. 1988. "Peace research, complex causation, and the causes of war." In *Peace research: Achievements and challenges* (pp. 57–69). Boulder, CO: Westview.

Sadkovich, James J. 2006a. "Franjo Tudjman and the Muslim-Croat War of 1993." *Review of Croatian History* 2 (1):207–45.

   2006b. "Patriots, villains, and Franjo Tudjman." *Review of Croatian History* 2 (1):247–80.

   2006c. "Who was Franjo Tudjman?" *East European Politics and Societies* 20 (4):729–39.

Saeger, James S. 2007. *Francisco Solano López and the ruination of Paraguay: Honor and egocentrism*. New York: Rowman & Littlefield.

Sagan, Scott D., and Kenneth N. Waltz. 1995. *The spread of nuclear weapons: A debate*. 1st ed. New York: W.W. Norton.

Salehyan, Idean. 2008. "The externalities of civil strife: Refugees as a source of international conflict." *American Journal of Political Science* 52 (4):787–801.

Sandos, James A. 1981. "Pancho Villa and American security: Woodrow Wilson's Mexican diplomacy reconsidered." *Journal of Latin American Studies* 13 (2):293–311.

Sang-Hun, Choe. 2013. "Steely leader of South Korea is battle-ready." *The New York Times*. April 12:A1.

Sarkees, Meredith R., and Frank Wayman. 2010. *Resort to war: 1816–2007*. Washington, DC: CQ Press.

Saunders, Elizabeth N. 2011. *Leaders at war: How presidents shape military interventions*. Ithaca, NY: Cornell University Press.

Schwartz, Benjamin I. 1951. *Chinese communism and the rise of Mao*. Cambridge, MA: Harvard University Press.

Schweller, Randall L. 2006. *Unanswered threats: Political constraints on the balance of power*. Princeton, NJ: Princeton University Press.

Sechser, Todd S. 2004. "Are soldiers less war-prone than statesmen?" *Journal of Conflict Resolution* 48 (5):746–74.

Senese, Paul D., and John A. Vasquez. 2003. "A unified explanation of territorial conflict: Testing the impact of sampling bias, 1919–1992." *International Studies Quarterly* 47 (2):275–98.

Shah, M.C. 1992. *Consensus and conciliation: P.V. Narasimha Rao.* Delhi, India: Shipra Publications.

Shao, Jun. 1996. "Bootstrap model selection." *Journal of the American Statistical Association* 91 (434):655–65.

Shirkey, Zachary C., and Alex Weisiger. 2007. "An annotated bibliography for the Correlates of War Interstate Wars Database." *Journal of Peace Research.* Retrieved from www.correlatesofwar.org/cow2%20data/WarData/InterState/Shirkey%20&%20Weisiger%20War%20Bibliography.pdf

Simonin, Bernard L. 1999. "Ambiguity and the process of knowledge transfer in strategic alliances." *Strategic Management Journal* 20 (7):595–623.

Simons, Lewis M. 1987. *Worth dying for: A Pulitzer prize-winner's account of the Philippine revolution.* New York: William Morrow.

Singer, J. David. 1988. "Reconstructing the Correlates of War Dataset on material capabilities of states, 1816–1985." *International Interactions* 14 (2):115–32.

Singh, Sonali, and Christopher R. Way. 2004. "The correlates of nuclear proliferation: A quantitative test." *Journal of Conflict Resolution* 48 (6):859–85.

Sirota, David. 2011. "Why people become chickenhawks." Salon.com. June 29. Retrieved from www.salon.com/news/david_sirota/2011/06/29/chickenhawk_origins.

Snyder, Jack L. 1984. *The ideology of the offensive: Military decision making and the disasters of 1914.* Ithaca, NY: Cornell University Press.

Somit, Albert, Alan Arwine, and Steven A. Peterson. 1996. *Birth order and political behavior.* New York: University Press of America.

Stam, Allan C., Alexander Von Hagen-Jamar, and Alton Worthington. 2012. "Combat environment and long-term costs of war: Evidence from Vietnam-Era twins." Unpublished manuscript. University of Michigan, Ann Arbor.

Stanton, Jessica. 2009. "*Strategies of violence and restraint in civil war.*" Dissertation, Columbia University.

Starobin, Paul. 2003. "The French were right." *National Journal* 35 (45): 3406–3412. Retrieved from www.metu.edu.tr/~utuba/Paul%20Starobin.doc.

Steelman, Lala Carr, Brian Powell, Regina Werum, and Scott Carter. 2002. "Reconsidering the effects of sibling configuration: Recent advances and challenges." *Annual Review of Sociology* 28:243–69.

Steinberg, Blema S. 2008. *Women in power: The personalities and leadership styles of Indira Gandhi, Golda Meir, and Margaret Thatcher.* Montreal, Canada: McGill-Queen's University Press.

Stewart, Louis H. 1992. *Changemakers: A Jungian perspective on sibling position and the family atmosphere.* New York: Routledge.

Stewart, Wayne H. Jr., and Philip L. Roth. 2001. "Risk propensity differences between entrepreneurs and managers: A meta-analytic review." *Journal of Applied Psychology* 86 (1):145–53.

Sulloway, Frank J. 1996. *Born to rebel: Birth order, family dynamics, and creative lives.* New York: Pantheon Books.

Taubman, William. 2003. *Khrushchev: The Man and his era.* New York: W.W. Norton.

Tetlock, Philip E., and James M. Goldgeier. 2007. "Psychological approaches complement – rather than contradict – international relations theories." In C. Reus-Smit and D. Snidal (eds.), *The Oxford handbook of international relations* (pp. 462–80). New York: Oxford University Press.

Thakur, Ramesh. 1996. "India and the United States: A triumph of hope over experience?" *Asian Survey* 36 (6):574–91.

Thatcher, Margaret. 1995. *The Downing Street Years*. New York: HarperCollins.

Thompson, George. 1869. *The war in Paraguay*. London: Spottiswoode and Co.

Thompson, J.A. 1985. "Woodrow Wilson and World War I: A reappraisal." *Journal of American Studies* 19 (2):325–48.

Thompson, Mark R. 2002. "Female leadership of democratic transitions in Asia." *Pacific Affairs* 75 (4):535–55.

Tickner, J. Ann. 1992. *Gender in international relations: Feminist perspectives on achieving international security*. New York: Columbia University Press.

Tompson, William J. 1995. *Khrushchev: A political life*. New York: St. Martin's Press.

Tremblay, Richard. E., Daniel S. Nagin, Jean R. Séguin, Mark Zoccolillo, Philip D. Zelazo, Michel Boivin, Daniel Pérusse, and Christa Japel. 2004. "Physical aggression during early childhood: Trajectories and predictors." *Pediatrics* 114 (1):e43–e50.

Tremblay, Richard E., and Daniel S. Nagin. 2005. "The developmental origins of physical aggression in humans." In R. E. Tremblay, W. W. Hartup, and J. Archer (eds.), *Developmental origins of aggression* (pp. 84–106). New York: Guilford Press.

Trinkunas, Harold A. 2001. "Crafting civilian control." In David Pion-Berlin (ed.), *Civil-military relations in Latin America* (pp. 161–93). Chapel Hill: University of North Carolina Press.

Tsebelis, George. 1995. "Decision making in political systems: Veto players in presidentialism, parliamentarism, multicameralism and multipartyism." *British Journal of Political Science* 25 (3):289–325.

Turner, Henry A. 1957. "Woodrow Wilson and public opinion." *Public Opinion Quarterly* 21 (4):505–20.

Van der Kiste, John. 1999. *Kaiser Wilhelm II: Germany's last emperor*. Stroud, UK: Sutton Publishing.

Van Evera, Steven. 1984. "The cult of the offensive and the origins of the First World War." *International Security* 9 (1):58–107.

Vasquez, John A., and Marie T. Henehan. 2001. "Territorial disputes and the probability of war, 1816–1992." *Journal of Peace Research* 38 (2):123–38.

Voors, Maarten, Eleonora E. Nillesen, Philip Verwimp, Erwin H. Bulte, Robert Lensink, and Daan Van Soest. 2010. "Does conflict affect preferences? Results from field experiments in Burundi." *MICROCON research working paper* 21. Retrieved from www.researchgate.net/publication/46443646_Does_Conflict_affect_Preferences_Results_from_Field_Experiments_in_Burundi/file/79e4150f3bd43511f1.pdf.

Waldman, Amy. 2004. "P.V. Narasimha Rao, Indian premier, dies at 83." *The New York Times*. December 24:C8.

Walt, Stephen M. 1987. "The search for a science of strategy: A review essay." *International Security* 12 (1):140–65.

Waltz, Kenneth N. 1959. *Man, the state, and war*. New York: Columbia University Press.

1979. *Theory of international politics*. Reading, PA: Addison-Wesley.

Washington, Ebonya L. 2008. "Female socialization: How daughters affect their legislative father's voting on women's issues." *American Economic Review* 98 (1):311–32

Waugh, Colin M. 2004. *Paul Kagame and Rwanda: Power, genocide and the Rwandan patriotic front*. Jefferson, NC: McFarland.

Weeks, Jessica. 2012. "Strongmen and straw men: Authoritarian regimes and the initiation of international conflict." *American Political Science Review* 106 (2):326–47.

2014. *Dictators at war and peace*. Ithaca, NY: Cornell University Press.

Weisiger, Alex. 2013. *Logics of war: Explanations for limited and unlimited conflicts*. Ithaca, NY: Cornell University Press.

Weisiger, Alex, and Keren Yarhi-Milo. 2015. "Revisiting reputation: How past actions matter in international politics." *International Organization* 69(2): 473–495.

Wendt, Alexander. 1999. *Social theory of international politics*. New York: Cambridge University Press.

Werner, Suzanne, and Amy Yuen. 2005. "Making and keeping peace." *International Organization* 59 (2):261–92.

Werts, Charles E., and Donivan J. Watley. 1972. "Paternal influence on talent development." *Journal of Counseling Psychology* 19 (5):367.

Whang, Taehee. 2010. "Empirical implications of signaling models: Estimation of belief updating in international crisis bargaining." *Political Analysis* 18 (3):381–402.

Whigham, Thomas L. 2002. *The Paraguayan war: Causes and early conduct*. Lincoln: University of Nebraska Press.

Whigham, Thomas L., and Barbara Potthast. 1999. "The Paraguayan Rosetta Stone: New insights into the demographics of the Paraguayan War, 1864–1870." *Latin American Research Review* 43 (1):174–86.

Wills, Chuck. 2009. *Jack Kennedy: The illustrated life of a president*. San Francisco, CA: Chronicle Books.

Wood, Lara A., Rachel L. Kendal, and Emma G. Flynn. 2013. "Copy me or copy you? The effect of prior experience on social learning." *Cognition* 127 (2):203–13.

Wright, Quincy. 1955. *The study of international relations*. New York: Appleton-Century-Crofts.

Xue, Gui, Zhonglin Lua, Irwin P. Levind, and Antoine Becharaa. 2010. "The impact of prior risk experiences on subsequent risky decision-making: The role of the insula." *Neuroimage* 50 (2):709–16.

Yager, Edward M. 2006. *Ronald Reagan's journey: Democrat to Republican*. Lanham, MD: Rowman & Littlefield.

Yoshikawa, Hirokazu. 1994. "Prevention as cumulative protection: Effects of early family support and education on chronic delinquency and its risks." *Psychological Bulletin* 115 (1):28.

1995. "Long-term effects of early childhood programs on social outcomes and delinquency." *The Future of Children* 5 (3):51–75.

Zafonte, Matthew, and Paul Sabatier. 1998. "Shared beliefs and imposed interdependencies as determinants of ally networks in overlapping subsystems." *Journal of Theoretical Politics* 10 (4):473–505.

Zubizarreta, Carlos. 1961. *Cien vidas Paraguayas*. Asunción, Paraguay: Ediciones Nizza.

Zuckerman, Marvin, and D. Michael Kuhlman. 2000. "Personality and risk-taking: Common biosocial factors." *Journal of Personality* 68 (6):999–1029.

Zuckerman, Marvin, and Michael Neeb. 1980. "Demographic influences in sensation seeking and expressions of sensation seeking in religion, smoking and driving habits." *Personality and Individual Differences* 1 (3):197–206.

Index